COMPETING FOR GLOBAL TALENT

COMPETING FOR GLOBAL TALENT

Editors

Christiane KUPTSCH and PANG Eng Fong

Contributors

Manolo ABELLA
Rupa CHANDA
Christopher R. COUNIHAN
Allan M. FINDLAY
Graeme HUGO
Chieko KAMIBAYASHI

Christiane KUPTSCH
Philip L. MARTIN
Mark J. MILLER
PANG Eng Fong
Niranjana SREENIVASAN
David ZWEIG

International Institute for Labour Studies
International Labour Office, Geneva

Wee Kim Wee Centre
Singapore Management University

Published by the International Institute for Labour Studies

The *International Institute for Labour Studies* (IILS) was established in 1960 as an autonomous facility of the International Labour Organization (ILO) to further policy research, public debate and the sharing of knowledge on emerging labour and social issues of concern to the ILO and its constituents — labour, business and government.

Copyright © International Labour Organization (International Institute for Labour Studies) 2006.

Short excerpts from this publication may be reproduced without authorization, on condition that the source is indicated. For rights of reproduction or translation, application should be made to the Director, International Institute for Labour Studies, P.O. Box 6, CH-1211 Geneva 22, Switzerland.

ISBN (Print) 92-9014-776-8
ISBN (Web PDF) 92-9014-779-2

First published 2006

The responsibility for opinions expressed in signed articles, studies and other contributions of this volume rests solely with their authors, and their publication does not constitute an endorsement by the International Institute for Labour Studies of the opinions expressed.

Copies can be ordered from: ILO Publications, International Labour Office, CH-1211 Geneva 22, Switzerland. For on-line orders, see www.ilo.org/publns

Photocomposed in Switzerland   BRI
Printed in France   SAD

Table of contents

List of contributors

Manolo I. ABELLA
   former Director, International Migration Programme
   ILO

Rupa CHANDA
   Professor, Indian Institute of Management, Bangalore
   India

Christopher R. COUNIHAN
   University of Delaware
   United States

Allan M. FINDLAY
   Professor of Population Geography, University of Dundee
   United Kingdom

Graeme HUGO
   Federation Fellow, Professor of Geography and
   Director of The National Centre for Social Applications of GIS,
   The University of Adelaide
   Australia

Chieko KAMIBAYASHI
   Professor of Industrial Sociology, Hosei University
   Japan

Christiane KUPTSCH
   Senior Research Officer, International Institute for Labour Studies
   ILO

Philip L. MARTIN
   Professor of Agricultural and Resource Economics,
   University of California-Davis
   United States

Mark J. MILLER
> Editor of International Migration Review and Emma Smith Morris
> Professor of Political Science and International Relations,
> University of Delaware
> United States

PANG Eng Fong
> Practice Professor and Director, Wee Kim Wee Centre
> Lee Kong Chian School of Business
> Singapore Management University
> Singapore

Niranjana SREENIVASAN
> Research Associate, Indian Institute of Management, Bangalore
> India

David ZWEIG
> Director, Centre on China's Transnational Relations, and
> Chair Professor
> Hong Kong University of Science and Technology
> Hong Kong, China

Foreword

Global talent has never been more mobile, thanks to changes at the national, regional and international levels which have eased their flow across borders. Many countries, developed as well as developing, have designed policies and programmes to attract talented people as students, temporary workers and immigrants. Many of these countries are also encouraging the return of skilled nationals who are working abroad. All are persuaded of the positive contributions skilled people can make to their development progress.

The quest for global talent was the theme of an international conference organized in January 2005 by the Wee Kim Wee Centre of Singapore Management University, a new university set up in 2000. The two-day conference brought together migration researchers and policy analysts from Asia, Europe and North America. Participants from Singapore included academics, policymakers and diplomats. The meeting discussed country experiences as well as wider regional and theoretical issues related to the growing flows of global talent. One issue that arose from the discussion was the asymmetric effects of the growing global talent flow on sending and receiving countries. Migrants and receiving countries gain but the short and longer-term effects on sending countries are less clear. Many poor countries have long complained about the negative effects of "brain drain" on their social and economic development. Another issue concerned the relative paucity of high-quality data on the flows of global talent. Better and more timely data, the meeting agreed, would help to produce more robust analyses of the impact of the growing movements of skilled people on both sending and receiving countries. They could help the design of policies and programmes to enhance the benefits of global talent flows while minimizing their adverse impact on poor countries.

This volume of papers presented at the conference is the result of a collaborative effort by the International Institute for Labour Studies of the ILO and the Wee Kim Wee Centre of Singapore Management University. It includes general and theoretical papers on skilled migration and also papers on the country experiences of Australia, India, Japan, Singapore, the United Kingdom, and the United States. The volume, it is hoped, will contribute to a better understanding of the growing competition for global talent.

Gerry Rodgers
*Director, International Institute
for Labour Studies, ILO*

Introduction

Christiane Kuptsch and Pang Eng Fong

Two centuries ago, the dominant economic theory was mercantilism, which held that governments should amass large quantities of gold and silver by encouraging exports and discouraging imports, that colonies should be sources of raw materials as well as captive markets for mother country products, and that emigration should be discouraged in order to keep wages low and export goods competitive. Today, theories of economic growth stress the importance of human capital to knowledge-based economies, and many countries aim to increase their stock of brainpower via immigration.

If governments change their goal from maximizing stocks of gold and silver to maximizing the brainpower within their borders, will economic growth, trade, and migration trajectories be altered? The optimistic view is that increased flows of talented people will forge closer links between developing and developed countries, which will spur trade and investment, leading to convergence in economic performance and less migration over time. The pessimistic view is that the global quest for talent will be won by countries that are already prosperous, which will widen the economic gaps that spur migration, and turn some developing countries into 'emigration nurseries' that produce migrants for foreign jobs.

A good way to think about the new global quest for talent is to reflect on how people migrate. During the great Atlantic migration in the century before World War I, some 60 million Europeans left for North and South America, arriving in New York or Buenos Aires and hoping to begin anew in lands of opportunity. There was no distinction between tourists, guest workers, and immigrants, and many Europeans soon wanted to leave Old Europe for a better life in the New World. Today, all countries have at least three major doors for arriving foreigners. Most arrive as tourists, business visitors, and other non-immigrants in the

1

country for a specific time and purpose. These guests are expected to leave when their visas expire. Another group of people slip across borders and become unauthorized foreigners. Finally, there is the door for immigrants, foreigners who are given work and residence rights and who, at least in traditional countries of immigration, are expected to become citizens eventually.

Each of these doors can be imagined as opening to a room, and the major 21st century change in migration is that foreigners do not necessarily stay in the room where they first arrived. Some tourists become unauthorized by staying longer than their visa permits or by going to work. Some foreign students become workers and immigrants, just as some unauthorized foreigners may become legal guest workers and immigrants as well. Thus, global talent may not arrive through that part of the immigrant door set aside for the world's best and brightest. Instead, talent may arrive as guest workers who can be sponsored for immigrant status by employers or as students who can be hired after graduation. Developing a deeper understanding of the indirect ways in which talent crosses borders is one objective of this book. Another objective is to understand the factors that contribute to the effective design and implementation of policies and programmes to attract global talent. Just as skilled foreigners can end up in a country via a variety of routes, there are also various successful ways to attract foreign talent and maximize their contributions to a country's development. The national experiences in this book underscore the fact that there are different approaches countries have used to attract skilled individuals.

New forms of competition

Part I of this volume raises some general questions regarding the competition for global talent. *Manolo Abella* provides an overview of the issues, highlighting developments that have spurred fundamental shifts in policies among the countries that wish to attract the world's best trained and most skilled workers. Abella reviews the nature and directions of these policy shifts, looks at the evidence of their impact on migration flows, and examines their consequences on host and source countries. He finds that in order to attract foreign specialists and professionals, non-immigration countries are increasingly under pressure to change their policies and to offer talented foreigners a more secure migration status. He also observes that the growing competition for the highly skilled has led to a rethinking of the way foreign worker policies are best administered. The main change appears to be a move from simply easing restrictions, e.g. on changing employers or quotas on sectors, to providing incentives, such as lower income taxes. Abella offers a typology of different approaches to attracting skills (human capital; labour market needs; business incentives; and academic gate approaches), noting that they are not mutually exclusive, and distinguishes different levels of policy making for attracting skills, namely the level of the nation state, regional accords and multilateral treaties.

Christiane Kuptsch focuses on the competition for foreign students and outlines why countries are interested in foreign students, including commercial and economic considerations as well as cultural, development and foreign policy reasons. Kuptsch underscores that students are often probationary immigrants. She examines the link between institutional settings and talent flows in reviewing options for host countries that wish to attract foreign students. A country's academic structure and business issues, such as costs, are central to the ability to gain and retain talent, as are labour market regulations and migration policy. Kuptsch analyses the flow of students from developing and transition countries to Europe, focussing on the steps France, Germany and the United Kingdom have recently undertaken to increase their appeal to foreign students such as changes to curricula, and new regulations for moving from student to worker status. Kuptsch also examines two recent European Union Council Directives, one on the status of third-country nationals who are long-term residents and the other on the admission of third-country nationals for, inter alia, study purposes. She concludes that "Castle Europe" has definitely been opened to foreign students, but has not yet become "Harbour Europe" for the students of the world.

National perspectives

Part II of the present book offers national perspectives, covering a selection of high-income countries from four continents, with different approaches to attracting skills, as well as the newly industrialized economies of China and India and their policies to encourage the return of successful emigrants.

Allan Findlay outlines the United Kingdom's switch from brain exchange to brain gain and draws attention to the social challenges that follow from pursuing a more positive immigration policy. These include the provision of social rights to immigrants, many of whom neither enjoy nor seek UK citizenship, but who nevertheless need support in terms of access to a social infrastructure during their time in the country. Findlay reviews the literature on globalization and international skill mobility: the 'brain drain' literature; research on 'brain exchange', notably within large companies and between global cities; and the 'transnationalism' literature that focuses on networks of ethnically and culturally distinctive people. He reviews the UK experience in competing for global talent relative to that of other economies and asks how the UK which has neo-liberal policies on most matters relating to provision of services to its own citizens, provides for migrants living within its borders. He finds that the current UK government, in line with its 'Third Way' political philosophy that stresses the strategic importance of civil society for social cohesion, has been particularly keen to have voluntary organizations, also termed as 'shadow state' institutions, play a role in supporting migrant communities. He calls for more research to establish just how this differential citizenship will impact on migrant welfare and rights.

Philip Martin believes that the experience of the United States with immigration demonstrates that opportunity attracts talent. The US allows foreigners to enter via three major channels: as immigrants, non-immigrants, and as unauthorized foreigners, and permits the non-immigrants and unauthorized to become immigrants if they find US employers to sponsor them. He notes that this happens often: in recent years about 90 percent of the foreigners receiving immigrant visas for employment reasons were already in the US. Martin states that the US system for attracting global talent can thus be seen as a probationary or Darwinian process, one that restricts the rights of foreign students and guest workers for at least several years, but holds out the hope of an immigrant visa and freedom in the US labour market as the eventual prize. A central recommendation of several recent US commissions has been to raise the share of immigrants admitted for employment and economic reasons, but the political strength of advocates for family unification, refugees, and other types of immigrants has prevented reductions in their numbers in order to expand employment and economic immigration. According to Martin, the US quest for global talent is therefore centred on expanding opportunities for skilled foreigners to enter as non-immigrant students or workers, which he qualifies as 'side-door expansion'.

Graeme Hugo analyses the contemporary Australian experience with respect to global competition for skilled workers, noting that Australia's position in this global market is a complex one: On the one hand, Australia has more experience than most nations in attracting skilled immigrants; on the other hand, while being a developed and mature economy, it occupies a peripheral position in the global economy. For much of the postwar period Australian migration policy concentrated on recruiting settlers from selected countries but a paradigm shift took place in 1996 when attempts began to bring skilled workers to Australia on a temporary basis. Hugo discusses these initiatives and their labour market effects and reviews recent policies aimed at retaining substantial numbers of temporary workers in Australia. He emphasizes that in purely numerical terms Australia is experiencing a "brain gain" of skilled workers but also notes that the tempo of emigration of skilled Australians has accelerated in recent years and assesses the scale and effects of this phenomenon. Finally, Hugo looks to the future and speculates about likely directions in Australian policy relating to the global competition for talent.

Pang Eng Fong discusses the experience of Singapore, a country that has derived substantial benefits by importing skilled and unskilled workers. Foreign workers are nearly a third of Singapore's 2.2 million labour force, and the city-state has recognized that, in a natural resource-poor and low-fertility nation, labour migration must be managed if it is to contribute to Singapore's stability and long-term prosperity. According to Pang, Singapore has been largely successful because, as a high-income, English-speaking and meritocratic society that welcomes foreign talent, Singapore offers migrants opportunities for economic advancement. Political stability, policy continuity and growing employment opportunities have encouraged immigrant workers with the right background and skills to work and settle permanently. In Singapore, as in other countries competing for mobile talented people, attracting talent involves economic benefits and costs as well as political decision that can be the subject of heated debates. Pang notes concern about the impact on locals of the growing influx of skilled foreigners, but support for the government's liberal immigration policy remains strong. An important factor in Singapore's success in attracting talent is the use of English as the main language of government and business.

Chieko Kamibayashi examines Japan's recent policies to attract foreign workers, essentially from Asia and mostly in the IT sector. Japan has introduced changes in its immigration control that make it easier for qualified foreigners to work in the country. For example, special and/or technical visa applications that employers have to make are now being handled within two weeks instead of a few months. Japan also entered into agreements on the mutual recognition of certain qualifications with a number of countries. However, in Kamibayashi's analysis, entry barriers to the Japanese labour market remain high, especially for cultural reasons. As long as Japanese customers ask IT firms for specific kinds of products in Japanese and for products that conform to their organization and business practices, knowledge of Japanese is necessary for high level engineers. Miscommunication is not only limited to language problems and Japanese employers have indicated that the main obstacle to hiring foreign IT engineers is the latter's limited communication with Japanese co-workers, in a culture that is strongly geared to team efforts instead of individual work. Foreigners tend to remain in lower level positions, which is a disincentive for global talent to go to Japan. Nonetheless, Kamibayashi predicts that in a few years time Japan will have succeeded in attracting more foreign IT engineers and the job content and level of positions available to foreigners will have improved, essentially since public opinion on foreign workers in Japan is changing in favour of their acceptance.

In analysing China's efforts to encourage a 'reverse brain drain', *David Zweig* highlights the variety of levels of governments and institutions that promote returnees. He categorizes and describes some of the policies adopted by the central government to promote the return of highly qualified Chinese, including financial incentives, improving the flow of information and bringing people back for short-term visits. He examines measures that local governments take to attract talent in competition with other cities and regions, as well as institutional efforts, e.g. by universities, government-funded research units and state-owned enterprises. Zweig reviews paradigm shifts in national level policies, reporting, for example, about the latest acknowledgment that, while return is highly valued, migrants can even "serve the nation" from abroad. Based on different surveys that he conducted, Zweig also assesses whether government policy is key in encouraging people to return and finds that market forces, facilitated by national government reforms, are the most important factor bringing people back in the private sector: A tremendous market awaits those who learned a valuable skill or received access to advanced technology while overseas. Moreover, China has created an environment conducive to foreign direct investment which has attracted many multinational companies, creating excellent jobs for overseas mainlanders who return. The Chinese Academy of Sciences seems to be succeeding as well, although there are questions about the quality of the talent that they attract: do only the 'second best academics' return?

Rupa Chanda and *Niranjana Sreenivasan* give an overview of the nature of skilled migration from India, such as its occupational and sectoral composition, before focussing on India's experience with skilled inflows, i.e. returnees and foreign migrants. They evaluate the contribution of skilled migration to notably the IT and health care sectors, and present government policy towards skilled migration. Chanda and Sreenivasan come to the conclusion that the Indian government increasingly attempts to realize the benefits of its considerable diaspora population through investments, technology and skill transfer, networking and collaboration. The government's main focus appears to be on attracting diaspora investment and Chanda and Sreenivasan find no concerted and direct efforts to attract back talent or retain it. Surveys of returned migrants and diaspora members suggest that much more needs to be done to address many of the institutional and governance related problems faced by returning Indians and diaspora investors. In Chanda's and Sreenivasan's analysis, economic liberalization and growing employment and business opportunities are currently the main forces driving return migration to India.

International Relations and global talent

The quest for global talent may affect the ways in which states interact with one another. It may strain their relations, e.g. when they act as competitors or where active recruitment by one country is perceived as aggressive and creating a 'brain drain' in another. It may also foster relations, e.g. through the signing of bilateral agreements that may result in less unemployed specialists in one country and the provision of essential skills to another. However, these are by far not the only consequences of cross border talent flows for international relations, as these flows can also change and shape societies and production systems.

The final chapter of this volume takes the reader into the realm of International Relations theory. *Christopher R. Counihan* and *Mark J. Miller* recommend moving away from all too state-centric models and from reliance on overly rationalist conceptions of decision-making processes when analyzing the migration of highly skilled workers. Instead, they propose to use a theoretical framework called Global Governance that sees both state and non-state actors as participating equally in the mutual construction of the political, economic and cultural landscapes within which they operate. In this theory, reality is 'intersubjective', i.e. it exists somewhere between the subjective realm of ideas and the objective realm of material things. Norms are constructed out of the prior experiences and lessons of the actors who inhabit a particular social space, thereby becoming substantially altered by the migration of agents across cultural boundaries. Counihan and Miller point out that in the Global Governance approach to highly skilled migration, the historical processes of skilled international migration and the parallel evolution of global business should not be presented as a jagged progression of separate and distinct "phases" of development. Instead, these processes should be thought of as a smooth progression that builds upon the social learning and the mutual construction of social reality created by the interplay of all actors. Highly skilled migration is shaped and is being shaped by the simultaneous globalizing and localizing forces at work in the global system.

Conclusion

Global talent has never been more mobile or sought after. A complex phenomenon that takes many forms, it comprises many groups of people - temporary skilled migrants moving to take jobs of limited duration, refugees, skilled immigrants, students and even tourists - whose movement across borders augments a receiving country's stock of human and technological skills. Opportunities for such workers have expanded with globalization, and barriers to their cross-border movement have fallen as countries actively promote inflows to redress domestic skill shortages and to quicken economic growth. Though less politically contentious than the movement of unskilled migrants, the flow of talented people across national borders has the potential to reduce or widen North-South divides. Receiving countries and the migrants themselves have benefited, but the benefits for sending countries are less clear, and some sending countries may be adversely affected by the outflow of their most talented citizens.

Not all countries focus their primary policy attention on attracting talented non-nationals. A few countries have developed policies to encourage the return of their educated nationals with some success, especially if they are experiencing rapid economic growth fuelled by foreign investors seeking employees with international experience. China and India fit this profile, having been able to attract overseas nationals back to the native labour market.

Global talent flows will likely expand for economic reasons, but may be slowed by politics. Coordination and cooperation among countries, both at the regional and international levels, can produce a more equitable distribution of the benefits resulting from the migration of talent, a task that will be made easier with better and more timely data that contributes to a deeper understanding of global talent flows and their impacts.

Part I: New forms of competition

Global competition for skilled workers and consequences

Manolo Abella

In an era of diminishing barriers to the movement of goods and capital there are increasing anxieties about the movements of people, controlling borders and preventing illegal migration. However, state policies have historically been favorable towards the movement of the highly skilled and they have became even more so over the recent decade due to several developments. One is the growth of global supply chains as liberalization of trade policies has made it possible for transnational companies to move production to the most economic locations. The emergence of these global production structures have been everywhere accompanied by greater movements or transfers of technical and managerial personnel. Another important development has been the growth of informal as well as flexible forms of employment, opening markets for foreign workers willing to enter occupations or sectors abandoned by natives. Still another factor is the rapid expansion of the knowledge economy and the demand it has created for a ready supply of young IT professionals. At the same time greater and greater numbers are seeking further education in other countries, many eventually not returning home and becoming migrants. And finally, the rapid ageing of populations in certain regions is generating demand for the services of medical and care personnel which the local workforce can no longer supply in sufficient numbers.

These developments have spurred some fundamental shifts in policies among countries in order to attract into their shores the world's best trained and most skilled workforce. This paper reviews the nature and directions of these policy shifts, looks at the evidence of their impact on migration flows, and their consequences on host and source countries. It finds that in order to attract foreign specialists and professionals non-immigration countries are increasingly under pressure to change their policies and to offer foreign talents more secure migration status than they have heretofore been willing to offer. In this growing competition for the best and the brightest, traditional countries of immigration which offer permanent residence or at least a path to permanent settlement clearly have an advantage over other rich countries, even if the latter also offer equally hospitable environment of personal security, well developed social welfare systems, and high standards of living. The stakes are clearly high for all. Countries which fail to attract foreign talents and skills risk not only falling behind in the in the global competition for new intelligent products and services, but also maintaining the standards of living their populations have been used to.

Experience has richly shown that human capital, rather than natural resource endowments, is the key to economic development. The current competition for the highly skilled has naturally raised alarms that it will further aggravate the problems of developing countries in creating a critical mass of professionals and technical workers needed to raise productivity in agriculture and industry, to manage public policies for more effective governance, and to expand education. Infusions of capital alone do not suffice to break out of under-development. A critical mass of native people with the skills necessary to create new knowledge or to transform imported knowledge into viable technologies for production, to design and create new products and services, and to make these competitive in the global market is an essential condition for progress. The huge investments already made by many developing countries to develop such human capital are now at risk because of the new migration phenomenon.

On the other hand, in countries with slow growing workforces governments are facing pressures to respond in a strategic fashion to the skilled labour requirements of business and industry without adding to popular anxieties about immigration. Recent changes in policies and legislation in Europe and in Asia suggest that there is now more recognition than before of the necessity to use immigration to achieve economic ends as well as meeting the demands of aging societies. Earlier policies adopted to assuage fears about displacement of native workers are giving way to employer-driven immigration schemes to bring in foreign managers and specialists on grounds that they are needed to spur research and innovation. At the same time many governments have taken measures to reduce bureaucratic impediments to processing applications for immigration and are launching active recruitment programmes to target countries.

Significant policy shifts are particularly notable in the admission of foreign medical personnel. While physicians and nurses have always been among the most internationally mobile of professions, the scale of organized recruitment and placement of nurses has already raised alarms about its impact on health care in developing countries of origin. The phenomenon is however likely to grow rather than diminish in the coming decades as average ages of medical and health workers are rising. Fewer and fewer of native youths in the rich countries are pursuing nursing as a profession. As populations age in many parts of the developed world and health care continues to be socialized, the demands for institutional care of the aged are already straining capacities of health delivery systems. Increasing labour force participation of women and declining size of families are aggravating the problem. In these societies it is understandable why the employment of foreign health professionals is increasingly being viewed as an inevitable solution to rising costs and unresponsive local labour markets.

Trends in the migration of the highly-skilled

Has the international mobility of the highly-skilled risen significantly beyond its past trajectory? Although statistics on migration are notoriously poor, and weaknesses of the past make comparisons over long periods of time particularly problematic, most observers seem agreed that this is the case. Much depends of course also on definitions on who should be included under this term, and what criteria should be used to evaluate significance. This paper does not intend to enter into the complexities of measurement and adopts the widest possible definition of highly-skilled to include not only persons with tertiary education but also those who have acquired specialized knowledge and skill through work experience or specialized training. Migration authorities have also used the same eclecticism in judging who qualifies as highly-skilled by relying on certifications by employers or by peer groups.

Recent estimates of the differential rates of emigration among the skilled and the less skilled show that the former are moving across borders in ever growing numbers. Docquier and Rapoport (2004) estimated, for example, that the worldwide average emigration rates amounted to 0.94 percent for the low skilled, 1.64 percent for the medium skill and 5.47 percent for the high skill workers. [1] Over the period 1990 to 2000 they reckoned that the worldwide average rate of emigration of skilled

---

[1] Docquier, F. and H. Rapoport (2004) "Skilled migration: the perspective of developing countries" Discussion Paper, Department of Economics, Bar-Ilan University, June 2004.

workers had risen by 0.75 percentage point, against only 0.06 percentage point for low skill and 0.41 for medium skill workers.

Table 1 below shows that over the decade of the 1990s the annual admissions of skilled immigrants to the traditional countries of immigration (Australia, Canada, New Zealand and the United States) as well as to Sweden and the United Kingdom have grown very rapidly. The admissions to the US grew 14.6 times over the decade while that to the UK rose ten times. However the two north American countries of immigration, the US and Canada, together accounted for as much as 70 percent of the admissions of skilled immigrants into these six countries.

Table 1   Admission of skilled immigrants in selected countries, 1991, 1999 and 2001

Country	Number (thousands)			Share of all immigrants (percentage)		
	1991	1999	2001a	1991	1999	2001
Australia[b]	41	35	54	37	42	60
Canada[c]	41	81	137	18	47	55
New Zealand		13	36		47	68
United States[d]	12	57	175	18	22	17
Sweden	0	3	4	6	8	10
United Kingdom	4	32	40	7	33	32

[a] Data for the United States referring to 2002.

[b] Skilled category including family members with certain tested professional qualifications and linguistic aptitudes.

[c] Skilled workers category including assisted relatives who are not point tested.

[d] Employment-based preferences category including family members of skilled workers.

Source: See Table II.12 in UN Department of Economic & Social Affairs, **World Economic and Social Survey 2004 International Migration**, New York, which cites OECD's SOPEMI as source.

The last three columns of Table 1 show that immigrant admissions progressively became more and more skilled, accounting for more than half of all admissions by 2001 in Australia, Canada, and New Zealand. In the case of the United Kingdom their share of annual admissions almost quintupled from 7 to 32 percent. For a more complete picture this table must be seen together with Table 2 which brings together data on admissions of temporary workers under skill-based categories. While the percentage share of the skilled in US immigration has not risen despite large absolute increases in numbers, the growth of admissions under temporary schemes shown in Table 2 has been huge. Much of the growth has been due to temporary admissions under H-1B visas. In 2000 the US accounted for over 56 percent of admissions to these countries under similar temporary schemes. The difference between France and the UK, as well as with the other immigration countries, is particularly notable.

The construction of a more complete picture of movements still awaits improvements in data collection and comparability of concepts used. For those countries which have more detailed information it is clear that trends already indicate sharp rises in numbers even over the short period of one decade. It may however be true that growth is largely concentrated in some areas. The limitations on globally comparable data are just too severe to allow a more complete assessment of trends. It is not unlikely however that what is happening in migration at the global level is analogous to, but does not reflect, what is happening to global trade. The globalization of merchandise trade has not really been truly global – growth has been largely concentrated in the trade among the industrialized countries and between them and China and a handful of other newly industrialized economies (NIEs) in Asia and Latin America.

Table 2   Temporary workers admitted under skill-based categories, selected countries, 1992-2000

Country	Thousands				
	1992	1997	1998	1999	2000
Australia	41	82	93	100	116
Canada	70	75	80	85	94
New Zealand		27	30	39	48
United States*	143		343	423	505
France	5	5	4	6	8
United Kingdom	54	80	89	98	124

* Number of admissions under H-1B visas, not the number of persons

Source: Table II.13 in UN Department of Economic & Social Affairs, **World Economic and Social Survey 2004 International Migration**, New York. The UN cited as source OECD's SOPEMI report *Trends in International Migration, annual Report* 1992-2001 and 2003 Editions and US Department of Homeland Security, Office of Immigration Statistics (2003).

What do we know about the direction of these growing movements of people? Are movements largely related to flows of trade and direct foreign investments and thus involve largely north-north and north-south movements? Since much of the world's least developed regions have very little share of the global markets for goods and capital, one would in theory expect them to supply more labour in general, and of the unskilled variety in particular. But how are these regions participating in the global market for the highly-skilled?

The largest flows of the highly-skilled appear to be between and among the developed countries, that is to say, among the EU countries and between the EU and North America. However, as a percentage of their work forces these movements do not appear very significant because they have large educated and skilled work forces to start with. Where the movements become very significant in terms of the origin work force is in the small developing countries. Although admittedly fragmentary, the available evidence tends to suggest that the origins of highly skilled migration include many of the world's least developed countries (LDCs). This has justified concerns about "brain drain" and reopened the debate about its consequences on the ability of LDCs to catch up.

The most complete and the most up to date estimates on the educational attainment of those reported in the 2000 round of censuses as foreign-born in 29 OECD countries were recently reported by OECD (Dumont and Lemaitre, 2005).[2] In the 29 OECD countries some 36.3 million persons (46 percent of the total foreign-born populations) come from another OECD country. Some 6.4 million or 17.6 percent are reported to have tertiary level of education but the proportions vary greatly from one country to another. The UK has 3.3 million expatriates in other OECD countries and among them 1.26 million (or 41 percent) are tertiary education graduates. Germany has 2.93 million expatriates in other OECD countries and of these 865,255 (or 30.4 percent) are tertiary education graduates. The US has a smaller number of expatriates in OECD countries, some 809,540, and among them half are tertiary education graduates. The other countries with large populations of tertiary educated expatriates in OECD countries are Canada (417,750), Mexico (472,784), France (348,432), Poland (328,058), Italy (300,631), and Japan (281,664). Those with small percentages of tertiary education graduates are Mexico (only 5.6 percent), Turkey (6.4 percent), and Portugal (6.7 percent).

Origin countries outside the OECD account for almost 47 million of the total number of the foreign-born in the OECD region. The biggest communities originate from the former USSR, former Yugoslavia, India, the Philippines, China, Vietnam, Morocco, and Puerto Rico. According to the OECD study, the former USSR accounted for the largest expatriate

---

[2] Dumont, Jean-Christophe and Lemaitre, Georges (2005) "Counting immigrants and expatriates in OECD countries: A New Perspective".

community with tertiary level education with 1.3 million, followed by India with 1 million.

Other studies and indicators provide further insights into what is happening in the movement of the highly skilled. It was for example estimated that about 80 percent of global admissions under the category of intra-company transferees take place among members of the OECD. In a Trans-Atlantic Round Table on High Skilled Migration in 2001 in Brussels it was cited that some 83,000 scientists and engineers left Europe for the US during the 1990s. Still another study reported that the UK accounted for 32 percent of foreign trained physicians in Canada and 39 percent of those in Australia.

Statistics are very scanty on south-south movements of the highly-skilled although it is often assumed that the flows are also significant, and especially so in regions where some agreement already exist on free movement for purposes of employment. In the Caribbean the CARICOM accord provides for the free movement for employment of university graduates. Similar selectivity of concessions on free movement is provided for in the protocols to regional cooperation agreements in the Andean countries, in MERCOSUR, and in ECOWAS in West Africa. Anecdotal evidence also indicates that south-north movements like flows of African doctors and nurses have triggered secondary south-south movements to make up for emerging shortages including from other regions (e.g. Cuban doctors in South Africa).

In sum, what we find is rapid growth of volumes and spread of the migration of the highly-skilled. The statistics available indicate that north-north flows have risen but lacking comparable statistics for developing countries we are unable to say where growth has been stronger. How closely movements relate to the other drivers of globalization like trade in goods and services, or direct foreign investments still remain to be answered. However it is already clear that whereas the poorest countries participate very little in the global growth of trade and investments, they appear to have a bigger stake in the flows of the highly skilled.

Approaches to attracting skills

What is an optimal policy for a country seeking to use immigration as a means to meet supply deficits for the highly-skilled? Are some governments pursuing optimal policies by introducing employer-driven schemes for attracting the world's best trained professionals? Given the known positive externalities that come from inflows of human capital to what extent should states facilitate and even subsidize such forms of immigration?

In the following we briefly survey how states are presently addressing the question of how to attract foreign skills. The approaches adopted by countries to attract foreign skills can be broadly distinguished from each other according to their objectives.

a. *Human capital* approach: associated with the traditional immigration countries particularly Canada, it aims to enrich a country's stock of skilled human resources over the long term. It typically provides the prospect of permanent residence as an incentive, together with the right to full mobility in the labour market and eventually naturalization when one acquires all social and political rights enjoyed by citizens. Countries differ on how they translate the approach into specific admission policies or programmes or in the criteria used for deciding on admissions, with some adopting transparent criteria that allocate specific points for various human capital characteristics, others specifying the need for applicants with "extraordinary abilities" in certain fields, and still others leaving the matter to administrative discretion of immigration authorities.

b. *Labour-market needs* approach: the most common adopted, it aims to provide a solution to cyclical shortages for skills in the labour market by the temporary admission of foreign workers with the requisite experience and qualifications. While countries differ on whether employers or the government determines needs and how much flexibility they offer for adjusting length of stay, the common element in this approach is the time-bound character of the admission, without settlement of the worker and his or her family envisaged. Most Asian labour-receiving countries view the issue only from this standpoint, and see the need for the option to repatriate foreign workers when unemployment rises.

c. *Business incentives* approach: is one aimed at encouraging trade and foreign investments by facilitating the entry and stay of investors, executives and managers, including their family members. Some countries have offered permanent residence status to investors who bring in a minimum amount of capital and employ a certain number of workers, but most countries simply offer facilitated temporary admission.

d. *Academic-gate* approach: is one aimed at drawing talents from the pool of foreign students graduating from local educational institutions and encouraging them to stay and work or do research. This is seldom formally stated as a policy but some countries notably the United States have been very successful in tapping into this rich pool of self-selected talents, most having done undergraduate schooling in their origin countries but completed PhDs in American universities.

These are not mutually exclusive approaches as many countries already have diverse portfolio of policies, but differences lie in the importance they attach to each approach. The traditional countries of immigration, in particular Canada and Australia, have adopted preference schemes which attach explicit value to human capital, but over the last decade they have also experimented with using immigration to attract financial investments.

What may be optimal policies depend on the benefits states seek to maximize. If the objective is to satisfy *labour market needs* it would be necessary to cap admissions at levels that do not cause displacement or unemployment in any particular occupation. Even here there are complications because 'needs" are not evenly distributed throughout geographic space. In Canada, some isolated communities in the north are very short of medical doctors and nurses, but not so in the big metropolitan centers like Toronto. On the other hand it will be more difficult to use other criteria like wage stability for setting caps on admissions. If the objective is to build up human capital stock, how does one use wages as a criterion for establishing a supply deficit?

From restrictions to facilitation

The growing competition for the highly skilled has brought about a rethinking of the way foreign worker policies should be administered. The main change appears to be a shift away from simply easing restrictions (referred to as facilitation) to one of offering incentives (i.e. lower income taxes). Since most countries started with restrictions – quotas on sectors, occupations or firms, short duration of work permits, labour market certification, minimum salaries, restrictions on changing employers, restrictions on employment of spouses, limits to extension of permits, obligation to return before change of status, language skills, etc. – the first steps to reform is to remove the restrictions. Hence today one sees that more and more countries are exempting the highly-skilled from various forms of such restrictions. A popular one is that of doing away with labour market tests or certifications and leaving the policy to be driven by employers. Another is giving the spouses of skilled workers equal access to the jobs market.

In response to industry pressures the US Congress, towards the end of 1998, passed the "American Competitiveness and Work Force Improvement Act" which provided a provisional increase in the number of H-1B visas from 65,000 to 115,000 per year in 1999 and 2000. It made H-1B visas fully portable meaning that workers may switch employers as soon as a new employer files a petition with the Immigration and Naturalization Service (INS).[3] The former law necessitated the approval of a petition before a worker could change employers. The new law allows H-1B workers to stay beyond 6 years if their green card applications have been under "process" for at least a year. One year extensions may be granted until the employment visa is approved and adjustment of status is final. It also raised the training fee levied on employers from US $500 to US $1000 which go to support the programmes of the Department of Labor and National Science Foundation on education and training for native born students and workers.

In 1998 Germany started a series of reforms to its immigration laws and regulations which included exemptions of foreign managers and specialists (who are not European Union citizens) in the employ of a multinational corporation operating in Germany from the requirement of prior labour-market tests. In 2000 Germany introduced its *Greencard Scheme* which required certain high standards for education and credentials or a salary offer of DM 100'000 (Euro 51,000) or more. The scheme has not attracted the number of applicants expected and has since been widely considered a failure. In the same year France passed a law that established the new categories of "scientist visa" and "scientist resident". An applicant must obtain a "protocol d'accueil" (welcome protocol) from an accredited French institution which must guarantee that it will cover the social insurance of the applicant during his or her period of stay. Once such a protocol is obtained the formal process of obtaining a visa is limited to a medical examination. Canada has defined 7 areas where workers are particularly needed and provided blanket labour certification for all who qualified. It also allowed spouses of "strategic" workers to work without labour certification. Canada has lost through emigration many of its qualified citizens to the US. To tempt them to return, the Government at one time exempted returnees from paying income taxes for three years, but the policy has since been changed because of suspicion that the policy actually encouraged people to work south of the border for a while to avail of the tax exemption later.

---

[3] As of 1 March 2003, the INS was abolished and its functions and units incorporated into a new Department of Homeland Security (DHS).

Incentives and active recruitment

The use of incentives rather than simply easing restrictions is still new and recent, and may also reflect the relative attractiveness of a country vis-à-vis other candidate destinations for the highly skilled. Norway introduced a novel scheme in 2002 which gave foreign specialists or skilled workers a "job seekers permit" valid for three months to come to Norway to look for work. The Province of Quebec in Canada is presently offering five-year income tax holidays (credits) to attract foreign academics in health sciences to teach in the province's universities. In some Scandinavian countries where long established welfare systems are supported by relatively high rates of income taxes, reduced income tax rates are now being offered to foreign specialists.

Active international recruitment especially by state bodies is another strategy for getting a steady supply of highly skilled workers. In November 2000 the UK and Spain signed an Inter-Governmental Agreement for the recruitment of Spanish nurses, and this was later expanded to include Associate Specialists and General Practitioners (GPs). The UK today targets specific countries including Switzerland, Italy, Greece, Bulgaria and India in its recruitment programme using similar inter-governmental agreements.

Other incentives offered by countries are to facilitate integration of the skilled workers through such means as recognition of their professional qualifications, and individualized language learning assistance for the workers and their family members. In France, the *Fondation National Alfred Kastler* assists foreign scientists to adjust to everyday life.

An optimal policy?

What is required for an optimal policy aimed at building human capital is more difficult to assess. If inflows of human capital have positive externalities, what should determine the level of admissions that would maximize benefits?

These issues assume concrete form when policies are translated into programmes. For example, Singapore has a blueprint for bringing the country into the 21st Century through the development of high tech industries. The problem is that 40 percent of its workforce still has less than secondary education. The Government has already set a target to bring up the current ratio of scientists and engineers per 10,000 workforce (currently estimated at 66) up to comparable levels elsewhere like 98 for Japan and 74 for the US. For the life sciences alone the Government has already set aside a S$ 60 million Life Sciences Manpower Development Fund. The Government nevertheless still foresees the need to bring in foreign research scientists.

Academic gates to pool foreign talent

Some countries notably, the US, the UK and France, have made good use of their established reputation as centres for higher education and research to attract the world's best and brightest. The advantages to such a strategy are evident. First is the lower cost of entering the labour market. Foreign students and scholars constitute a substantial pool of current and prospective highly skilled migrants, and are self-selected. They would already possess the language skills to qualify as students. Secondly, foreign graduate students, unlike native graduate students with better work opportunities, provide a ready supply of cheap research assistants. And to top it all, many foreign students in North America and the Pacific are made to pay the full cost of their education and hence provide universities with an additional source of finance.

Table 3 below shows the density of foreign students enrolled in OECD countries. It shows that many European countries have high ratios of foreign to total student population. However, foreign students tend to be concentrated in large numbers in only a few countries. It has been estimated that 80 percent of all foreign students in the OECD countries go to only five countries (the US, UK, Germany, France, and Australia).

Table 3 Density of foreign students in selected countries

Country	Foreign students per 1000 enrolled students	Country	Foreign students per 1000 enrolled students
Australia	125.9	Japan	6.0
Austria	114.9	Korea	1.0
Belgium	40.1	New Zealand	36.7
Canada	27.9	Norway	31.6
Denmark	60.1	Switzerland	159.5
France	73.0	United Kingdom	108.1
Germany	81.6	United States	32.4
Italy	12.4	OECD mean	60.3

Source: See Table II.2 in SOPEMI Trends in International Migration 2001, OECD, Paris.

Countries are endeavoring now to encourage the best foreign graduates to stay and work through various adjustments in their student visa regulations. It is now possible for students to change their student visas to work permits in countries like Australia (may even apply on-line), Canada, France, Ireland, Japan, Korea (up to maximum of 3 years), New Zealand (added points if the qualification is gained in New Zealand), Czech Republic, Switzerland and the US. Some countries have been offering loans and subsidies to finance the completion of graduate studies by the more promising candidates. Understandably, study abroad is rapidly becoming a precursor to migration. In the US the National Science Foundation reported that 88 percent of Chinese PhD recipients were still in the US five years after they graduated. There are however interesting differences. Among the Korean PhD graduates only 11 percent have stayed.

Attracting skills at different levels of policy-making

Christian makes a useful distinction among three levels of policy-making on immigration: at the level of the nation-state, regional accords, and a multilateral treaty regime.[4] Each level is not necessarily separate from another since a policy independently adopted by a state may at a later time be adopted by others in the context of regional agreements or multilateral treaties. A national policy may, for instance, be adopted because of an obligation to harmonize policies under regional agreements like NAFTA or CARICOM, or because of commitments to multilateral treaty regimes. In the European Union, member states can still pursue their respective independent admission policies for third country nationals as for example Germany's "green card" programme, even as they bind themselves to allow free movement within their territories of citizens of other member states. And they may at the same time be signatories to a multilateral regime like the General Agreement on Trade in Services (GATS) which aims to liberalize the movement of service providers including professionals from all state parties. Today, individual states typically engage in policy making at all three levels simultaneously as more and more states are signatories to regional treaties and to GATS.

Mobility of the highly skilled under regional trade agreements

There are today a number of regional accords which have a significant impact on reducing the barriers to the free movement of labour, especially the highly skilled, across national borders. The movement of

---

[4] Bryan P. Christian "Facilitating High Skilled Migration to Advanced Industrial Countries: Comparative Policies" Institute for the Study of International Migration, Georgetown University, Washington, D.C.

Table 4   Provisions for the highly skilled in selected regional accords

	Coverage	Key provisions	Support programmes and limitations
European Union			EURES – employment services Exchange programmes
NAFTA	Business visitors Traders & investors ICTs Professionals		
AFTA (Asean Free Trade Area)	Trade in services as in Mode 4	ASEAN members committed to negotiate freer movement of capital, skilled labour and professionals, and technlogy	
ANZCERTA		Full market access, national treatment Must be viewed together with "Trans Tasman Travel Arrangement" which provides for free movement for work	
COMESA (Common Market for Eastern & Southern Africa)	Broad based treaty establishing by 2025 full monetary union and free movement of goods, services, capital and labour	Interim protocol on gradual elimination of visa requirements and a protocol on the free movement of labour, services, and right of establishment	
CARICOM (Caribbean Community)		Freedom of travel and exercise of profession; no need for work permits (Protocol II Establishment, Services, Capital 1998) National treatment guaranteed	Government may limit coverage to protect public morals, public order and national security.

Sources: Bryan Paul Christian "Facilitating High-Skilled Migration to Advanced Industrial Countries: Comparative Policies" Institute for the Study of International Migration, Georgetown University, 13 March 2000.

Nielson, J. "Current regimes for temporary movement of service providers: Labour mobility in regional trade agreements", paper presented at Joint WTO-World Bank Symposium on Movement of Natural Persons (Mode IV) under the GATS, Geneva, April 2002.

The Australian Chamber of Commerce & Industry "Advancing the Liberalization of Trade in Services: Enhancing GATS Mode 4 the Movement of Natural Persons" Nov. 2002.

labour is approached in a wide variety of ways. Table 4 provides a brief on some regional accords, their coverage, key terms of agreement regarding the movement of workers, and supporting programmes as well as limitations. Of these the most developed in terms of free movement of labour are those of the European Union and the lesser-known Australia New Zealand Closer Economic Relations (ANZCERTA). By obliging states to follow and observe treaty commitments some, though not all, of these regional treaties do impinge on state rights to regulate entry and stay of individuals and to unilaterally change policies on admission and treatment of nationals of other state parties. However the more general situation is where treaties still provide considerable scope for state parties to regulate access to employment and the conditions of employment.

Table 4 above shows that some agreements cover the mobility of labour in general, while others are limited to facilitated movements for certain kinds of trades or under certain investment-related activities. Note that the right to free movement of people does not always automatically entail a right to provide specific services. According to Nielson these different approaches reflect a "…range of factors including the degree of geographical proximity of the parties and the extent of similarities in their levels of development, as well as other cultural and historical ties." More liberal approaches would seem to depend on geographical proximity and similarity in level of development.

A multilateral framework for policy-making (GATS trade in services)

The GATS agreement from the Uruguay Round represents the first multilateral and legally enforceable agreement on the international trade in services. Its central objective is the progressive liberalization of trade in services which is seen by many developing countries as a promising avenue for expanding exports where they have some comparative advantage. They have particularly in mind Mode IV on the provision of services through the movement of natural persons, in other words workers. Table 5 below illustrates how GATS provides a multilateral framework for policy making on the movements of the highly skilled.

Up to the time of this writing commitments of countries to GATS Mode IV have been little different from what the countries already offer under different schemes to facilitate the movement of executives and managers, specialists, engineers and other skilled service providers. The developing countries have not succeeded in getting further commitments

Table 5   Example of multilateral framework: GATS

Key elements	Principles	Present status
General concepts (Part I) obligations and disciplines (Part II)	States must guarantee market access and national treatment; Most-favoured nation treatment (MFN); Transparency; Progressive liberalization.	Majority of commitments simply confirm status quo, or guarantee only some form of minimum trading rights. Market access and national treatment defined on a sector by sector basis.
Schedules of specific commitments (Part III)	Horizontal Sector-specific Obligations in all services – business, communication, construction and engineering, distribution, educational, environmental, financial health-related and social, tourism and travel related recreational, cultural and sporting, transport; – and modes of supply.	
Modes of service delivery	I Cross-border supply II Consumption abroad III Commercial presence	
	General migration laws - outside GATS Labour market regulations – under GATS but not access to labour market	
		Definitions – Senior executives? Length of stay allowed Economic need / labour market test?

Sources: Bryan P. Christian "Facilitating High Skilled Migration to Advanced Industrial Countries: Comparative Policies" Institute for the Study of International Migration, Georgetown University, Washington, D.C.
The Australian Chamber of Commerce & Industry "Advancing the Liberalization of Trade in Services: Enhancing GATS Mode 4 the Movement of Natural Persons" Nov. 2002.

from the advanced countries to liberalize admission of less skilled service providers.

The commitments of the EU, the US, Canada, and Australia with respect to admission of skilled migrants under GATS are shown in Table 6. The developed countries have more commitments in GATS under Mode I (cross-border supply), Mode II (consumption in the territory of the supplier), and Mode III (commercial presence abroad); while developing countries, notably the Philippines, Thailand, China and Brunei, have more commitments to liberalization under Mode IV (the delivery of services abroad).

Table 6   Categories of skilled entrants under the GATS

Country/Region	Business visitors	Intra-company transferees	Professionals	
EU	90 days	Variable	90 days	Professionals engaged on a contractual basis in 16 fields; some countries require labour market test
Canada	90 days	3 years	90 days	Professionals limited to legal, urban planners, senior computer specialists
Australia	6 months	Variable	2-4 years	Specialists (subject to labour market test)
United States	90 days	5 years	90 days	B-1 for business -visitors; L-1 for ICTs. H-1B for professionals (US Congress set "floor" of 65,000)

Source: Table 1 in Bryan P. Christian "Facilitating High Skilled Migration to Advanced Industrial Countries: Comparative Policies" Institute for the Study of International Migration, Georgetown University, Washington, D.C.

In brief, the GATS framework provides no guaranteed access for Mode IV suppliers. Its added value is to transform the policies countries are already pursuing with respect to facilitating admissions of the highly skilled into multilateral commitments. By and large Mode IV allows countries to keep or impose restrictions, and by itself contains no specific provisions for facilitated entry.

Consequences of highly-skilled migration

The increasing mobility of workers has rekindled interest in its consequences on growth and development of host and origin countries. There are political and social consequences that are also only recently receiving some attention. In the case of the migration of the highly skilled there is already considerable consensus on the positive growth effects of additional human capital on receiving countries. The consequences for income distribution are also deemed largely favorable as it leads to a narrowing of real income gaps. The increased supply of the highly skilled components of the work force reduces or slows down the growth of their nominal wages while increased productivity in the production of goods consumed by lower skill workers lead to lower prices.

However, for analogous reasons, there is still some concern about its net effects on source or origin countries. There are many consequences which have been postulated, most importantly the problem of brain drain, but migration research as a whole is still very fragmentary and lacks a firm statistical base. Annex Table A illustrates how different measures of brain drain can lead to sharp differences in the list of countries affected. Most countries do not monitor the departure of their citizens, let alone record their qualifications. The notoriously poor quality of data on remittances, for instance, has weakened attempts to assess the overall impact of emigration on growth. With respect to the developmental consequences, the more recent controversy centers around the fact that while source countries may lose human capital, migration on the other hand also has beneficial consequences in the form of knowledge gained and transferred and significant remittances from broad. There is still little consensus on whether the highly skilled have a higher propensity to remit their savings compared to the less skilled. By and large the issues are not ones of weak conceptual models but the lack of solid empirical evidence.

While it is not our intention to go over a well-trodden path, it may be useful to consider those questions regarding consequences on origin countries on which there is still little agreement in the literature.

- *What constitutes a brain drain?* In the brain drain controversy there is an implicit assumption that countries are likely to be permanently damaged by loss of their educated citizens. Under what conditions will this hold true? Once assumptions of autarchy in the supply of skills is removed, the degree of vulnerability changes. Even poor countries seem to import foreign personnel from other low-wage countries.

- *Impact on GDP growth* The expectation is that GDP growth will be negatively affected because the emigration of the highly skilled depletes an origin country's stock of human capital. However development performance of origin countries seems not to be linked to levels of skilled emigration. Is the expectation of negative impact unwarranted?

- *Impact on trade*   To what extent has the loss of human capital undermined the potential of source countries to develop comparative advantage in high tech industries? Again, this expected consequence needs closer evaluation since countries that have suffered from brain drain like Chile, Mexico, the Philippines, Argentina and Costa Rica have been successful in shifting from traditional to more sophisticated industrial products.

- *Impact on investments in education*   It has been hypothesized that the possibility of emigrating to higher wage countries stimulate individuals to invest in higher education in anticipation of bigger returns. What is the evidence that this hypothesis is supported by experience? If the hypothesis is valid, is there an "optimal level of emigration" that stimulates the pursuit of higher education in developing countries?

- *Diaspora investments*   As high income earners highly skilled workers should have higher savings rates and may even be investors themselves. Because of this some governments have launched programmes like offering *matching* grants to encourage their nationals abroad to invest more in their home countries and communities. On the other hand they are also likely to become permanent residents in countries where they are employed. Under what conditions are they more likely to invest?

- *Technology and knowledge transfer*   Backward linkages to countries of origin can increase the available knowledge and technology that boost productivity. Have source countries actually benefited from such knowledge transfers? Does transfer involve permanent return?

Annex Table A **Countries or areas experiencing brain drain according to different reports**

A Adams (2003) a	B Carrington and Detragiache (1998) b	C Bein, Docquier and Rapoport (2002)
Dominican Republic	Dominican Republic	Argentina
El Salvado	El Salvador	Bolivia
Guatemala	Fiji	Chile
Jamaica	Gambia	Costa Rica
Mexico	Ghana	Dominican Republic
Philippines	Guatemala	Ecuador
Sri Lanka	Guyana	El Salvador
Tunisia	Honduras	Guyana
Turkey	Iran	Jamaica
	Jamaica	Mexico
	Kenya	Nicaragua
	Mexico	Panama
	Nicaragua	Peru
	Panama	Philippines
	Sierra Leone	Republic of Korea
	Taiwan Prov of China	Thailand
	Trinidad & Tobago	Trinidad & Tobago
	Uganda	Uruguay
		Venezuela

ª R.H. Adams, Jr. (2003) under the assumption that the migration of more than 10 percent of the tertiary educated population from a country causes brain drain.

ᵇ Classification based on the 10 percent benchmark applied by Adams.

References

Adams, R.H., 2003. International Migration, Remittances and Brain Drain: Study of 24 Labor Exporting Countries. World Bank Policy Research Working Paper, No.3069, April, Washington, D.C.

Alburo, Florian and Danilo Abella, 2001. "Brain Drain from the Philippines", International Migration Papers, ILO Geneva.

Barro, Robert and Xavier Sala-I-Martin, 1995. *Economic Growth*, New York: McGraw-Hill.

Beleva, Iskra and Mariana Kotzeva, 2001. "Bulgaria: Country Study on International Skilled Migration," Bulgarian Academy of Sciences and University of National and World Economy in Sofia.

Beine, Michel, Frederic Docquier, and Hillel Rapoport, 1999. "Brain Drain and Economic Growth: Theory and Evidence", Seminaire par l'Axe éthique et développement durable du Centre d'Economie et d'Ethique pour l'Environnement et le Développement, Université de Versailles St Quentin en Yvelines (http://www.cybercable.tm.fr/~jarmah/public_html/Hrapoport11.htm).

Bertelsmann Foundation, 2000. *Migration in the New Millennium: Recommendations of the Transatlantic Learning Community*, Gütersloh: Bertelsmann Foundation Publishers.

Bhagwati, Jagdish and Koichi Hamada, 1973. "The Brain Drain, International Integration of Markets for Professionals and Unemployment: A Theoretical Analysis," *Journal of Development Economics*, 1, 19-42.

Bhorat, Haroon, Jean-Baptiste Meyer and Cecil Mlatsheni, 2001. "International Skilled Migration: The Case of South and Southern Africa", Development Policy Research Unit, School of Economics, University of Cape Town, South Africa.

Carrington, William J. and Enrica Detragiache, 1998. "How Big is the Brain Drain?" A Working Paper of the International Monetary Fund. Washington, D.C.

Chang, Howard F., 1997. "Liberalized Migration as Free Trade: Economic Welfare and the Optimal Immigration Policy". *University of Pennsylvania Law Review* 145 (May): 1147-244.

Christian, Bryan Paul, 2000. "Facilitating High-Skilled Migration to Advanced Industrial Countries: Comparative Policies" Institute for the Study of International Migration, Georgetown University, 13 March.

Docquier, F. and Rapoport, H. "Skilled migration: the perspective of developing countries" Mimeo, The World Bank.

Dumont, Jean-Christophe and Lemaitre, Georges, 2005. "Counting immigrants and expatriates in OECD countries: a new perspective", OECD Social, Employment and Migration Working Papers No. 25, Paris, OECD.

Findlay, Allan M., 2001a. "From Brain Exchange to Brain Gain: Policy Implications for the UK of Recent Trends in Skilled Migration from Developing Countries," University of Dundee.

— 2001b. "Policy Proposals Relating to the Impacts on Developing Countries of GATS Negotiations over the Temporary Movement of Natural Persons," University of Dundee.

Haque, Nadeem Ul and M. Ali Kahn, 1997. "Institutional Development: Skill Transference Through a Reversal of 'Human Capital Flight' or Technical Assistance," Working Paper of the International Monetary Fund, July.

Haque, Nadeem Ul and Se-Jik Kim, 1995. "Human Capital Flight: Impact of Migration on Income and Growth," *IMF Staff Papers*, 42(3), 577-607.

ILO (International Labour Organization), 1997. *Protecting the Most Vulnerable of Today's Migrant Workers: Tripartite Meeting of Experts on Future ILO Activities in the Field of Migration*, ILO: Geneva, http://www.ilo.org/public/english/90travai/migrant/papers/protvul/index.htm.

Khadria, Binod, 2001. "India: Country Study - Skilled Labour Migration (the 'Brain Drain') from India: Impact and Policies," Jawaharlal Nehru University, New Delhi.

Korale, Raja B. M., 2001. "Skilled Labour Migration (the 'Brain Drain') from Developing Countries: Sri Lanka Case Study," Colombo.

Lowell, B. Lindsay, 2001a. "Policy Responses to the International Mobility of High Skilled Labor," Georgetown University.

— 2001b. "Some Developmental Effects of the International Migration of the Highly Skilled," Georgetown University.

Martin, Philip L., 1990. "Labor Migration and Economic Development," pages 647-664 in Commission for the Study of International Migration and Cooperative Economic Development, 1990. *Unauthorized Migration: Addressing the Root Causes. Research Addendum, Volume II.* Washington, D.C.

Mountford, A., 1997. "Can a Brain Drain be Good for Growth in the Source Economy?" *Journal of Development Economics*, 53(2), 287-303.

Nielson, J., 2002. "Current regimes for temporary movement of service providers: Labour mobility in regional trade agreements". Paper presented at Joint WTO-World Bank Symposium on Movement of Natural Persons (Mode IV) under the GATS, Geneva, April.

OECD, 2001. *Trends in International Migration 2000.* Paris: OECD.

OECD, *International Migration of Physicians and Nurses: Causes, Consequences and Health Policy Implications*, DELSA/ELSA/WP1/WKF (2002)3.

Pellegrino, Adela, 2001. "Skilled Labour Migration from Argentina and Uruguay," Centro Latinoamericano de Demografia.

Puris, Shivani and Tineke Rizema, 1999. "Migrant Worker Remittances, Micro-Finance and the Informal Economy: Prospects and Issues". International Labour Organization, Working Paper 21.

Rothboeck, S., V. Vijaybhaskar and V. Gayathri, 2001. "Labour in the New Economy". *Background paper for the World Employment Report*, ILO, Geneva.

Salt, John and Allan Findlay, 1989. "International Migration of Highly-Skilled Manpower: Theoretical and Developmental Issues", pages 159-180 in Reginald Appleyard (ed.), *The Impact of International Migration on Developing Countries*, Paris: OECD Publications.

Stalker, P., 2000. *Workers Without Frontiers: The Impact of Globalization on International Development*, Geneva: International Labour Office.

Staubhaar, Thomas, 2000. "International Mobility of the Highly Skilled: Brain Gain, Brain Drain or Brain Exchange", HWWA Discussion Paper No. 88, Hamburg, ISSN 1432-4458.

Straubhaar, T. and A. Wolter, 1997. "Globalization, Internal Labour Markets and the Migration of the Highly Skilled." *Intereconomics*, 32(4): 174-180.

Thomas-Hope, Elizabeth, 2001. "Skilled Labour Migration from Developing Countries: The Caribbean Case", University of the West Indies.

Wickramasekara, P., 2003. "Policy responses to skilled migration: retention, return, and circulation", Perspectives on Labour Migration, ILO, Geneva.

Wong, Kar Yiu and Chong Kee Yip, 1999. "Education, Growth, and Brain Drain", *Journal of Economic Dynamics and Control*, 23(5-6): 699-726.

Students and talent flow – the case of Europe: From castle to harbour?

Christiane Kuptsch

Introduction

Today, students have incentives to move across borders for at least part of their studies. In a "knowledge economy" (World Bank, 1999) muscle to work land or shovel coal becomes less and less important whereas abilities such as quickly adapting to new production processes or being able to communicate with people from other linguistic and cultural backgrounds are increasingly valued. Adaptability and innovation require knowledge. Demand for higher education is likely to increase as people will want to succeed in the knowledge economy and education acquired in different contexts can be expected to be valued particularly highly with the internationalization of production and increased cross-border trade.

Flows of students exist in all directions, from one advanced to another advanced country, from developing to advanced countries, etc. Figure 1 summarizes the different possibilities and some of the policy issues involved.

Figure 1   Possible flows and policy issues

From \ To	Advanced countries (ACs)	Developing countries (DCs) *(including countries in transition)*
Advanced countries	– competition for talent	– main flows likely within specifically designed (exchange) programmes
Developing countries *(including countries in transition)*	– competition among ACs for these flows – "brain drain" for developing countries	– flows from lesser to more developed DCs – cooperation between DCs to avoid "brain drain" to ACs ("economies of scale")

This paper will highlight only one type of flow, namely the one from developing and transition countries to advanced countries and it will focus on Europe as destination. The host country perspective will be analysed and the brain drain question for developing countries left aside.

Evidence will essentially be drawn from recent developments in France, Germany and the United Kingdom as the three largest recipients of foreign students in Europe (see Table 1). In addition, the paper will analyse the latest changes at the level of the European Union, i.e. report on proposals that have been made by the European Commission and review recent European Council Directives concerning students and long-term residents who are third-country nationals.

Table 1   Foreign students in selected European countries ("top ten"), 2001

	Foreign students	Share of foreign students
Austria	31,682	12.0 %
Belgium	38,150	10.6 %
France	147,402	7.3 %
Germany	199,132	9.6 %
Italy	29,228	1.6 %
Netherlands	16,589	3.3 %
Spain	39,944	2.2 %
Sweden	26,304	7.3 %
Switzerland	27,765	17.0 %
UK	225,722	10.9 %
Big 3	572,256	
Top 10	781,918	
Total Europe	856,733	

Source: OECD, 2004, Table 3.2.

Data on foreign students in Europe must be interpreted with care. On the one hand, many European countries do not include as foreign students those enrolled in programmes that last less than one year. Exchange students who pay fees to institutions in their home countries fall in this category and those enrolled in a branch of the home university located abroad. On the other hand, in countries such as France, Germany and Switzerland, one has to distinguish between (a) students who hold foreign passports but who received their schooling in the host country and whose presence is based on legal grounds other than education, often family ties ("educational inlanders"); and (b) students who entered the country for strictly educational purposes, whose legal title to stay in the country is linked to their studies ("educational foreigners") (Kuptsch, 2003). During the winter semester 2000/2001, some 187,000 foreign students were registered in institutions of higher learning in Germany. Of them 32.8% were graduates of German high schools, i.e. "educational inlanders" (Isserstedt/Schnitzer, 2002, p. 5). France also has about one third of its foreign students falling into the category of "inlanders" (Gisti, 2000, p. 5). In Swiss universities, 12,192 "educational foreigners" and 5,714 foreign nationals who had gone to school in Switzerland were registered in 1997/98; 13,981 (5,377) in 2000/01; and 16,446 (5,594) in 2002/03 (Office fédéral de la statistique, mai 2003).

What essentially interests us in this paper are foreign students who came as migrants and not those who were residents prior to their higher education. Therefore, we will use data on "educational foreigners" wherever possible and when using the term "foreign students", it is to this category that we refer if not otherwise specified.

The above OECD table refers to *all* students with a foreign passport, no matter where they received their primary and secondary education. Britain, France and Germany would however also be the three largest recipients of foreign students in terms of numbers if one looked at "educational foreigners" exclusively.

The run for foreign students: some evidence and reasons

While Europe is concerned with brain drain to other advanced countries, in particular to the United States, and has encouraged intra-European flows of students, the greatest concern in the recent past has been to open the doors of Europe's institutions of higher learning to students from the developing world, including transition countries.

As the International Centre for Migration Policy Development (ICMPD) has pointed out, all governments of the European Union (EU) were in principle happy to receive foreign students because they wished to establish or improve political or economic relations with the countries of origin. Belgium, France, Portugal, Spain and the UK maintained their relation as former colonial powers through a considerable intake of students from the former colonies, while countries like Austria, Denmark, Finland, Germany and Sweden largely provided access to their study facilities for persons from transition countries in Central and Eastern Europe to intensify the relationship with these nations (ICMPD, 2000, p. 6).

In the late 1990s Germany embarked on an active policy of attracting foreign students, as part of a package of measures designed to strengthen Germany's economic competitiveness. Policy documents now spoke of "internationalizing studies in Germany" and no longer of "being international" as a general feature of science. In October 2000, representatives from business, academia and political parties launched a campaign to promote Germany world-wide as a centre for science and education (*"Konzertierte Aktion internationales Marketing für den Bildungs- und Forschungsstandort Deutschland"*) [1] (Isserstedt/Schnitzer, 2002, p. 11).

In the United Kingdom, a worldwide campaign to augment the number of overseas students was launched in 1999. Prime Minister Tony Blair announced to the press that he had set a target of attracting 75,000 extra students to the UK by 2005. He hoped to foster this by streamlining visa arrangements; providing better and more accessible information to potential students; and making it easier to combine study with work (Press Notice 1999/0278).

In January 2000, the French government announced that it would like to double the number of visas delivered to foreign students; and the Ministry of National Education expressed the hope that in the long run about 20% of the students in higher education in France would come from abroad (Gisti, 2000, p. 5). [2]

There was thus a clear desire by the German, French and UK governments to attract foreign students.

Expanded efforts to recruit foreign students are also reflected in official websites that serve as a portal to higher education opportunities in particular countries, such as www.edufrance.fr/ for France, www.daad.de and http://campus-germany.de/ for Germany, www.studyinsweden.se for Sweden and www.hero.ac.uk as well as www.educationuk.org for the United Kingdom. Most of these sites focus on the opportunities and costs of studying in the country and highlight particular advantages. For example, the Swedish site points out that Sweden is a "safe and modern country" where "innovation and creativity run deep" and "standards are high", a country that offers choice with "over 200 master's programmes in English" and where "education is free". Some sites also emphasize that foreign students may work while they study and after they graduate. "And because it costs to live in Sweden, foreign students can work while studying" (www.studyinsweden.se).

---

[1] This initiative also included the establishment of offshore universities (e.g. the German University Cairo), an innovative move for Germany.

[2] It is not clear whether this statement about the long-run referred to all students with a foreign passport or to only those who had done their schooling abroad.

The European Commission also took steps and tabled a proposal in October 2002 for a *Council Directive on the conditions of entry and residence of third-country nationals for the purpose of studies, vocational training or voluntary service.*[3] It wished to promote the Member States together as a world centre of excellence for education, to create synergy and possibly economies of scale. In the explanatory memorandum that accompanied the proposal, the Commission put forward that "welcoming large numbers of third-country nationals to Europe's educational establishments, especially at master's and doctorate levels, can have a beneficial effect on the quality and dynamism of Europe's own training systems. Establishments will have an incentive to develop more and more high quality courses meeting the demand for internationalisation in education and for greater student mobility" (EC, 2002, Explanatory memorandum, p. 3).

Where the cost of providing training is not recuperated by fees that the students have to pay, States make considerable investments on which they may have little or no direct return when they allow foreigners to study in their universities. According to the German Federal Statistical Office, in 2000 Germany spent about 1.06 billion Euros to finance the studies of people from developing and transition countries, 68.7% of which were allocated for students who had received their schooling outside of Germany (educational foreigners). When only looking at the cost of studies with developmental relevance according to OECD guidelines, i.e. when not taking into account the cost of studies in languages, cultural sciences, arts and sports, the total cost amounted to approximately 0.57 billion Euros, of which 77.9% was spent for newly arrived students with foreign nationalities (Kultusministerkonferenz, 2003, p. 26-29). The French government supports higher education, for French and foreign nationals alike, by about 6,000 Euros per student per year (http://www.edufrance.fr/en/a-etudier/etudes02-6.htm).

Students cost; they also pay little or no taxes. However, in a 2001 work on student mobility, the OECD pointed out that the growing internationalization of educational systems clearly had beneficial effects for the host countries. One had to take into account not only the larger educational offer thanks to rising numbers of students but also the foreign students' contribution to domestic demand. Possibly, foreign students even created a more flexible domestic labour force as more people studied in an international environment (OECD, 2001, p. 112, 113).

---

[3] The content of the final Council Directive will be discussed below, under "Europe's future".

Besides the reasons given by the European Commission (more dynamism and better quality education) and the OECD (increased educational offers and positive effects on domestic markets for labour, goods and services), there are several others why governments and institutions in Europe have encouraged the arrival of non-European students. There are cultural, commercial and economic reasons, as well as considerations related to development policy (development assistance) and migration policy. For obvious reasons, foreign policy concerns appear to be less pronounced than during Cold War years.[4]

Having students participate in programmes that involve study in another country can promote mutual understanding. Many governments assume that exposure to their country's people and institutions will influence foreign students who return to think favourably about their former host country and lead to commercial links through the students' use of products and working methods from the host country. Where former students become politically active in their country of origin, this has the potential of fostering foreign policy ties.

Host countries are also interested in generating revenues for educational institutions via this form of export of educational services. In Europe such considerations are particularly relevant for countries where university fees are higher for foreign than domestic students. Many European countries offer "free" higher education and countries such as Denmark, Germany, Norway and Sweden do not charge tuition to domestic or foreign students. Other countries require students to pay at least some fees, but do not charge foreign students more than domestic students, including France, Italy and Spain. Finally, some countries such as Austria, the Netherlands, Switzerland and the UK require all students to pay tuition and fees, and charge foreign students more than local students.[5]

In official discourse, development policy considerations are also an important reason for encouraging students from developing countries to study in Europe. The return of students who studied abroad can be a

---

[4] In a publication of 2004 that analyses the internationalization of higher education worldwide, the OECD distinguishes between four different approaches to cross-border post-secondary education: the *mutual understanding* approach that encompasses political, cultural, academic and development aid goals; the *capacity building* approach that encourages the use of post-secondary education as a quick way to build an emerging country's capacities; the *revenue generating* approach that offers higher education services on a full-fee basis without public subsidies; and the *skilled migration* approach that emphasizes the recruitment of selected international students and tries to attract talented students to work the host country. The OECD study does not limit itself to the flow of students. It defines cross-border education as three-fold: persons going abroad for educational purposes (people mobility) – the category that we look at here; educational programmes going abroad (programme mobility) and institutions or providers investing abroad (institution mobility). Internationalisation and Trade in Higher Education – Opportunities and Challenges, OECD 2004.

[5] For a classification of other, including non-European countries see OECD 2004, table 1.2, p. 26.

powerful means of development assistance by rapidly building up the local human capital stock in the country of origin.

When proposing the Council Directive on students from non-Member States, the European Commission was careful to emphasize that making it easier for foreign students to study in the EU should not aggravate the South-North brain drain. One would need to seek partnerships with the countries of origin; and the proposed Directive fitted into the strategy of stepping up cooperation with developing and transition countries (EC, 2002, Explanatory memorandum, p. 3). In France, the Cohen report, submitted to the Ministries of National Education and Foreign Affairs in 2001 titled "Action plan to improve the acceptance of foreign students in France", warned that neither competition with other countries nor development cooperation ("international solidarity") should be made the single goal of France's educational policy (Cohen, 2001). In a similar vein, the German government proclaimed that besides a better competitive position in the international "run for brains" in a knowledge economy, increased numbers of foreign students would be a means of cultural policy as well as an instrument of development cooperation and European integration.

Europe thus strives to attain different objectives simultaneously when bringing in students from developing countries. One final reason is of particular interest in the context of competition for global talent: to attract skilled students who may become skilled immigrants.

Students' migration as probationary immigration and the interest in students as qualified immigrants

Leaving considerations of equity such as the brain drain issue aside, one may assume that it would make sense for advanced countries to attract highly skilled persons as immigrants for whose education the host countries have not paid. Why is it then that advanced countries take a particular interest in foreign students as potential immigrants? Is this a rational choice?

According to structuration theory, one has to look at the information gathering processes involved in coming to a rational decision. Years of studies provide an excellent occasion and sufficient time for both the foreign student and the host country to probe the other.

Students can gather information on the host country during their study years, on incomes, job opportunities, working and living conditions as well as "psychic income" such as climate, scenery and other non-quantifiable factors.

Host country authorities, in turn, can gather information on the potential immigrant. Security considerations are high on the agenda for host countries these days. Students convicted for committing crimes, who were members of forbidden associations or engaged in activities that run counter the host country's constitution, etc. stand small chances of becoming accepted as a migrant for employment after graduation – if they are allowed to stay that long. The authorities can also decide to let only those people join their society who successfully terminated their studies or let those students stay longer. Most educational systems have built-in tests as for the latter: students, including domestic ones, can only pursue higher (such as doctoral) studies if they obtained a certain average on their exams.

To study successfully in the host country usually requires mastering the local language. From the perspective of linguistic ability, foreigners who studied in the host country are therefore on average a safer bet for host country employers than newcomers to the country. The same will hold true in respect of knowledge about working methods, work ethics, etc. Have datelines to be taken "dead serious"? What is the right tone for speaking with colleagues, superiors, clients, etc.? While newcomers might rapidly grasp the rules of society and the workplace, students who have been in the host country for several years can be expected to already have acquired this type of social knowledge and competence.

Social competence and linguistic skills also help where an adaptation to new employer demands is needed or an adjustment to changing labour market conditions. Where changes in the long run can be expected, foreign students who wished to remain in the host country after graduation and were allowed to do so for having shown willingness and signs of integration and adaptation will therefore be more appealing than highly skilled migrants who were admitted to the host country for the purpose of fulfilling one particular job. Indeed, in most contexts, foreign students do not fall in the category of "unwanted immigrants". Initially, they are socially acceptable because they come for a temporary stay and do not compete on the labour market where they "take away" jobs from the local population. Their success in finding employment after graduation is then often indicative of their adaptation to the rules of the host country society – so that they remain socially acceptable.

The fact that they hold a host country degree is an advantage for the students in finding a job in their host country. But in addition to making them attractive for host country employers as employees (employers know what they are "buying into"), the degree also makes them attractive for host country authorities as immigrants. The problem of educational equivalencies across borders does not exist in relation to host country students. This problem of transfer and recognition of credits and diplomas between countries often results in professional immigrants taking jobs for which they are over-trained and in their deskilling over time, a situation to the detriment of both the migrant and the host society which cannot benefit fully from the additional human capital that it imported.

For host countries, students can also be more attractive than other highly skilled migrants from the perspective of retaining "brains". For advanced countries that are convinced that human capital will support economic growth and competitiveness, the retention of talent becomes a serious issue. Brain gain that is short term is not enough, and brain drain of both local talent as well as freshly gained foreign talent has to be avoided or minimized. While the return of highly skilled migrants to their country of origin might be desirable from the perspective of that country's development, return may be viewed differently by the host country that attracted the migrant in the first place.

There are reasons to believe that, on average, people who undertook their studies in the host country and then stayed on will be less inclined to return to their country of origin then others. A 2004 Massey University study that looked at New Zealanders abroad found differences in values/motivation between people intending to return and those attracted to remain overseas. The potential returnees put great emphasis on family and friendship, whereas those inclined to stay abroad had high values for achievement and influence (http://masseynews.massey.ac.nz/2004/Press_Releases/05_27_04.html). Study years are an important phase in life for building friendships and relations and for some people these are also the years for starting families of their own. Family and friendship-oriented people among the student migrants are likely to have developed personal attachments in the host country. They have, therefore, fewer incentives to return to the country of origin than family and friendship-oriented people among the general population of highly skilled migrants who built their personal ties before moving to the host country. Admittedly, cultural dimensions also play a role in this respect. Care for elderly parents back home may be a "must". There may be pre-arranged marriages with partners who remained in the country of origin. Or there may be pressures to marry among one's own cultural/ethnic group. [6] Where the latter is the case and a student meets someone from their group in the

---

[6] Every second Turkish woman in Germany, for example, got married to a man who was chosen by her family and not herself (Kelek, 2005, p. 31-37).

host country and there are no other obligations or attachments, the "retention via personal ties" argument holds again. Incentives to go back would lie essentially in economic opportunities in the home country.

Institutional settings and the flow of students – How to attract foreign students? Policy options for host countries

The above reflections make it clear that retention is linked to institutional settings in the host country (in a wide sense of the term "institution", i.e. including sets of rules and regulations), for example, the question of whether a student can bring their spouse or parents. The students' decision to come to a particular country in the first place is equally influenced by the institutional framework of the potential host country.

Obviously, a student's decision to study abroad and his/her choice of destination depend on a multitude of monetary and non-monetary factors beyond institutional settings.[7] However, host country governments have no control over the geographical location, climate or scenery of their country or push factors such as lacking accessibility to or a narrow range of post-secondary studies in the students' countries of origin. The OECD cautions that, while tuition fees play a significant role for students, cost aspects should not be overestimated either and points to the Nordic countries where tuition fees are low or non-existent but which do not receive large numbers of foreign students (OECD, 2004, p. 30, 31). Host countries, therefore, will have to watch institutional settings that they can shape if they look for options of attracting and retaining foreign talent.

Issues such as a country's academic structure and technical business issues are central to its ability to gain talent and retain it, as are labour market regulations and migration policy.

Academic attractiveness tends to be related to the culture and history of a country and is more country specific. The academic issues often result from the internal structures and local traditions of universities and other establishments. For example, UK universities are known to enjoy a high degree of autonomy in their hiring policies and make larger use of temporary academic staff than their counterparts in France and Germany where academic career structures are highly regulated (Mahroum, 2003,

---

[7] The OECD provides a comprehensive list of the most important student rationales for moving abroad and choice of destination. See Internationalisation and Trade in Higher Education – Opportunities and Challenges, OECD 2004, p. 30.

Figure 2 Summary of institutional issues

Academic issues	Business issues	Immigration legislation	Labour market regulations (in conjunction with migration policy)
Is the host country's research community sufficiently "internationalized" to pull talent from overseas? Do local institutions of higher learning appear as "centres of excellence"?	Are there financial rewards and career returns that attract people? How efficient are a country's marketing campaigns?	How difficult is it for a student to enter the country? Can family members join and, if yes, when?	Are students allowed to work in parallel to their studies? How difficult is it for students to stay after graduation and have access to the labour market?

p. 1). The roles played by institutions of higher learning in countries' national innovation systems and academia-industry mobility are also crucial, e.g. in shaping career prospects.

The perception of what constitutes a problem or the major problem in each country influences the policies that governments implement. Is a country seeing itself as lagging behind with "internationalization"? Should it provide easier access for students to its labour market to pull talent? Countries may work on only one of the above issues specifically or on several or all issues.

European countries have opted for multi-pronged approaches as the following evidence from France, Germany and the United Kingdom will show.

Recent developments and regulations in France, Germany and the United Kingdom

Marketing

We have already noted that all three countries, France, Germany and the UK, launched marketing campaigns to attract foreign students, using for example the internet. The German government works with business and academia and stresses Germany's combination of old traditions with modern technologies, its strengths both in theory and practical application (http://campus-germany.de/english/1.5.35.html). The UK emphasizes possibilities for students to work (http://www.dfes.

gov.uk/international-students/wituk.shtml), and France advertises its tradition of non discrimination in underlining that no distinction is made between French and international students. "Under French law, the requirements for admission are the same, as are the degrees awarded. The country that coined the phrase human rights rejects all forms of discrimination." (http://www.edufrance.fr/en/a-etudier/choisir02.htm).

In November 1998, the French Ministries of National Education and Foreign Affairs, together with the Ministry of Culture and Communication and the State Secretariat of Foreign Trade, established the *EduFrance Agency* with the task of promoting French higher education abroad (*Journal officiel de la République Française*, 22 November 1998). Among other things, EduFrance organizes education fairs abroad and has 40 offices worldwide to offer information and advice to potential students and help them with their applications to French institutions of higher learning.

For purposes of helping students with their applications to German universities, the German Academic Exchange Service (DAAD) and the Conference of Deans (Hochschulrektorenkonferenz – HRK) founded the "Application Services for International Students (*uni-assist*)" which began operations at over 50 universities in May 2004. *Uni-assist*, offers the opportunity to apply for admission to several universities with only *one* set of documents. *Uni-assist* pre-checks all documents to make sure that they are complete and fulfill all necessary formal requirements before they are forwarded to the universities concerned. Applicants are charged 50 Euros for the first application and 10 Euros for each additional application.[8] From February 2005 *uni-assist* will offer international applicants the option of submitting their applications online (http://www.uni-assist.de/english/index.html).

France and Germany as non-English speaking countries, more than the United Kingdom, have felt the need to assist potential students with their applications. As part of their marketing campaigns, all three countries made available additional scholarships for foreign students. For example, in the UK the *Chevening* programme currently provides around 2,300 new scholarships each year for postgraduate studies or research at UK institutions of higher education. These scholarships, funded by the Foreign and Commonwealth Office and administered by the British Council, are offered in over 150 countries (http://www.chevening.com/).

---

[8] The service is less expensive for EU nationals: 25 and 10 Euros respectively.

"Internationalization" of studies

"Internationalization" and academic harmonization across the world has meant for many countries "anglophying" local academic systems. In Europe this was formalized in the 1999 Bologna Declaration that sets out an agenda for the future harmonization of structures of higher learning (Mahroum, 2003, p. 4). Initially signed by 29 European Ministers of Education, the Bologna process counted 40 members following a 2003 ministerial meeting in Berlin (OECD, 2004, p. 96).

France and Germany have created numerous new university programmes in English language and now offer bachelor and master programmes. For Germany the introduction of the BA degree was a small revolution as students traditionally received only one university degree after completion of their entire period of higher education. Traditionally, students in Germany worked towards the equivalent of their MA or PhD from the first day that they enrolled in university. In the winter semester 2000/2001 Germany had more than 280 BA and over 150 MA degree programmes (http://campus-germany.de/english/1.40.168.html).

Germany also reserves a certain number of study places in restricted admissions disciplines such as medicine and pharmacology for international applicants (www.daad.de). Certain curricula are so popular that there are not enough study places throughout the country. All students are then subject to a selection process in which the average marks obtained in the "Abitur" or the equivalent foreign school leaving certificate determine admission. This quota for foreign students is clearly indicative of the country's determination to internationalize its offer of higher education. It has the potential of creating agitation among German candidates who are not admitted but would have been were it not for their foreign counterparts.

Entering the host country

In France, students from outside Europe (that is students from countries other than the European Economic Area[9], plus Andorra, Monaco, San Marino, Switzerland and the Vatican) must obtain a visa. After the first year of study, visas are automatically renewed, provided the student is able to produce the required documentation. On *EduFrance's* website, students are warned that if they plan to complete two programmes in succession (such as a programme in French as a foreign

---

[9] The European Economic Area (EEA) comprises the countries of the European Union and Iceland, Liechtenstein and Norway.

language, followed by an academic programme), admission to both programmes should be obtained before applying for a visa so that their visa would be valid for the entire duration of studies. French visas cannot be extended in France.

All non-European students must obtain a residence permit, including people who need no visa. International students who intend to study in France for more than three months are required to see the local *préfecture* (government centre) within two months after their arrival to obtain a temporary residence permit showing their student status. This permit is valid until the expiration date of the applicant's passport or until the date of completion of the applicant's academic programme, whichever comes first. The permit must be renewed annually.

In Germany students from outside the European Union have to apply for a visa with the exception of nationals from Australia, Canada, Honduras, Israel, Japan, Monaco, New Zealand, San Marino, Switzerland and the United States. Three types of visa exist for international students: (1) a language course visa which cannot be subsequently converted into a student visa and is valid only for the duration of the course; (2) a three-month study applicant's visa for people who have not yet obtained university admission. After admission, it must be converted as quickly as possible into a resident permit for student purposes at the office for foreigners' affairs; and (3) the regular visa for study purposes, valid for one year. For the latter the student has to provide proof of university admission and financial resources for the duration of study.

On 1 January 2005 Germany's new Immigration Act came into force and certain procedures were facilitated for students. An internal approval process of the authorities replaced the previously used dual approval procedure for work and residence permits. Students now benefit from a one-stop procedure: a possible work permit will be issued by the foreigners' authority concurrently with the residence permit, provided the employment authorities have agreed to this.

The United Kingdom, more than France and Germany, advertises easy entry to the country, and has indeed amended visa regulations for students and introduced service targets for processing visa applications. For example, the targets for dealing with straightforward and non-straightforward student visa applications are 24 hours and 10 working days respectively. International students can expect to have a decision made on a straightforward application to extend or change their permit ("leave" in UK terminology) within two weeks of receipt by the Home Office's unit which initially considers the case. Moreover, partnership arrangements between Visa Sections and the British Council have been introduced in some countries where large numbers of student applications are received. These are to ensure that students submit properly documented applications which can be processed quickly. Such arrangements are in place in New Delhi, Islamabad and Beijing and there are plans to introduce them in Moscow, Istanbul and Bangkok.

When an international student applies for a visa or seeks entry to the UK, the Entry Clearance Officer and/or Immigration Officer will need to be satisfied that the student can afford to support him/herself and any dependants without recourse to public funds. The Government has introduced a new facility whereby earnings from any guaranteed part-time work at a publicly funded institution of further or higher education in the UK at which the student will be studying will be taken into account when the student's financial means are assessed. [10]

Employment during studies

Increasingly there is recognition everywhere in Europe that foreign students might need to work to finance their studies, the same as nationals do.

International students in France have the right to work if they hold a residency permit and are enrolled in an institution that participates in the student health plan of the French social protection system (*Sécurité Sociale*). French law allows international students to work no more than 884 hours in a given year which translates into 19.5 hours per week during the academic year and full-time employment during vacations.

Before the entry into force of the new German Immigration Act foreign students were allowed to take on a limited amount of paid employment without having to obtain a work permit, namely a maximum of 90 days per year up to 4 hours per day. The new law made the "90 days per year"-rule more flexible. Students can now also work for 180 half-days without a work permit. [11] As for jobs in relation to university work such as positions as assistants at university or other scientific or research institutions, these can be taken on without time limits. Any activities that extend beyond this continue to be dependent on approval by the employment authorities.

Largely publicized as part of their campaign to attract foreign students, the UK has eased restrictions on international students taking paid employment since 1999. Foreign students who are not nationals of a

---

[10] For more details see: http://www.dfes.gov.uk/international-students/vaetuk.shtml

[11] In practice this was often allowed even before the introduction of the new rule. http://www.daad.de/deutschland/en/2.2.1.17.html

European Economic Area (EEA) country, and who have in their passports a stamp prohibiting them from working "without the consent of the Secretary of State", have no longer been required to obtain the Secretary of State for Education and Employment's permission on an individual basis for work during studies. This means that they no longer had to apply to their local job centre or to the Overseas Labour Service in order to: take vacation and spare time work; undertake a work placement with an employer which is part of their course of study ("sandwich students") or undertake a paid internship. There were no changes to the conditions applying to the hours and types of work that students may undertake. These are: (1) the student should not work for more than 20 hours per week during term time, except where the placement is a necessary part of their studies and is undertaken with the education institution's agreement; (2) the student should not engage in business, self employment or provide services as a professional sportsperson or entertainer and (3) the student should not pursue a career by filling a permanent full-time vacancy.

In 2004 the government also proposed to make it easier for the dependants of foreign students to work by linking a dependant's entitlement to work to the student's permit. If the international student is granted leave of 12 months or more then a dependant will be permitted to work, irrespective of the length of their own grant or leave. [12]

Employment after studies – from student to worker status

In the past, the change from student to worker status has been difficult in European countries. The criteria have changed for specific students.

In 1998, France announced that foreign students holding a French IT degree would now be able to change their status from student to worker, no longer subject to a labour market test. [13] In 2002 students "presenting a technological and commercial interest to French enterprises" received the same privilege. [14]

Similarly, even before the entry into force of the new Immigration Act, foreign students in Germany could change their residence concession (*Aufenthaltsbewilligung*) for the purpose of studies into a concession for employment, provided they found employment as a "scientifically

---

[12] For more details see http://www.dfes.gov.uk/international-students/wituk.shtml

[13] See Ministerial circular DPM/DM 2-3/98/429 of 16 July 1998.

[14] See Ministerial circular DPM/DMI 2 2002/25 of 15 January 2002.

qualified person". [15] The new law consolidated this in stating that where in justified individual cases a public interest exists in the employment of a qualified person, a residence permit may be issued for the purpose of employment (§ 18, IV AufenthG / Article 18, IV Residence Act).

Particularly successful students may also be able to benefit from the fact that highly qualified migrants in Germany now have immediate access to settlement permits. For example, high-ranking academics, researchers and teaching staff will be among the target group (www. daad.de). The settlement permit automatically entitles the holder to take up gainful employment and cannot be made subject to any additional conditions.

What is more, foreign students may now stay up to one year after graduation to search employment in Germany. Previously, most non-EU students had to leave within 90 days.

The UK, too, has made it easier for international students to remain in the UK for a short period after the end of their course. Students who took courses of 12 months or more will now be given permission to remain in the UK until 31 October following the end of their course. This is to enable them to "consider whether to progress to a further level of study in the UK, arrange training or work experience with an UK employer ... or simply to say goodbye..." (www.dfes.gov.uk). Similar to the people under the Highly Skilled Migrant Programme [16], students are offered the opportunity to be free agents in the labour market for some time after their graduation.

Scotland, with economic indicators below UK average, has reached an agreement with the Home Office which allows overseas graduates from Scottish universities, who express the intention of living and working in Scotland, to stay on for two years beyond the October date. Students will be allowed to seek any type of job in Scotland and they can switch into work permit employment or other legal migration routes for which they may qualify during or after the two years. The scheme will be in operation from summer 2005. Since October 2004 Scotland also seeks to attract foreign students through a scholarship scheme that combines a

---

[15] With the new Immigration Act, the previous five titles of residence were reduced to two, a short-term residence permit (*befristete Aufenthaltserlaubnis*) and a settlement permit (*unbefristete Niederlassungserlaubnis*).

[16] The Highly Skilled Migrant Programme (HSMP) is a scheme launched in 2002 which seeks to attract individuals with exceptional personal skills and experience. This programme represents a major departure from others UK schemes since no prior offer of employment is necessary and it is the migrant and not the employer who is the applicant. Successful applicants are free agents in the labour market for one year. An elaborate point system scores applicants.

year of post-graduate study with a year of work experience (Scottish Executive, 2004, p. 12, 13).

The UK government also highlights opportunities for foreign students to take up employment in the UK after completion of their studies under the Training and Work Experience Scheme (TWES). The TWES is a special arrangement within the work permit scheme that allows people to do work-based training for a professional or specialist qualification, a graduate training programme or to undertake work experience. Permit applications are made by employers. Employers name a person to do specific training or work experience with them on a full-time basis. The person (student) cannot use the permit for different work experience/training or to work for a different employer.

Promotional measures with effect: rising numbers of foreign students

In the UK the number of foreign students has tripled since 1990 (OECD, 2004, p. 21). The continuing upward trend can be illustrated by the fact that some 369,000 students were admitted to the UK in 2002, 9% more than in 2001. There were considerable rises in the number of students especially from the Indian sub-continent and the rest of Asia while the number of students from Europe and Oceania decreased between 2001 and 2002. More information on the trend since the late 1990s is provided in Table 2. The numbers exclude nationals of the European Economic Area (the EU plus Iceland, Liechtenstein, and Norway) as well as dependants.

Table 2   Admissions of students to the UK, 1998 – 2002

	1998	1999	2000	2001	2002
All nationalities of which:	266,210	272,330	321,500	339,195	368,795
Europe	71,510	62,340	69,820	75,320	74,985
Americas	82,800	87,530	99,115	98,985	101,040
Africa	16,400	17,920	20,325	25,165	27,625
Indian sub-continent	7,805	8,505	10,375	14,650	20,575
Rest of Asia	84,340	92,515	109,955	121,725	141,060
Oceania	1,885	1,995	2,015	2,390	2,320
Other nationalities	1,460	1,530	900	960	1,190

Source: Dudley, Turner & Woollacoot, 2003, table 2.3, p. 22.

In France, the number of student visas doubled between 1997 and 2000, reaching 46,000; and went up another 25% in only 12 months, for a total of 58,000 visas delivered in 2001.[17] In comparing the numbers for 2000 and 2001, the *Groupe permanent du Haut conseil à l'intégration chargé des statistiques*[18] found that 13.3% more Asians, 12.9% more Africans and 24.1% more nationals from the Maghreb requested and received student visas. At the same time, there was a decrease in students originating from countries of the European Union that were registered in France (Groupe permanent, 2002). In referring to all students with foreign passports, the Ministry of Foreign Affairs reported over 180,400 persons enrolled in French universities in 2003, which represented an increase of 13% over the previous year. Prior increases had been as follows: 6% from 1999 to 2000, 9.5% from 2000 to 2001 and 12.6% from 2001 to 2002 (http://www.diplomatie.gouv.fr/ education/etudiants_etrangers/). The marked difference between the increase in student visa delivery from 2000 to 2001 (25%) and the increase in total number of foreign students (9.5%) indicates that growth rates are more pronounced for "educational foreigners" than "educational inlanders" in France.

The same trend can be observed in Germany. If we analyse changes in Germany between 1997 and 2000, we find that the number of "educational inlanders" went up by 12.1% whereas that of "educational foreigners" increased by 21.2% (Isserstedt/Schnitzer, 2002, p. 9). Data on changes between 1993 and 2001 which distinguish between 1st year students and all students enrolled also confirm the "internationalisation" of studies in Germany in the form of an increase in the number of foreign newcomers to the educational system. Increases in 1st year students were 103% for "educational foreigners", 17% for foreign students with schooling in Germany; and 15% for German students, and the respective changes for all students enrolled were 65%, 23% and –4% (Kultusministerkonferenz, 2003, p. 30).

From winter semester 1997/98 to winter semester 2000/2001, only 2.1% more foreign students with schooling outside of Germany came from EU countries, while the number of these students from Eastern and Central Europe increased by over 80% (80.7%; 1997: 15,371 students;

<hr>

[17] Lacking data for France that distinguishes between foreigners who are "educational inlanders", i.e. went to school in France, and others, student visas will be taken as indicator. Visa delivery says nothing as such about the number of foreign students present in a given country at a given moment but is indicative of a trend.

[18] Permanent Group on Statistics of the High Council for Integration.

51

2000: 27,776 students). More students also came from Africa (23.1%) as well as from Asia (22.3%) during the same time period. The increase of students from the Americas was more modest with about 5.6% (Isserstedt/Schnitzer, 2002, p. 5, 9).

Table 3   Foreign 1st year students ("educational foreigners") in Germany, 2001

Rank	Country of origin	Number
1	China	6,180
2	France	3,225
3	Poland	3,208
4	Bulgaria	2,678
5	Spain	2,625
6	Russian Federation	2,504
7	United States	2,363
8	Italy	2,274
9	Austria	1,553
10	Ukraine	1,393
11	United Kingdom	1,203
12	Hungary	1,089
13	Romania	1,057
14	Czech Republic	1,049
15	Turkey	976
16	Morocco	968
17	India	902
18	Cameroon	813
19	Greece	754
20	Dem. Rep. of Korea	692

Source: Kultusministerkonferenz, 2003, p. 34.

The above data show that France, Germany and the United Kingdom all have succeeded in attracting more and more foreign students to their educational systems and especially students from developing and transition countries.

More students but remaining labour market gaps?

It remains to be seen whether this increase in foreign students will also lead to filling labour market gaps. In 2001, more than half of the foreign students in France and Germany studied languages, cultural sciences, sports, law, economics and social sciences and no more than 20% subjects such as engineering, mathematics or natural sciences. The exact percentages and ranking of disciplines are shown in Table 4.

Table 4   Distribution of foreign students according to discipline, 2001

Germany			France		
1	languages and cultural sciences, incl. sports	27.6%	1	languages and cultural sciences	35%
2	law, economics and social sciences	25.6%	2	law (12%) and economics (18%)	30%
3	engineering	18.3%	3	sciences	20%
4	mathematics and natural sciences	16.9%			
5	arts	4.8%			
6	health	4.5%	4	health	10%
7	agriculture, forestry, nutrition	1.8%	5	other (IT, etc.)	4%

Source for Germany: Kultusministerkonferenz, 2003, p. 35.

Source for France: Coulon & Paivandi, 2003, table 5, p. 16. The figures for France refer to *all* foreign students, i.e. they include people with French primary and secondary education.

The UK government established that the country suffered from a shortage of physical science, engineering and mathematics students at university as well as skilled workers in these disciplines and launched the Science and Engineering Graduate Scheme (SEGS) in response. The scheme which became operative in October 2004 allows non-EEA nationals who have graduated from UK higher or further education establishments with good degrees (2.2 or higher) to remain in the UK for 12 months after graduation in order to pursue a career. Applicants must intend to work during the period of leave granted under the scheme and be able to maintain and accommodate themselves and any dependants without recourse to public funds. The scheme rules also provide that applicants must intend to leave the UK at the end of their stay, unless granted leave as a work permit holder, highly skilled migrant, business person or innovator.

Europe's future: Policy choices at European Union level

Students earning a long-term resident status

In many countries, regular migrants may demand the conversion of their temporary residence permit into a permanent or long-term resident status after a given period. Students, despite their regular status, have traditionally been excluded from this right almost everywhere. [19] However, it can be a powerful means of retaining and possibly also of attracting highly skilled migrants, including students, to give them a residence status that makes them equal to nationals in many respects and especially on the labour market. Such a status offers the migrant security and choice.

The European Commission apparently shared this opinion when proposing that periods as a student should count towards a long-term resident permit. In August 2001 the Commission tabled a draft Directive designed to grant an EU status of long-term resident to third country nationals who legally resided for five years in a Member State. Under this draft, students would earn a right to remain in the host country based on their student status.

Article 5 of the proposed Directive specified under letter (b) that periods of residence for study purposes should be taken into account fully where someone undertook studies towards a doctorate and as half only in all other cases. This latter provision is evidence of the Commission's conviction that the Union should give priority to granting settlement status to particularly qualified foreigners, including the students among them. This corresponds to what the OECD has identified as the "skilled migration approach" to cross-border secondary education. [20] Under this approach two classes of foreign students may develop, "brains" and "clients". The "brains" are the highly skilled, successful students, often at doctoral level or people with special skills, such as IT specialists. All others are "clients", those who bring fees to private institutions of higher learning or augment numbers in public establishments so that the educational offer might be upgraded and rendered more competitive. The stress is put on the "best" among the students and not everyone. The "clients" are supposed to leave after their temporary stay for educational purposes.

---

[19] See for example in France Ord. 45, art. 15, 12.

[20] See footnote 4 above.

"Putting down roots in a Member State is a sine qua non for acquiring the status provided for in the Directive", explained the European Commission (EC, 2001, Explanatory memorandum, p. 7). One does not see why a regular student should put down fewer roots than someone pursuing doctoral studies and apparently the distinction made between doctoral and other students seemed artificial also to the EU Member States. When *Council Directive 2003/109/EC on the status of third-country nationals who are long-term residents* was adopted on 25 November 2003[21], the distinction had disappeared.

What is more, whereas the Commission proposal automatically calculated years of study as counting towards the period necessary to acquire resident status (for doctoral students in full, for others in half), under the final Directive this is no longer the case. "Member States shall grant long-term resident status to third-country nationals who have resided legally and continuously within its territory for five years immediately prior to the submission of the relevant application" (Article 4). However, in Article 3 point 2. of the final Directive one can read "This Directive does not apply to third-country nationals who: (a) reside in order to pursue studies or vocational training". Under the Directive as adopted, student years are now only taken into account where someone subsequently acquired some other title of residence which enables him to be granted resident status. If this is the case, years of residence for study purposes (or vocational training) will count half towards the five years needed (article 4, point 2., sentence 2). A person who studied for six years in a Member State of the European Union and changed status after graduation as she found employment would be able to apply for a long-term resident status after two years in her job, and not five years as a foreign colleague without studies in the host country.

"Cautious" Council Directives

While this approach represents an improvement for foreign students in the EU over the provisions that existed in most Member States, the regulations that were adopted are not as radical a change as the initial Commission proposal. As concerns another Directive, one specifically on students and similar groups of people, the Commission's more "service-oriented" proposals did not either find consensus among EU Member States.

---

[21] It went into force one month later, on 23 January 2004. Member States must comply with the Directive by 23 January 2006 at the latest (Article 26).

Suffice it here to give one single example. Concerning the mobility of non EU-students within the Union, the Commission had proposed that where a third-country national already held a student residence permit in one Member State, a second Member State should issue a permit for its territory *within 30 days*, provided the student met the necessary conditions. *Council Directive 2004/114/EC of 13 December 2004 on the conditions of admission of third-country nationals for the purposes of studies, pupil exchange, unremunerated training or voluntary service* gives more leeway to the EU Member States and provides that the student should be admitted by the latter Member State "within a period that does not hamper the pursuit of the relevant studies, whilst leaving the competent authorities sufficient time to process the application" (Article 8).

The final Council Directive on students from third countries is also more oriented towards security issues than the proposal that the Commission had tabled in October 2002. Under point (14) of the preliminary considerations, it is clarified that admission can be refused on duly justified grounds, in particular if the non-EU student is regarded a potential threat to public policy or security. Member States have to assess the facts and the "notion of public policy and public security also cover cases in which a third-country national belongs or has belonged to an association which supports terrorism, supports or has supported such an association, or has or has had extremist aspirations".

Point (15) mentions the fight against abuse and misuse of the procedure set out in the Directive, a point missing from the Commission proposal. As for fees, Article 20 of the Council Directive simply provides that Member States may require applicants to pay fees for the processing of applications, whereas the draft Directive had specified that fees should not exceed the actual administrative costs incurred (Article 22 of the draft Directive).

Several elements of the final Directives, both on the long-term resident status and on the admission of students, are thus less favourable to foreign students than the proposals made by the European Commission. They may therefore have less of a potential to attract third country nationals to study in the EU and make them stay after graduation.

Council Directive on students: some highlights

Since the Council Directive on the admission of third-country nationals for the purposes of studies represents the frame for future policies on foreign students in the countries of the European Union, with the exception of the United Kingdom, Ireland and Denmark[22], we will highlight some of the Directive's main provisions.

General conditions for admission of a student are the following: valid travel documents; parental authorization for minors and sickness insurance coverage in respect of risks normally covered for nationals of the host Member State. The student must not be a threat to public policy and security or public health and provide proof that s/he paid the fee for processing the application, if the Member State so requests (Article 6). Students must have been accepted by an establishment of higher education to follow a course of study and provide evidence of sufficient resources to cover their subsistence. In addition they must show that they have paid the fees charged by the establishment and have sufficient knowledge of the language of the course that they intend to follow (Article 7).

Article 12 stipulates that a renewable residence permit shall be issued to the student for the period of at least one year, except where the course duration is less than a year. This permit may be withdrawn when a student does not make acceptable progress in his/her studies or does not respect the limits imposed on access to economic activities.

Indeed, the countries of the European Union agreed that students from third countries should be given access to the labour market to cover part of the cost of their studies (see point (18) of the Directive's preamble). The Directive's Article 17 even confers them a right, in using the term 'entitlement': "Students shall be entitled to be employed and may be entitled to exercise self-employed economic activity" (point 1.). However, this right is limited at the same time, with Article 17 also stating that the "situation of the labour market in the host Member State may be taken into account". In addition, access to economic activities may be restricted during the first year of studies (point 3.).

It will be up to the Member States to determine the maximum number of hours per week or days or months per year that the students can work but this must be no less than 10 hours per week or the equivalent of it (point 2.). In comparison, the situation as of 2000 in the countries of the EU is summarized in Figure 3 below.

As can be seen, the Directive's provisions on work outside study time give more options to foreign students than some of the previous national legislation. Where they are less favourable, the Directive has a safeguard clause in any case. Article 4 stipulates that the Directive shall

---

[22] These countries did not take part in the adoption of the Directive and are not bound by it or subject to its application. See points (25) and (26) of the preamble to the Directive.

be without prejudice to the right of Member States to adopt or maintain provisions that are more favourable to the persons to whom it applies.

Article 18 gives procedural guarantees to students such as where applications are turned down, possible redress procedures should be indicated as well as the time limit for taking action.

Finally, the Directive is careful to make a cross reference to the one on the long-term resident status of third-country nationals before pointing out that Member States, for the purpose of granting further rights under national law, are not obliged to take into account the time during which someone with a student status has resided in their territory (Article 24).

The Directive entered into force on 12 January 2005 and Member States have to comply with it by 12 January 2007 (Article 22). Only for the issuing of residence permits, do they have an additional grace period of two years, i.e. up to 2009 (Article 23).

Figure 3   European Union, 2000 – Employment regulations for students from third countries

Austria	employment not permitted
Belgium	up to 22 hours/week and during academic holidays
Denmark	during academic holidays; after 18 months residence: up to 15 hours/week
Finland	up to 20 hours/week and during academic holidays
France	half-time work permitted
Germany	up to a total annual period of 3 months; during holidays; other exceptions
Greece	employment not permitted
Ireland	employment not permitted
Italy	up to 20 hours/week for a max. total of 1,040 hours/year
Luxembourg	employment not permitted
Netherlands	up to 10 hours/week
Portugal	supplementary work permitted
Spain	employment not permitted
Sweden	during academic holidays
United Kingdom	up to 20 hours/week during term time and full time during vacations

Source: ICMPD, 2000, p.22

Conclusions

In our interpretation, the fact that the final European Council Directives were somewhat more cautious than the Commission proposals, more oriented towards security issues and offering a little less incentive for foreign students to come to the EU, stems from the nature of the actors and their respective roles in the international system. While it is in the interest of the Commission that more and more competencies go to the Union, States want to keep their prerogatives and especially maintain control over who enters and remains in their territories. The Commission would like to underline the EU's integration in global markets and strengthen its competitive edge no matter how, while the Member States still operate in a recruitment stop mode to some extent. After all, facilitating the entry of foreign students might clash with another policy objective that most European governments pursue today: to avoid the (permanent) immigration of unskilled workers. The student status could be used as a stepping stone to a stay for other purposes and in particular for low-skilled work. This, in the eyes of most European governments, must be prevented.

While European countries might pursue marketing campaigns, internationalize their educational systems and change national immigration and labour market regulations to attract foreign students, and do so successfully as this paper has shown, they remain cautious at the same time, as developments at EU level indicate. The policy towards foreign students in Europe of today touches upon three policy areas: migration policy, commercial policy and international development policy. It is influenced by at least three objectives:

- the desire to get ready for the "knowledge economy", competing for the pole position in the run for brains;

- a restrictive immigration policy when it comes to low-skilled workers; and

- helping countries of origin with the education of their nationals, in a gesture of international solidarity.

Under such conditions, a maximum position of openness can hardly be adopted and, indeed, the countries of the European Union will probe their foreign students before they make them immigrants. Those who find employment will see their study years credited.

"Castle Europe" has definitely opened up for foreign students but has not turned into "Harbour Europe" for the students of the world.

References

Cohen, Elie, 2001. "Un plan d'action pour améliorer l'accueil des étudiants étrangers en France – Diagnostic et propositions", Rapport au Ministre de l'éducation nationale et au Ministre des affaires étangères. 19 July.

Commission of the European Communities, 2001. "Proposal for a Council Directive concerning the status of third-country nationals who are long-term residents", Official Journal C 240 E, 28/08/2001 P.0079-0087.

Commission of the European Communities, 2002. "Proposal for a Council Directive on the conditions of entry and residence of third-country nationals for the purposes of studies, vocational training or voluntary service", COM (2002) 548 final – 2002/0242 (CNS), Brussels, 7.10.2002.

Coulon, Alain & Paivandi, Saeed, 2003. Les étudiants étrangers en France: l'état des savoirs. Rapport pour L'Observatoire national de la Vie Etudiante (OVE), Université de Paris 8, Centre de recherches sur l'enseignement supérieur, March.

Council Directive 2003/109/EC of 25 November 2003 on the status of third-country nationals who are long-term residents. Official Journal of the European Union L016, 23/01/2004, p. 44-53.

Council Directive 2004/114/EC of 13 December 2004 on the conditions of admission of third-country nationals for the purposes of studies, pupil exchange, unremunerated training or voluntary service. Official Journal of the European Union L375, 23/12/2004, p. 12-18.

Dudley, Jill; Turner, Gill & Woollacoot, Simon, 2003. Control of Immigration: Statistics United Kingdom, 2002. Home Office, National Statistics, August.

Gisti (groupe d'information et de soutien des immigrés), 2000. "Les droits des étudiants étrangers en France" (les cahier juridiques). September.

Groupe permanent du Haut conseil à l'intégration chargé des statistiques, 2002. Rapport pour l'année 2001. November.

ICMPD (International Centre for Migration Policy Development), 2000. "Study: Admission of third-country nationals to an EU member state for the purposes of study or vocational training and admission of persons not gainfully employed", carried out on behalf of the European Commission. Final report. August.

Isserstedt, Wolfgang and Schnitzer, Klaus, 2002. "Internationalisierung des Studiums – Ausländische Studierende in Deutschland, Deutsche Studierende im Ausland". Ergebnisse der 16. Sozialerhebung des Deutschen Studentenwerks (DSW) durchgeführt durch HIS Hochschul-Informations-System, Bonn, Bundesministerium für Bildung und Forschung.

Kelek, Necla, 2005. Jede zweite Türkin in einer Zwangsehe. Emma 1/2005, Januar/Februar, p. 31-37.

Kultusministerkonferenz, 2003. Studierende ausländischer Herkunft in Deutschland von 1993 bis 2001. Statistische Veröffentlichungen der Kultusministerkonferenz. Dokumentation Nr. 165 – Januar 2003. Bearbeitet im Sekretariat der Kultusministerkonferenz.

Kuptsch, Christiane, 2003. Foreign students in Europe: between red carpet and red card. Note prepared for the IILS/ILO workshop "Temporary migration – Assessment and practical proposals for overcoming protection gaps", Geneva, 18-19 September 2003.

Mahroum, Sami, 2003. Brain Gain, Brain Drain, an international overview. Background paper for the Austrian Ministry for Transport, Innovation and Technology (bmvit). Alpbach Technology Dialogue, 22-23 August 2003.

OECD, 2001. Trends in International Migration, Part II: "Student Mobility Between and Towards OECD Countries: A Comparative Analysis", Paris, OECD.

OECD, 2004. Internationalisation and Trade in Higher Education – Opportunities and Challenges, Paris, OECD.

Press Notice 1999/0278. "Tony Blair launches drive to attract overseas students to UK". 18 June 1999.

Scottish Executive, 2004. Attracting Fresh Talent to Meet the Challenge of Growth, Edinburgh, February.

World Bank, 1999. "Knowledge for Development" (World Development Report). Oxford University Press.

Part II: National perspectives

Brain strain and other social challenges arising from the UK's policy on attracting global talent

Allan M. Findlay

Introduction

The United Kingdom (UK) has come to recognize that highly skilled international migration is part of globalization, and that globalization is both inevitable and potentially desirable (Glover et al, 2001). To quote the UK prime minister, Tony Blair, "we have a chance in this century to achieve an open world, an open economy and an open global society with unprecedented opportunities for people and business." [1] Such "openness" in the arena of migration is however both hard to achieve and thoroughly problematic both from the perspective of a government that wishes to make "globalization work for the poor" (DFID, 2000) and from the perspective of the migrants who, as well as offering their talents to the host economy, wish access to the carefully guarded services and social infrastructure of the state.

Previous work (Findlay, 2002, Lowell et al 2004), some of it undertaken with colleagues at the International Labour Office, provides considerable empirical detail of the way in which the UK has shifted over a relatively short period from engaging in quite limited exchanges of highly skilled international migrants with other OECD countries to a position of becoming a major net recipient of international skills. The timing of change in the UK's migration regime seems to closely mirror the new migration policies introduced following the switch in 1997, from a right of centre Conservative government broadly opposed to labour immigration, to a centrist Labour government with a more positive perspective

---

[1] Tony Blair, Davos, January 2000.

towards recruiting global talent. Since 1997 the UK's position within the international migration system has been transformed (Figure 1). This has resulted in the growth of skill flows from many developing countries as well as an increased intensity of linkage with the labour markets of other developed economies. Some evidence of this switch from brain exchange to brain gain is included in this chapter, but attention also focuses on the social challenges that follow from pursuing a more positive immigration policy. These include provision of social rights to immigrants, many of whom neither enjoy nor seek UK citizenship, but who nevertheless need support in terms of access to a social infrastructure during their time in the country.

Figure 1   International migration flows to and from the United Kingdom

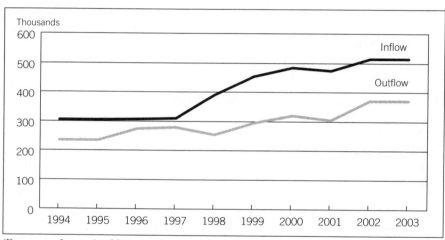

(Data source: International Passenger Survey, 1994-2003)

The paper is organized into three sections. The first section considers the literature relating to globalization and international skill exchanges as well as the neo-liberal mechanisms which deliver services to temporary migrants such as work permit holders and asylum seekers. The second section reviews the UK experience in competing for global talent relative to that of other economies. The third section asks how a state such as the UK, that espouses neo-liberal policies on most matters relating to provision of services to its own citizens, provides for migrants living within its borders.

Skilled migration, brain strain and differential citizenship

There is both an academic literature and a policy debate on talent migration that inform the material included in this paper. The academic literature has three main strands that merit attention here. First, there is the long-established tradition of economic researchers who view talent transfer from one economy to another as a net loss of investment by one state (Bhagwati and Hamada, 1973; Bundred and Levitt, 2000) to the benefit of another state that reaps the value added by deploying these skills within their economy. The assumption that inter-state talent transfers are an unambiguously negative phenomenon in economic terms has, however, been questioned by those who recognize that the global trade in goods and commodities often produces net benefits to both senders and receivers (Stalker, 2000).

Second, research on international skilled transient flows within large companies and between global cities (Salt and Findlay, 1989; Findlay 2001) led to a recognition that economic globalization required international brain exchanges to take place and that barriers to such skill movements could be damaging to states insisting on highly restrictive immigration policies. Some economists have produced evidence that there is an optimal level of talent emigration that should be sought in certain developing countries. This is on the basis that increased investment in education and training in relevant global skills take place if there is a probability that a proportion of a country's human resources may subsequently migrate to take up high salary jobs (Stark and Wang, 2002; Stark, 2003; Beine et al 2003). To date there have been very few studies to test the central hypothesis that emigration encourages more skill creation than skill loss. Lowell et al (2004) have suggested however that managed migration policies can ensure the "brain strain" associated with the global recruitment of talent can prevent international skill flows becoming a deleterious brain drain.

Third, a literature has emerged that suggests that population mobility should no longer be viewed through the modernist lenses of states and of populations "belonging" to "nation-states". Instead, transnationalism has emerged amongst diasporic networks of ethnically and culturally distinctive peoples (Cohen, 1997; Vertovec, 1999; Braziel and Mannur 2003). Talent embedded in these networks is often highly mobile and may not even be particularly visible because of the hetero-local nature of these populations (Zelisky, 2001). Nevertheless intense talent exchanges occur within these networks taking economic advantage of the global reach of diasporic groups.

Turning to the policy debate, it is interesting to note the curious contradictions of contemporary migration policy statements. At a time when European governments seem to be competing with each other to emphasise how firmly their borders are closed to so-called "bogus" asylum seekers, there also appears to be a new scramble to recruit highly skilled workers. Thus, while the electorate in most West European democracies are wooed with messages about the front door of the state being firmly bolted to clandestine migrants and unwanted entrants (Niessen, 2000), governments have performed a remarkable change of policy over the last ten years with regard to highly skilled migration (Dumont and Lemaitre, 2005). Promoting skilled immigration it has been argued is not only highly appropriate because of low levels of demographic growth, but more significantly it is a prerequisite to sustained economic growth in a competitive global economy. In these circumstances it is argued that any national economy needs to have attractive and flexible immigration policies to obtain the best global skills (Spencer, 2003). Critics campaign against such policies on diverse grounds. In the UK an oft-cited argument in the early 21st century has been that policies favouring global talent recruitment risk establishing uncontrolled immigration and an increased social burden on state provision, for example, in the national health service. Proponents have responded by promoting the idea that skilled migrants in the global economy are transient, spending relatively short periods of time in any one location before returning home or moving on to other niches in the global labour market.

Some of this policy debate can be captured from the public pronouncements on immigration made by British politicians. Consider, the words of Britain's former e-commerce minister, Patricia Hewitt. In the context of an IT recruitment fair in Bangalore, where delegates from Britain, the USA and Japan, inter alia, were seeking to recruit skilled Indian IT workers, she commented:

"Of course we've relaxed our immigration laws. We want to make it clear that Indians are welcome in Britian." (http://news.BBC.co.uk, 2000)

The relaxation to which she refers relates to the September 2000 statement by the then UK Immigration Minister, Barbara Roche:

"Britain has always been a nation of immigrants. ...It is British openness and tolerance, and migrants' ability to adapt and thrive, that I believe will help us to meet the challenges of the 21st century... The market for skilled migration is a global market - and not necessarily a buyer's market. ...The UK needs to have a policy that meets modern needs... it is important that we preserve and enhance the flexible and market-driven aspects of the current work permit system." (www. homeoffice.gov.uk, 2000)

These are not statements that one would have been likely to hear from UK government ministers in the early 1990s (Kleinman, 2003). Those defending the policy of the second Labour government led by Blair between 2001 and 2005, were quick to point to the safeguards attached to the government's approach to labour market "openness" within the global economy (Spencer, 2003). Following the re-election of Blair for a third term, the system of admittance came under scrutiny because of the politicization of immigration in the election with the Labour government promising a continued open policy, but one organized using a points system similar to that found in the USA. However, between 1997 and 2005, it was the employer-led work permit system which proved to be the main channel by which skilled migrants entered the country. Checks within this system sought to ensure that the position of resident workers was not undercut (Dobson et al, 2002). Employers were not allowed to bring in migrants if it was believed local labour sources were sufficient and employers were not permitted to employ migrants at a lower wage rate than domestic labour. The scheme, therefore, in many ways proved that there was demand within the UK economy for skills that domestic labour sources could not provide. There was also evidence that work permit holders were likely to put much more into the economy than they cost in terms of the social and welfare services that they used (Glover et al, 2001; Gott and Johnston, 2002).

However, it is also evident that many of the skilled migrants who came to the UK after 1997 were neither transient nor invisible, and that their engagement within the UK labour market was quite problematic. Parallels have been drawn, for example, with the guest worker schemes of the 1960s in the way in which migrants ended up in undesirable locations both sectorally and geographically. It was the "difficult" schools in the UK's inner cities that recruited foreign teachers to take up posts that local staff did not want. In the health service it was the low level of wages that were blamed for the failure to recruit and retain enough local nurses and it has been claimed that it was the least pleasant positions in hospitals to which foreign doctors were recruited (Bundred and Levitt, 2000). One result of the UK's "employer-led" policies may therefore have been segregation within skilled labour markets of many immigrant staff.

Another dimension of the policy that has been criticized is that it implied fostering a new brain drain from developing countries to meet the needs of already developed nations. In developing countries, emigration of some skilled workers represents for them an important route out of poverty with significant positive impacts upon the livelihood and well being of their families (Black, 2003; Stark, 2003), but for many developing countries the scale of skilled emigration is so great as to deplete their economies of key skills. One study of 55 developing countries provided evidence that a third of them lost more than 15% of their tertiary educated population through migration (Lowell et al, 2004). Extreme examples include Turkey and Morocco losing 40% of this group and the Caribbean economies where it is estimated a half of tertiary educated adults have left. In addition there is some evidence that migrants seldom repatriating remittances to anything like the value of the initial investment that has been made in their education (Commander et al, 2002). The new demand in developed countries for foreign skilled workers at the very least needs to be recognized as creating a "brain strain" in much of the developed world (Lowell et al, 2004), but one that can be countered by appropriate migration policies. Others are opposed to further international skill transfers and see the last decade as a new era of brain drain from south to north (Bhagwati, 2003).

Despite the social concerns that have been identified, it can be argued from a social justice perspective that there are many good reasons why the UK, like other West European governments, should adopt policies that favour skilled immigration (Niessen, 2000). Most forceful of these is the case that voluntary migration is a fundamental human right and that, while policies are required that regulate migratory processes, policies should facilitate rather than complicate the transfer of skilled workers. This is especially the case where migrants are seeking to move from countries where national governments do not respect individual human rights (Ruhs, 2003). Rather than criminalising and marginalising such people as "bogus asylum seekers", as is a danger at present for many professional migrants entering the UK from countries of the former Yugoslavia, it can be argued that international law is being upheld by permitting the migration of skilled workers in these situations. These matters have been assessed in much more detail elsewhere (Lowell and Findlay, 2002), and guidelines set out to indicate how positive immigration policies in the developed world can limit the "brain strain" for developing economies. Indeed careful analysis of the research literature leads Lowell et al to advocate that countries stick to a carefully managed temporary worker programme by attempting to strengthen mechanisms that favour return migration of skilled people once their temporary work permits expire. Equally, they argue that longer term skill exchanges should be linked to policies that capitalize on the development opportunities arising from expatriate diasporas (Lowell et al, 2004). These are not issues that are explored further here. Instead attention at the end of this paper focuses on the issue of how the UK has engaged the "shadow" state to provide care and services to migrants within the new era of skilled immigration that has emerged.

As noted above, the UK has sought as a western democracy to benefit from migrant skills without extending permanent citizenship (with its associated costs) to most of those delivering the extra skills that it needs (Geddes, 2003). It is in this context that the UK government has been particularly keen for voluntary organisations (or, as they have been termed, "shadow state" institutions (Wolch, 1990)) to play a role in supporting migrant communities. Keen to distance itself from both the "Old" Labour Left (pro-state, anti-market) and the Conservative Right (pro-market, anti-state), the Blair government embraced a so-called Third Way political philosophy which stressed the strategic importance of civil society for social cohesion. For New Labour, voluntary organisations represent the organised vanguard of civil society. There are, however, very few studies of the role that voluntary organisations play in encouraging self-help among migrant communities through local development initiatives, or of the specific services for economic migrants and refugees that are provided in areas like health, housing, language training, and employment.

The connections between voluntary associations and citizenship are well established in social and political theory. Hirst (1994) and Turner (2001), for example, both articulate a positive view of how voluntary associations "provide opportunities for social participation, for democratic involvement at the local level, and thus for active citizenship" (Turner, 2001, 200). From the perspective of a government keen to engage skilled migrants as "active citizens", the voluntary sector is therefore of pivotal importance. Research in Canada has highlighted how the neo-liberal political agenda of the 1980s and 1990s, that witnessed the rolling back of the welfare state, has meant that language training and interpretation services, help with finding employment, and public and citizenship education programmes for recent immigrants are largely the responsibility of local shadow state organisations (Creese, 1998; Mitchell, 2001).

While some endorse the state's withdrawal from service provision to migrants, others are critical of these policies. In the context of voluntary sector organisations it has been suggested that the result is the development of passive rather than active forms of citizenship, with service users treated as the "clients" of welfare services delivered by a largely professionalised workforce (Brown, 1997). In short, the use of voluntary sector organizations, produces circumstances of "differential citizenship" that suit the purposes of the receiving state and its government, but may serve less well the needs of the migrant. From the utilitarian economic perspective promoted by many governments seeking to attract global talent, this shift in social policy is therefore a natural complement to other dimensions of their position that seeks to maximize the economic gains from encouraging international brain gains while minimizing the costs to the receiving country of such movements. To those sustaining a social justice perspective on migration, the reduced social rights that this policy implies are much less acceptable.

From skill exchange to brain gain

The UK experience of competing for global talent

While the United States had been a world leader in the global competition to recruit skilled foreign workers since the 1950s, it was not until the mid-1990s that the UK began to consider the possibility of adopting a positive approach to international skill recruitment. In the UK foreign workers from outside the EU qualify for entry mainly through the work permit scheme and can become permanent residents if they work in the country long enough. Programmes include the main work permit scheme (including the Training and Work Experience Scheme (TWES)), the Seasonal Agricultural Workers Scheme, (SAWS), the Sectors Based Scheme (SBS), and the Highly Skilled Migrant Programme (HSMP).

The UK's changing position in global migration exchanges can be measured from a range of official datasets such as the UK's International Passenger Survey (IPS), the Labour Force Survey, Work Permit statistics produced by Work Permits UK (formerly called the Overseas Labour Service), and Asylum and Settlement statistics published annually by the Home Office. All these sources are subject to error and major backward corrections often have to be applied as was the case for example for the International Passenger Survey following the appearance of the 2001 UK Population Census.

The International Passenger Survey[2] shows that in 2003 the UK made a net gain of 236,200 non-British citizens. This is a significant net gain by contrast with the very modest net gains of the 1970s, 1980s and

---

[2] The international passenger statistics quoted here show flows to the EU as it was constituted in 1995 and excluding the 10 states that were admitted to the EU in May 2004.

early 1990s. From 1997 there was a strong upward shift in the number of people entering the country (Table 1) with figures for the inflow of non-British citizens exceeding 300,000 every year since 1999. The peak of 418,200 in 2002 was only slightly more than the 2003 figure.

Outflows of non-British citizens from the UK have also been high, but since 1997 the scale of outflows have always been much less than the inflows, with net gains to the UK of over 170,000 persons in 2002 and 2003 by contrast with net gains of only 101,000 in 1995. The most significant source of growth in non-British citizen flows has been among New Commonwealth and other foreign non-EU citizen flows.

Table 1   Migration flows to/from UK by citizenship, 1995-2003 (thousands)

	1995	1997	1999	2001	2003
Inflows: all citizens	311.9	326.1	453.8	479.6	512.6
Inflows: non-British citizens	228.0	237.2	337.4	373.3	406.8
Of which New Commonwealth	58.3	58.7	66.5	83.9	103.1
Outflow: all citizens	236.5	279.2	290.8	307.7	361.5
Outflow: non-British citizens	101.0	130.6	151.8	148.5	170.6
Of which New Commonwealth	11.9	19.8	12.3	18.6	16.6
Net Flows: all citizens	+75.4	+46.8	+163.0	+171.8	+151.0
Net Flows: non British citizens	+127.0	+106.6	+185.8	+224.8	+236.2
Of which New Commonwealth	+46.5	+38.9	+54.2	+65.4	+86.5

Source: ONS, 2004

These flows need to be compared with movements of British citizens over the same time period. While inflows of British citizens have oscillated around the same level over the last decade, outflows have grown. This has meant an increase in the net loss to the country from UK citizen flows to other parts of the world. Even allowing for British citizen flows the overall impact of migration to and from the UK of people of all citizenships still produced significant net gains and ones that were much higher than in the past. In 2003 the net gain to the UK was 151,000 persons or roughly double the figure for 1995 (net gain of 75,400). These figures point overall to the UK being more connected to the global economy by migration than at any time in the recent past and with net gains by migration reaching a new and higher level than was the case under the migration policies that governed the countries between the 1970s and the mid-1990s.

The growing importance of skilled migration is readily demonstrated in empirical terms by examining time series occupational data contained in the International Passenger Survey. Table 2 shows the increasing volume of skilled immigration to the UK by non-British Citizens employed in professional or managerial posts. The 1990's was a decade when skilled international migration became ever more important. Numbers rose from 33,000 in 1992 to 76,000 in 1998 and 103,000 in 2002. As a proportion of all non-British citizen inflows, including those not in the labour force, professional and managerial migrants made up 23.7 per cent of the total between 1995 and 1998, while by 2002 the proportion had risen to 35.3 per cent. Calculated as a percentage of those in active employment, the proportion grows from 58.8 per cent in 1992 to 64.4 per cent in 2002.

Table 2 Professional and managerial migration to and from the UK of non-British citizens, 1992-2002 (thousands)

	Inflow	Outflow	Net flow
1992	33.1	25.6	+ 7.5
1994	44.1	18.0	+26.0
1996	52.4	22.6	+29.7
1998	76.4	30.3	+46.1
2000	108.6	52.8	+55.8
2002	103.0	46.0	+57.0

(Source : ONS, *International Migration*, Series MN, 1992-2004)

The outflow of professional and managerial persons of non-British citizenship was much smaller than the inflow from 1998 to 2002. Although inflows of professional and managerial workers seem to have stabilized at between 100 and 110,000 persons per annum, net gains have continued to rise because outflows have lagged far behind inflows. Between 1999 and 2002 the net gain was over 200,000 highly skilled workers in total, compared with only 60,600 during the four year period 1991-1994. These statistics seem therefore to confirm the view that the "UK has moved away from a position of brain exchange in the early 1990s to one where the country was making, in numerical terms, substantial brain gains" (Findlay, 2002, 7).

Britain's "favourable" location within the global labour market for skills is confirmed when one compares net non-British citizen professional and managerial migration gains for the 1990s with the pattern of

British citizen professional and managerial flows. In the early 1990s, net British citizen outflows of professional and managerial staff exceeded net non-British citizen inflows on two occasions (1991 and 1992). This pointed to some kind of balanced exchange between the UK and the world knowledge economy. By contrast since 1995, and especially from 1998 onwards, British citizen professional and managerial net outflows were smaller every year than net inflows of non-British citizens. Previous research by the author has shown that the UK's shift from a position of brain exchange to one of brain gain has not been achieved particularly as a result of increased skilled migration flows from developing countries relative to inflows from elsewhere (Findlay, 2002). However, what has been of concern is that while skilled migration from other parts of the world have displayed transient characteristics, skilled migration from developing countries have not been matched by significant return flows. The result has therefore been a more serious imbalance between inflows and outflows from developing countries.

To summarise, it appears from the International Passenger Survey that Britain has shifted from a position of engaging in an open and moderately equitable exchange of skills with other countries to one of being a net beneficiary of the international flow of human talent. Net gains of non-British citizens in professional and managerial occupations are no longer offset by equivalent net outflows of skilled British citizens. And net gains of talented people from developing countries are less likely to be transient in character and more likely to settle than skilled migration from other parts of the global economy. Claims that the academic literature on brain drain relating to the ideas of Bhagwati and Hamada (1973) is out-dated and should set aside in a favour of theories relating to situations of brain exchange or talent flow within ever-changing diasporic networks, therefore need to be treated with care. Clearly there remain some significant geographically and economically-specific circumstances in which international talent flows result in a relatively permanent redistribution of skills from one country to another, without any clear positive economic returns to the sending countries.

Channels of migrant entry to the UK

Discussion turns now from aggregate figures about the UK's position in relation to international labour migration flows to more detailed analysis of the migration channels which the government has shaped to organize movement to the UK. In recent years by far the three largest groups of non-British citizens migrating to the UK are students, asylum-seekers (and others given leave to remain in UK for asylum-related reasons) and work permit holders. Home Office statistics show that not only are these the largest channels of entry to the UK, but they are also the channels where numbers of migrants have increased most markedly over the last five years (student entrants up from 272,000 in 1999 to 319,000 in 2003; asylum seekers up from 110,000 to 185,000 over the same period).

Table 3   Selected channels of migrant entry to UK in terms of those given leave to enter (thousands)

	1999	2001	2002	2003(p)
Students	272	339	369	319
Asylum and other related cases	110	153	127	185
Working holiday makers	46	36	42	46.5
Spouses and fiancés	30	29	30	31
Au pairs	15	12	13	15
Settlement on arrival	2	3	2	3

Source: Home Office Statistical Bulletin, 2004, 17. The home office provides data for other channels not included in Table 3. For example data for work permits is excluded from this Table but listed in below Table 4.

Work permits. The growth in number of work permit holders is even more dramatic than that of other channels and especially when set in the context of the 1990s as a whole. In 1995 only about 33,000 applications for work permits were approved (Table 4). Since then the number has risen to over 130,000 (133,337 in the 12 months to 31st March 2003 and 135,333 to 31st March 2004), representing a massive four fold increase. The most dramatic rise has been in the number of persons granted permission to remain as a work permit holder as a result of an extension to an initial permit (Table 5). It is evident then, not only that UK government policy on skilled labour migration has been altered dramatically over recent years in a way that has been effective from the point of view of admitting ever-larger numbers of talented people to the UK within the Work Permit scheme. It also clear that many of these migrants are less transient than the Work Permit scheme might be thought to indicate. On the contrary, an ever-larger proportion of temporary migrants are being given permission to remain in the UK, increasing the prospects of their settlement and reducing the likelihood of their return to their countries of origin. This trend therefore raises concerns amongst those who argue that the "brain gain" being enjoyed by the UK is at the same time contributing to a "brain strain" in many of the countries sending skilled migrants abroad (Lowell et al, 2004).

Table 4   Work permit applications approved in the United Kingdom, 1995 to 2002

Applications approved	Total Approved	Per cent approved	Work Permits	First Permissions
1995	32,704	84.7	21,688	2,473
1996	36,132	86.6	23,596	2,849
1997	42,844	87.7	28,675	3,059
1998	51,613	88.1	33,659	3,906
1999	58,245	88.3	37,269	4,696
2000	85,638	91.5	56,484	8,257
2001	115,760	89.3	67,872	15,765
2002	129,041	83.1	65,579	20,046

Source : Findlay (2002, 14). Caution needs to be applied in interpreting these time series data because of the ways in which the immigration system has altered and been recorded over time. The total figure in the left hand column includes new work permits, first permissions, extensions, changes of employment and various other minor categories of approval. For more details see Findlay (2002) and Dobson et al (2002).

Table 5   Extensions of leave to remain as a work permit holder or trainee

	1999	2001	2002	2003 (p)
Work permit holder	13,790	43,240	53,170	73,295
Trainee	8,045	8,160	7,915	10,695
Total	21,835	51,400	61,085	83,990

Source: Home Office Statistical Bulletin, 2004, 19.

Analysis of work permits is particularly useful since it allows the researcher to analyse which sectors of the UK economy have been the particular destinations for new labour migrants. The top three occupation groups for 2002 were IT related occupations, health/medical occupations and managers and administrators (Findlay, 2002). Health and medical services have grown significantly over time in relation to the other sectors and occupations. As can be seen in Table 6, the largest national group in 2002 was Indians, with 18,999 issues (21 per cent), immigrants from the USA and South Africans. These figures compare with only 2000 work permits granted to Indians in 1995. India continued to top the league table in 2003 and 2004. Other nationalities with large increases in skilled migration to the UK over the last ten years have been Filipinos, South

Africans and Malaysians (Table 6). It is particularly noticeable that much of the increase in skilled migration to UK has been brought about by the establishment of sector-specific linkages: for example Filipinos to work in the health sector, and Indians to work in IT (Findlay, 2002).

Table 6 Analysis of UK work permits by nationality, 1995 and 2002

Nationality	1995		2002	
	Number	Per cent	Number	Per cent
Australia and NZ	1,575	6.5	7,819	8.8
Canada	923	3.8	2,080	2.3
South Africa	659	2.7	7,971	9.0
United States	7,876	32.6	9,537	10.8
Japan	2,423	10.0	2,661	3.0
Czech Republic	199	0.8	551	0.6
Poland	615	2.5	1,609	1.8
Russia	735	3.0	997	1.1
India	1,997	8.3	18,999	21.4
Philippines	66	0.3	6,831	7.7
China	657	2.7	2,567	2.9
Malaysia	296	1.2	3,353	3.8

Data source: Findlay, 2002, 14.

Highly Skilled Migrant Programme. Having drawn out the main trends evident in Work Permit datasets, it seems appropriate to comment on specific UK schemes and initiatives that have emerged too recently to have as yet produced any datasets by which they can be judged. For example, the Highly Skilled Migrant Programme (HSMP) was launched in January 2002 and uses a point score system similar to that in Australia and Canada. The individual migrant as opposed to the employer is the applicant. This may have implications for developing countries as it is difficult to stop individuals from coming to the UK. Indeed, it would be easier to legislate in relation to employers than to individual migrants. The top groups of occupations have been finance, business managers, ICT, telecommunications and medical occupations.

Registration Scheme for Migrants from EU Accession Countries. The United Kingdom, as a member of the EU, has traditionally exchanged skilled migrants with other EU member states without requiring in-migrants from these states to obtain a work permit. However, the expansion of the EU in May 2004 to include ten new countries from Eastern

Europe led to concerns about the scale of migration that would occur. As a result the UK government put in place a scheme to require workers from the new accession countries to register their arrival. By November 2004 some 91,000 migrants had registered, far exceeding the Home Office's expectations (that no more than 13,000 people would come per annum), and indicating something of the scale of demand for skilled migration to the UK.

National Health Service International Fellowship Scheme. Another recent development is the National Health Service international fellowship scheme launched in January 2002. This invites highly experienced health professionals (e.g. consultants) to work in the UK for up to two years. The aim of this scheme is to foster international co-operation and promote the NHS abroad by shared learning between different health care systems (Department of Health, 2002). However it has been noted that this scheme will exacerbate the brain strain emerging in many developing countries and may exacerbate inequalities in global health unless there are explicit measures to facilitate the flow of doctors back to developing countries (Patel, 2003). In principle temporary programmes can be beneficial. However this is dependent on the programme being, as it is described, "temporary".

Student mobility. As Table 4 indicated, temporary migration of talent to the UK also includes student migration. Not only have ever larger numbers of students been recruited to study in the UK, but new policy initiatives have recently attempted to increase the retention rate of these students after their studies are complete (Findlay, 2002 and King et al, 2004). Foreign nationals who have studied mathematics, science or engineering in the UK will in future be able to work in the country for 12 months following graduation under the new Science Engineering Graduates Scheme (Home Office 2003a). And Scotland has pioneered a scheme to persuade foreign students to stay after their studies as an attempt to boost the regional economy as well as tackling the problem of demographic decline. Researchers have already questioned whether students studying in the UK migrate to learn or simply use the experience to "learn to migrate" (Li et al, 1996). If the UK follows the patterns of the USA, student migration may become a major route to adding to the economy's stock of talent. It has been reported that amongst Chinese and Indian doctoral students in the US around 50 per cent plan to stay (Commander et al, 2002). Currently in the UK switching into work permit employment is allowed for student nurses and postgraduate doctors and dentists (McLaughlan and Salt, 2002).

Work permits and the UK health sector

The UK traditionally has offered work permits based on a list of recognised domestic skill shortages such as health, education and other professional sectors. Focusing specifically on the health sector, it has been estimated that by 2008 the UK will need 25,000 more doctors and 250,000 nurses (Dovlo, 2003). On this basis plans were laid during the second Blair administration to target the Indian subcontinent which was said to be "hugely populated" with doctors who would like to come to the Western hemisphere (Dougherty, 2003; Seguin, 2003).

As shown by doctor registrations in the UK, there are now equal levels of new registrations with the General Medical Council (GMC) between UK graduates and overseas graduates. Between 1993 and 2003 the proportion of overseas registrations grew year on year. By 2002, 31 per cent of all doctors practicing in the UK and 13 per cent of nurses were born overseas, and in London these figures were 23 per cent and 47 per cent respectively. Some 45 per cent of new registrations of nurses in UK are international. Six of the top ten countries for "work permits" issued to foreign nurses were African (Dovlo, 2003). There is therefore much evidence to suggest that the UK's policy of global talent recruitment in the health sector is having potentially deleterious effects on at least some developing countries (Table 7).

Table 7   Registered doctors in UK by country of qualification, selected developing countries, (2003)

Country of Qualification	No of Registrations		
	Full Registration Only	Full and Specialist Registration	Limited Registration
India	14,252	2,473	3,842
South Africa	6,418	989	–
Pakistan	2,939	621	707
Egypt	1,644	512	154
Sri Lanka	1,427	450	211
Iraq	955	400	198
Jamaica	732	66	–
Bangladesh	562	71	62
Burma	526	64	79
Ghana	207	71	46

Data taken from Dovlo, 2003.

The UK has however made some efforts to protect countries. For example, the Department of Health banned NHS trusts from recruiting from South Africa and certain Caribbean countries in 1999, following the recognition of severe nursing shortages. In the last few years NHS trusts have been encouraged to engage in nursing recruitment initiatives in other countries such as Spain and the Philippines. However research finding have questioned whether these policies are adequate. Despite the ban, the number of nurses who arrived in the UK from South Africa has continued to rise. The problem is that the ban does not apply to private recruitment agencies or private sector employers.

Despite praise worthy efforts by the UK Department of Health to develop and promote ethical guidelines for use in international recruitment of health workers (Findlay, 2002), severe problems remain for the developing countries who are paying for the training of health staff, yet who cannot afford to retain them in a globally competitive market place.

Skilled migration and differential citizenship

If the UK's efforts to be competitive in the global labour market have led to problems for some of the countries from which migrants have been recruited, it is equally true that the policy has also led to domestic challenges within the UK with regard to migrants" social rights. These challenges have been particularly apparent because of the government's desire for fiscal and political reasons to draw a line between the social rights of UK citizens and those of others living within the UK's borders.

Government ministers have gone to great lengths to emphasize that the economy needs foreign skills and that migrant workers are not a drain on the economy. Consider for example the comments of David Blunkett, Home Office Minister until December 2004 talking about recent migrants from the ten new EU accession states:

"Those (migrants) registered with us so far are... accountants, nurses and teachers. By contributing to our economy and paying into the system these accession state workers are supporting our public services, not being a drain on them. It is likely that those working here will do so for short periods of time before returning home..."[3]

This quote begs the question of how the UK has met its obligations with regard to the social rights of temporary skilled workers. In practice the government has chosen to "care" for migrants through the develop-

---

[3] David Blunkett announcing the first results of the EU accession states worker registration scheme on 7th July 2004.

ment of a "mixed economy" of local welfare services (covering areas such as housing and health) as well as the private and the voluntary sectors. It should not be implied that state provision for migrant workers and other new entrants to the UK, such as asylum seekers, is absent or inadequate, but rather that the UK government, not wishing to raise taxes to expand state services for new arrivals, has done a great deal to encourage expansion of voluntary organizations in this sector. This in turn has had significant implications for how the UK state now approaches its migrant population.

The implications of these developments have been the focus of research by Fyfe et al (2005 in press). This research points to four main conclusions. First, voluntary sector organisations dealing with migrants are in many senses "vulnerable", being small in size and recent in origin. The sector is immature and finds providing services to an ever-growing population of migrants very challenging. Second, the organisations are very dependent on government funding, leaving them open to manipulation by the state in the way that they operate. Third, relationships exist between organization size, age of establishment and the extent of government funding. Finally, the questionnaire survey of 105 voluntary organizations shows that while the activities of the organizations varied little in relation to sources of funding, those that received government funding were much more likely to see the state as impinging on their policies towards migrants and migrant communities (Fyfe et al, 2005 in press).

To be faithful to the survey results, it is important to recognize that although some organisations resented government surveillance of their activities others did not feel too constrained by the acceptance of government funding. Of course, simply because some organisations did not complain about the influence of government on their activities (other than in terms of the bureaucratic exercises required to gain funding), does not mean that the state was not having a profound influence on them. For example, voluntary organisations dealing with labour migrants reported spending much time on issues associated with helping migrants gain appropriate legal advice about work permits or employees rights within the NHS. Equally, as Wolch (1990) has suggested in her account of the "shadow state", the government can use changes in its funding of such organisations in ways which allow it to erode service provision but in ways which mask state responsibility for service cuts.

Conclusions

This study has shown some of the ways that UK immigration policies have changed over the last decade. There has been a major increase in immigration especially of students and skilled workers. Promoting temporary skilled migration through the UK's work permit scheme has been one of the main mechanisms by which the government has sought to achieve its goals of on the one hand delivering the skills that the economy needs while on the other hand appearing to limit the social, cultural and economic impacts of migration. However, openness to the world economy has not always been translated into openness of access within the UK labour market. Furthermore, recent statistics released by the UK government show that many of the "transient" migrants who entered under the Work Permit scheme have sought to extend their permits (Table 5) and may well seek to settle in the UK.

Several policy challenges arise from the migration policies examined in this paper. First, there is the risk that temporary skilled immigration could be used as an alternative to training local people for the skills that the UK economy needs. Skilled immigration should of course be a supplement not an alternative to extra investment in training domestic labour. The matter raises serious concerns in areas such as medicine, where clearly Britain over many decades has consistently failed to train enough doctors inside the UK as well as failing to pay nurses high enough wages to keep them in the profession. Bundred and Levitt (2000) note that developed countries not only need to make greater efforts to train sufficient doctors to meet their projected human resource needs, but they also should consider strategies for investing in the modernisation of the medical education systems of developing countries by way of compensation for tapping their very scarce medical resources through international migration of health professionals.

Second, introducing workers of whatever skill level on temporary contracts and expecting the majority of them to leave at the end of these contracts seems optimistic. History teaches that there is nothing so permanent as a temporary worker. That many of the UK's temporary foreign skilled workers wish to stay and settle should be anticipated and appropriate policies should be developed accordingly. As argued by Lowell et al (2004) and Ruhs (2003), countries like the UK need to work harder both to encourage return migration of temporary workers in order to avoid damaging the economies from which the migrants have been drawn and also to integrate those who do not return. As important as devising measures to encourage return, is the need to avoid criminaliza-

83

tion of those migrants who wish to stay in the UK. There is now strong evidence to show that migrants, especially highly skilled ones, are likely to command above average wages and to pay more taxes than the value of the services they collect from the state (Glover et al 2001). Thus policies to facilitate more skilled workers to come to developed economies need to be paralleled by new strategies to tackle discrimination and criminalization, which in the past have often deprived migrants of the opportunities to contribute as fully as they would have liked to both their sending and host nation. Not all would be as sure as Barbara Roche about "British openness and tolerance", although hopefully it is something to aspire to. The danger is that the "temporary" label attaching to the work permits by which skilled migrants are being encouraged to enter the country leads to a neglect amongst policy makers of policies that will ensure that this new wave of movers are given social rights as well as jobs (Fyfe et al 2005 in press). The differential citizenship offered by the UK government through its approach of fostering voluntary organizations to care for migrants within the shadow state needs to be further researched, before it can be endorsed as an adequate mechanism for supporting the UK's new migrant communities.

It remains uncertain what the full effects are for migrants of the UK government engaging the shadow state to provide for many aspects of their needs. It appears that the government in the UK has had a substantial impact through its funding regime in increasing the number of voluntary organizations geared to delivering a diverse range of services to migrant groups. Further research is needed to establish just how the conditions of differential citizenship that have resulted will impact on migrant welfare and rights. Many have good reason to fear the neo-liberal approach being adopted in the UK, believing that basic human rights as well as the provision of basic welfare services is best achieved by the state and should not be devolved to the voluntary sector.

References

Beine, M., Docquier, F. and Rapoport, H., 2001. Brain drain and economic growth, *J of Development Economics*, 64, 275-89.

Bhagwati, J. and Hamada, K., 1973. The brain drain, international integration of markets for professionals and unemployment: a theoretical analysis, *J of Development Economics*, 1, 19-42.

Bhagwati, J., 2003. Borders Beyond Control, *Foreign Affairs*, January/February.

Black, R., 2003. "Migration, Globalisation and Poverty: the new DFID-funded Development Research Centre on Migration", Department for International Development Seminar, 24 February 2003.

Braziel J. and Mannur A. (eds.), 2003. *Theorizing Diaspora*. Malden: Blackwell Press.

Bundred, P.E. and Levitt, C., 2000. "Medical migration: who are the real losers?", *Lancet*, 356, 245-246.

Cohen, R., 1997. *Global Diasporas*. London; UCL Press.

Commander, S., Kangasniemi, M. and Winters, L.A., 2002. "The Brain Drain: Curse or Boon? A Survey of the Literature", Paper prepared for the CEPR/NBER/SNS International Seminar on International Trade, Stockholm, 24-25 May.

Crease, G., 1998. Government restructuring and immigrant/refugee settlement work, *Metropolis Working Paper* 98.12 Vancouver: University of Vancouver.

DFID (Department for International Development), 2000. *Eliminating World Poverty* (White Paper on International Development) London: DFID.

Department of Health, 2002. *International Recruitment of Consultants and General Practitioners for the NHS in England*, Department of Health, London.

Dobson, J., Koser, K., McLaughlan, G. and Salt, J., 2001. International Migration and the United Kingdom: Recent Patterns and Trends, *RDS Occasional Paper*, 75, Home Office, London.

Dougherty, K., 2003. "Quebec look to Internet in MD quest", The Montreal Gazette, November 19, http://www.canada.com.

Dovlo, D., 2003. The Brain Drain and Retention of Health Professionals in Africa, Regional Training Conference on Improving Tertiary Education in Sub-Saharan Africa: Things that Work!, Accra, 23-25 September 2003.

Dumont, J.-C. and Lemaitre, G., 2005. "Counting immigrants and expatriates in OECD countries: a new perspective", OECD Social, Employment and Migration Working Papers No. 25, Paris, OECD.

Findlay, A., 2001. International migration and globalization. In M. Saddique (ed.) *International migration into the 21st century*. Elgar: Cheltenham, 126-52.

Findlay, A., 2002. From Brain Exchange to Brain Gain: Policy Implications for the UK of Recent Trends in Skilled Migration from Developing Countries, *International Migration Papers* 43, International Labour Office, Geneva. http://www.ilo.org/public/english/protection/migrant/download/imp/imp43.pdf.

Fyfe, N., Findlay, A. and Stewart, E., 2005 in press. Shifting regimes and meanings of citizenship: forced migration, welfare and the restructuring of social rights in Britain, *Environment and Planning A*.

Geddes, A., 2003. Migration and the welfare state in Europe. In S. Spencer (ed.) The *Politics of Migration* Blackwell: Oxford, 150-162.

Glover, S. et al., 2001. Migration: an economic and social analysis, *RDS Occasional Paper* 67, Home Office: London.

Gott, C. and Johnston, K., 2002. The migrant population in the UK: fiscal effects. *RDS Occasional Paper* 77, Home Office: London.

Hirst, P., 1994. *Associative Democracy*. Cambridge: Polity Press.

Home Office, 2003. Statistical Bulletin (Control of Immigration) Home Office: London.

Home Office, 2004. Statistical Bulletin (Control of Immigration) Home Office: London.

King, R., Findlay, A., Ruiz-Gelices, E. and Stam, A., 2004. International student mobility *HEFCE Issues Papers* 30, HEFCE: London.

Kleinman, M., 2003. The economic impact of labour migration. In S. Spencer (ed.) *The Politics of Migration* Blackwell: Oxford, 59-74.

Li, L., Findlay, A., Jowett, A. and Skeldon, R., 1996. Migrating to learn and learning to migrate, *International J of Population Geography*, 2, 51-67.

Lowell, B.L. and Findlay, A., 2002. Migration of Highly Skilled Persons from Developing Countries: Impact and Policy Responses, *International Migration Papers*, 44 ILO: Geneva http://www.ilo.org/public/english/protection/migrant/publ/imp-list.htm.

Lowell, L., Findlay, A. and Stewart, E., 2004. Brain Strain, *Asylum and Migration Working Paper* 3, Institute of Public Policy Research: London.

McLaughlan, G. and Salt, J., 2002. "Migration policies towards highly skilled foreign workers", Report to the Home Office, available at: http://www.homeoffice.gov.uk/rds/pdfs2/migrationpolicies.pdf.

Mitchell, K., 2001. Transnationalism, neo-liberalism and the rise of the shadow state, *Economy and Society*, 30, 165-89.

Niessen, J., 2000. *The management of managers of immigration.* Management Policy Group: Brussels.

ONS, 2004. International Migration Series MN, Office of National Statistics: London.

Patel, V., 2003. Recruiting doctors from poor countries, *British Medical Journal*, 327, 926-28.

Ruhs, M., 2003. "Temporary foreign worker programmes: Policies, adverse consequences, and the need to make them work", Perspectives on Labour Migration, International Labour Office, Geneva.

Salt, J. and Findlay, A., 1989. International migration of highly skilled manpower. In R. Appleyard (ed.) *The impact of international migration on Developing Countries*, OECD: Paris, 159-180.

Seguin, R., 2003. "Quebec to help foreign MDs pass exams", *The Globe and Mail* (Canada), November 19, http://globeandmail.com.

Spencer, S. (ed.), 2003. *The Politics of Migration* Blackwell: Oxford.

Stalker, P., 2000. *Workers without frontiers.* ILO: Geneva.

Stark, O., 2003. "Rethinking the Brain Drain", *Discussion Paper* 2003-04, Department of Economics, University of Calgary, Canada.

Stark, O. and Wang, Y., 2002. Inducing human capital formation: migration as a substitute for other subsidies, *J of Public Economics*, 86, 28-46.

Turner, B., 2001. The erosion of citizenship, *British J of Sociology* 52, 189-210.

Vertovec, S., 1999. Conceiving and researching transnationalism, *Ethnic and Racial Studies* 22, 447-62.

Wolch, J., 1990. *The Shadow State*, The Foundation Center: New York.

Zelinsky, W., 2001. *The Enigma of Ethnicity.* Iowa: Iowa University Press.

Competing for global talent: The US experience

Philip L. Martin

Summary

The US experience with immigration demonstrates that opportunity attracts talent. The US allows foreigners to enter via three major doors: as immigrants, non-immigrants, and as unauthorized foreigners, and permits the non-immigrants and unauthorized to become immigrants if they find US employers to sponsor them. This happens often: in recent years about 90 percent of the foreigners receiving immigrant visas for employment reasons were already in the US. The US system for attracting global talent can thus be thought of as a probationary or Darwinian process that restricts the rights of foreign students and guest workers for at least several years, but holds out the hope of an immigrant visa and freedom in the US labor market as the eventual prize.

The US probation-to-immigrant system raises a question often asked by economists: why not increase the economic benefits to the US of immigration by raising the share of immigrants admitted for employment and economic reasons from the current 10 to 15 percent to half or more, as in Australia and Canada? This has been the central recommendation of several US commissions in the past two decades, but the political strength of advocates for family unification, refugees, and other types of immigrants has prevented reductions in their numbers in order to expand employment and economic immigration.

With the ceiling on immigrant visas for employment stuck at about 140,000 a year for workers and their families, or 1/7 of the annual million a year immigrant flow, the US quest for global talent has been centered on expanding opportunities for foreigners with skills to enter as non-immigrant students or workers. The symbol of this side-door expansion was the H-1B program, which jumped from 65,000 visas a year to 195,000 during the 1990s economic boom. The IT-recession of 2001 has led to a debate over US policy toward attracting global talent. On the one hand, the H-1B ceiling was raised in Fall 2004 to 85,000 a year, at the request of employers who discovered that available visas were gone early in the year. On the other hand, major changes in the legal immigrant system have been blocked by a dispute over how to deal with the 10 million mostly unskilled and unauthorized foreigners in the US—should they be converted to guest workers expected to return home, legalized to become immigrants, or put in their own probationary earned immigrant system?

Introduction

The United States is a nation of immigrants. US presidents frequently remind Americans that, except for Native Americans, they or their forebears left another country to begin anew in the United States. The national motto e pluribus unum (from many, one) highlights the expectation that the US immigration system permits individuals to better themselves while also benefiting and strengthening the United States.

Foreigners enter the United States through three major doors: immigrant, non-immigrant, or unauthorized. During the 1990s, there were 9 million legal immigrants admitted, about 250 million non-immigrants (excluding Mexicans and Canadians crossing for short visits), and 15 million unauthorized foreigners apprehended. Each of these flows has continued at the average levels of the 1990s despite the terrorist attacks of September 11, 2001, so that in fiscal year 2003, the most recent data available, there were 706,000 legal immigrants, 28 million non-immigrants, and over one million apprehensions.

Foreigners admitted via one door do not stay in the channel associated with their entry. Legal immigrants may become naturalized US citizens or emigrate (perhaps 20 percent emigrate), non-immigrants may change their status from student or guest worker to immigrant or become unauthorized, and unauthorized foreigners may become legal non-immigrants or immigrants. In recent years, over half of the legal immigrants admitted in any year were already in the US, either in a non-immigrant or unauthorized status, when their immigration visas became available. The percentage of employment-related immigrants already in the US was even higher: 90 percent of legal immigrants admitted because of their outstanding skills or because US employers requested them were already in the US.

The US immigration system is best understood as one in which 35 million foreign-born residents "slosh around" in a country of 295 million. Roughly a third of these foreign residents are naturalized US citizens, a third are legal immigrants or non-immigrants, and a third are unauthorized. Understanding the quest for global talent in the American case means understanding how foreigners enter the US in a category other than immigrant or "intending American," and how they adjust their status to become immigrants and eventually naturalized citizens.

This paper first reviews the four front doors to the US immigration system, then turns to the programs that admit foreigners as non-immigrant students, guest workers, intra-company transferees, and Nafta professionals, and then highlights a few of the cases that have helped to shape the current US debate. The paper concludes that the US does not have a coherent strategy for attracting global talent, which means that other countries with focused strategies could become very competitive in attracting the world's best and brightest.

Highly skilled immigrants

The US accepts immigrants for four major purposes: family unification, employment (to fill vacant jobs), refugees and diversity. The number admitted each year through these four major doors is partially fixed by quotas, so that the global ceiling of 480,000 to 675,000 immigrants a year is exceeded because some types of immigrants are exempt from the ceiling.

Indeed, immigration averaged about 920,000 a year over the past decade, and would have been higher in 2003 if the government had been faster in dealing with the 1.2 million applications for immigrant visas that are pending (almost all are expected to result in the issuance of an immigrant visa). The rising number of immigrants and the significant backlog reflects primarily family unification, especially as more immigrants becoming naturalized US citizens and sponsor their immediate family members for admission. In recent years, about two-thirds of US immigrants have US citizen or legal immigrant relatives already in the US who petition for their admission. The largest share of these family unification immigrants are immediate family members of US citizens: between 40 and 50 percent, often resulting from Americans marrying foreigners in the US or immigrants becoming naturalized US citizens and bringing their spouses, children, and parents to the US. [1]

---

[1] In fiscal year 2003, the 333,400 immediate relative immigrants were 47 percent of the immigrant flow, and they included 185,000 spouses of US citizens, 78,000 children, and 70,000 parents.

Table 1   Immigration to the US, 1991-2003

Fiscal year	Admissions
1991	1,827,167
1992	973,977
1993	904,292
1994	804,416
1995	720,461
1996	915,900
1997	798,378
1998	654,451
1999	646,568
2000	849,807
2001	1,064,318
2002	1,063,732
2003	705,827
Average	917,638

Source: Immigration Yearbook. The 1.8 million in 1991 reflected legalization. http://uscis.gov/graphics/shared/aboutus/statistics/ybpage.htm
The backlog of foreigners in the US awaiting immigrant visas was 1.2 million in 2003.

About a seventh of US immigrants (including their family members) are admitted because they have extraordinary ability or because US employers sponsored them for immigrant visas. The third group of front-door immigrants is for refugees and asylum seekers, about an eighth of the flow, and the fourth includes diversity[2] and other immigrants.

There are three important points about the employment-related immigrant door. First, three-fourths of the employment-related visas involve a US employer proving to the satisfaction of the US Department of Labor that US workers are not available to fill the job for which the employer is seeking an immigrant; these certification decisions are often contentious, suggesting that global talent can be in the eye of the beholder.[3] Second, there are relatively few admissions of "global talent" such as foreigners with extraordinary ability, outstanding professors, and

[2] Diversity immigrants are persons who applied for a US immigrant visa in a lottery open to those from countries that sent fewer than 50,000 immigrants to the US in the previous five years.

[3] The 1965 Immigration Act says that foreigners can be admitted to fill vacant US jobs if (1) there are not sufficient workers who are able, willing, qualified and available at the time of application for a visa and admission to the United States and at the place where the alien is to perform such skilled or unskilled labor, and (2) the employment of such alien will not adversely affect the wages and working conditions of workers in the United States similarly employed.

executives and managers—the first preference category admitted without a test of the US labor market—fewer than 1,000 a month. Third, if the US share of global talent is about the same as its share of immigration, say half, then it appears that there is not a large number of highly talented people eager to migrate.

Most economists have had little to say about the overall level of immigration, [4] but much more to say about its composition; most advocate a higher percentage of immigrant visas for the highly skilled (Borjas, 1999). There are two major ways to select global talent: on the basis of supply or demand. Supply selection uses individual characteristics to pick those likely to succeed in the labor market, assigning points for age, education, language skills, and sometimes a job offer, and requiring applicants to score a minimum number of points to get an immigrant visa. The demand approach emphasizes the job offer, but can also set minimum supply or individual characteristic standards, e.g., the employer wants to fill a job with a foreigner who must have at least a college degree. Most countries (including the US) use a combination of supply and demand criteria for evaluating applications for employment-based immigrants, but the US emphasizes the demand approach to ensure that the foreigner has a job, while countries such as Australia and Canada emphasize the supply approach, making the job offer a small fraction of the points needed for an immigrant visa.

The 140,000 ceiling (raised from 54,000 a year in 1990) on employment-related immigrant visas includes family members, which means that an average 55,000 a year "principals" got employment-related immigrant visas after being screened or sponsored (Table 2). If we define "global talent" as those with "extraordinary ability," which the regulations suggest means a Nobel prize or a worldwide reputation, the US admits an average 2,200 a year (these foreigners can enter without a test of the US labor market and without a US employer). Outstanding professors and multinational executives, on the other hand, must have US job offers, but their US employers do not have to prove that US workers are not available (there is no test of the US labor market); their number averages 2,400 and 6,700 a year. In short, if US first-preference immigrants are considered global talent, the US attracts 11,000 a year, or about 1 percent of its annual immigration flow.

---

[4] Unlike Canada, the US does not have an immigration goal such as admitting enough immigrants to raise the population by one percent a year. Instead, most US legislation includes the general assertion that "immigration is in the national interest" without specifying levels.

Table 2 Employment-based US immigration, 1998-2002

	1998	2000	2002	Average	
Principals getting visas	33,771	50,135	79,802	54,569	Per Dist
1st preference	8,709	11,452	13,807	11,323	100%
Aliens with extraordinary ability	1,691	2,002	2,881	2,191	21%
Outstanding professors/ researchers	1,835	2,667	2,737	2,413	4%
Multinational executives/ managers	5,183	6,783	8,189	6,718	4%
2nd preference Professionals with advanced degrees	6,933	9,815	21,334	12,694	12%
3rd preference	15,143	24,373	41,238	26,918	23%
Skilled workers	8,515	13,651	17,788	13,318	49%
College graduates	3,927	8,771	21,679	11,459	24%
Other workers (unskilled workers)	2,701	1,951	1,771	2,141	21%
4th preference, religious	2,695	4,403	3,366	3,488	4%
5th preference, investors	259	79	52	130	6%
Principals-Per of US immigration	5%	6%	8%	6%	0%
Dependents of Principals	43,746	56,889	95,166	65,267	
Total US Immigration	654,451	849,807	1,063,732	855,997	

Source: Yearbook of Immigration Statistics, http://uscis.gov/graphics/shared/aboutus/statistics/ybpage.htm
Data are for calendar years; total can exceed 140,000 a year because visas can be used up to six months after being issued.

There are more second-preference immigrants, an average 13,000 a year, who are professionals with advanced degrees. They must undergo labor certification (http://atlas.doleta.gov/foreign/perm.asp), meaning that their US employers must prove to the satisfaction of the US Department of Labor that no US workers are available to fill the job for which the employer is seeking an immigrant visa.[5] Third-preference immigrants must also undergo labor certification, and the average 27,000 a year principals include significant numbers of H-1B workers whose employers

[5] State workforce agencies supervise employer recruitment, and the time between when they receive an employer's request for supervised recruitment and approval varies widely, often requiring three years or more (http://atlas.doleta.gov/foreign/times.asp#state).

sponsored them for an immigrant visa. [6] A maximum 10,000 immigrant visas a year are available to unskilled workers, so that the wait for Americans sponsoring their maids and gardeners for immigrant visas is often a decade or more.

Religious worker immigrants do not undergo labor certification—they are admitted on the basis of attestations by their US church employers. In most cases, foreign ministers and professionals working in a religious vocation are already in the US on the R-1 non-immigrant visas available to religious workers, and their US church or organization sponsors them for immigrant visas.

Foreign investors undergo a separate investment and job creation test to obtain immigrant visas. In most cases, they invest at least US$500,000 to create or preserve at least 10 full-time jobs (at least 35 hours a week) in a "targeted employment area," which includes rural areas and urban areas with unemployment rates that are 150 percent of the US average rate. After making the investment (most are passive investments in which the foreigner is not an active manager), the foreigner receives a two-year probationary immigrant visa which converts to a regular immigrant visa thereafter.

During the mid-1990s, when there was a debate about the labor certification process in the wake of recommendations to substitute a fee for supervised recruitment, the Inspector General of the Department of Labor (DOL) issued a report that was very critical of the process (US Department of Labor, 1996.). [7] An examination of the records of 24,000 requests for immigrant visas found that 99 percent of the foreigners were already in the US and that 74 percent were already employed by the employer requesting an immigrant visa for them. Some 165,000 US workers applied for these 24,000 jobs, almost seven US applicants per job, but in virtually every case, the US workers were found not qualified, and the foreigners were hired.

The central conclusion of the report was that US employers sponsored foreigners for immigrant visas to "reward" them, so that, even though the reason for issuing the visa was to fill a vacant job for which no US workers could be found, a third of the foreigners left the employer who sponsored them within a year of getting their immigrant visas, which made them free agents in the US labor market.

---

[6] There are two so-called Schedule A occupations for which US employers do not have to recruit US workers before being certified as needing immigrants: physical therapists and nurses who hold licenses to practice in the state where the employer who wants to hire them is located.

[7] Deborah Billings, "Audit by DOL Inspector General Faults Employment-based Immigration Programs," Daily Labor Report, April 15, 1996.

The Gannett News Service did a series of articles in August 1996 that echoed the Inspector General's findings, concluding that the US$270 million spent by employers on labor certification, and the US$50 million spent by the federal government supervising their recruitment, was largely a going-through-the-motions exercise.[8] Gannett emphasized that many of the foreigners receiving immigrant visas because their employers sponsored them were not highly skilled. Between 1988 and 1996, for example, some 40,000 housekeepers, nannies and domestic workers were sponsored for immigrant visas, as were 15,000 cooks and chefs, 3,000 auto repair workers, 252 fast-food workers, 199 poultry dressers, 173 choral directors, 156 landscape laborers, 122 short-order cooks, 77 plumbers, 68 doughnut makers, 53 baker's helpers, and 38 hospital janitors.

Almost all US employer requests for immigrant visas to fill vacant jobs are eventually approved, but US employers and the immigrants they sponsor are very critical of the delays. Most did not support mid-1990s recommendations to substitute a "significant fee" of US$10,000 to US$20,000 per visa requested, and then dispense with supervised recruitment, perhaps because a fee-based system may have threatened the work of the thousands of lawyers who specialize in helping employers to navigate the labor certification process (http://www.aila.org).[9]

Instead, DOL took two other steps to deal with employer complaints of lengthy supervised recruitment. First, DOL has for the past several years permitted employers who can prove that they tried to recruit US workers during the previous six months to forego supervised recruitment by submitting copies of ads for workers and other evidence of active efforts to locate US workers.

Second, DOL announced a new Program Electronic Review Management (PERM) system that would substitute H-1B attestation-type procedures for labor certification, meaning that employers would complete an online form with 56 questions, answering yes or no to whether the foreigner is currently employed by the employer, whether proficiency in a foreign language is required to perform the job, and whether US applicants were rejected for the job. If the answers to these questions are satisfactory, the employer should receive approval to ask for an immigrant visa for the worker in question within three weeks, but employers found

---

[8] Jim Sprecht, "Government has little control over job-based immigration," Gannett News Service, August 4, 1996.

[9] For a list of fees and processing times for various immigration statuses, see www.usavisanow.com/immigrationservicesprices.htm

to have lied in answering the questions to be required to return to supervised recruitment and its delays. Unions and critics of employer-sponsored immigrant visas say that the new procedures implemented to reduce delays make it impossible for DOL to satisfy its duties to ensure that US workers are unavailable and that the presence of foreign workers will not adversely affect similar US workers.

Employment-based immigration is a contentious but low-profile issue in the United States. Academic studies consistently conclude that the net economic benefits of immigration, estimated to add 1/10 of 1 percent to US GDP of about US$11.5 trillion, would be higher if the US shifted the composition of immigrants toward the highly skilled. Employers who seek immigrant visas for foreigners and the lawyers who advise them express dissatisfaction with the delays and costs of the current systems, but have been unwilling to shift toward a pay-to-prove-that-you-need immigrants system, with the funds collected used to subsidize training in labor-short occupations. Instead, budget cuts to the DOL have resulted in the proposed simplified PERM system that will give US employers easier access to immigrants without fees or certification.

Highly skilled migrants

Immigration is sometimes referred to as the front-door to the US, which makes non-immigrant admissions the side door and illegal immigration the back door. Non-immigrants are foreigners who come to the United States to visit, work, or study, that is, they are in the US for a specific time and purpose. The number of non-immigrants tripled in the past 20 years, primarily because of the growing number of tourists and business visitors, but there has also been significant growth in admissions of temporary foreign workers—over a million a year have been admitted in recent years, although the same individual could be counted several times in admission data.

The non-immigrant program that may be closest to "global talent" is offers of O-1 visas for foreigners with "extraordinary ability in the sciences, arts, education, business or athletics" further defined as "a level of expertise indicating that the person is one of the small percentage who have risen to the top of the field of endeavor." The supporting documentation for applicants for O-1 visas includes national and international prizes, scholarly publications, and/or "evidence that the alien has or will command a high salary." US "peer organizations" are consulted to ensure that the foreigner seeking an O-1 visa is truly outstanding.

O-1 visas are issued for one year, but can be renewed indefinitely; about 26,000 were issued in fiscal year 2001, plus 4,000 to accompanying persons.

A third of the temporary foreign worker admissions in the late 1990s were for foreign professionals with H-1B visas, half are from India, and over half of the H-1Bs work in IT-related fields while they stay in the US up to six years. The H-1B program allows most US employers seeking to have foreigners admitted to fill jobs to attest that they are paying prevailing wages and that there is no strike that has made a job vacant, and then foreigners with at least a BA are permitted easy entry for up to three years to fill a US job that normally requires its holder to have a BA degree. While in the US, H-1B workers can have family members with them and can become immigrants if their US employer sponsors them for an immigrant visa. The admissions process is straightforward. The US employer or petitioner completes an online DOL form and, with only minimal checks certifies the employer's request, which is then submitted to immigration authorities and to consular officials overseas, so that the foreigner or beneficiary can receive the H-1B visa inside or outside the US. [10]

The H-1B visa is unusual because (1) it permits dual intent: foreigners can say they want to become immigrants and still obtain a visa, while foreign students or tourists cannot, and (2) the US employer in effect controls the border gate, not the government. The attestation procedure means that the employer makes assertions, and there is normally no enforcement unless there are complaints. [11] Under the alternative certification procedure, by contrast, the government controls the border gate, and does not allow foreigners to be admitted until the employer satisfies the government that US workers are not available. As the number of H-1B visa holders in the US climbed in the late 1990s, there was considerable frustration as some foreigners who assumed that they would be able to obtain immigrant visas within the six year validity of their H-1B visas, had to leave as their six years ran out before they received immigrant visas.

---

[10] There is also a small H-1C program that admits up to 500 registered nurses a year (and up to 25 per US state) to serve in hospitals designated as "health professional shortage areas" (most are in Texas). The H-1C program was approved in 1999, and is based on a smaller 1989 H-1A visa program for nurses that expired. One unique feature is that hospitals applying for H-1C nurses must develop and submit plans to reduce their dependence on foreign nurses over time. Hospitals that hire nurses under the H-1B program do not have to file such a dependence-reduction plan.

[11] "Labor (DOL) can certify that an employer's application form for H-1B workers is error free, but it has no authority to verify the information on the form. Labor cannot take enforcement action even if it believes that employers are violating the law" unless it receives a complaint of violations, as from a competitor or a US worker (GAO, 2000).

Table 3   Employment-based immigration and H-1Bs, 1992-2003

	1992	1993	1994
Employment ceiling	140,000	140,000	140,000
Immigrants (including families)	116,198	147,012	123,291
Waiting list	140,000	161,207	143,213
H-1B Visa ceiling	65,000	65,000	65,000
H-1B Admissions	110,223	92,795	105,899
	1995	**1996**	**1997**
Employment ceiling	140,000	140,000	140,000
Immigrants (including families)	85,336	117,499	90,607
Waiting list	146,503	140,000	140,000
H-1B Visa ceiling	65,000	65,000	65,000
H-1B Admissions	117,574	114,458	200,000
	1998	**1999**	**2000**
Employment ceiling	140,000	140,000	140,000
Immigrants (including families)	77,517	56,817	107,024
Waiting list	160,898	142,299	194,074
H-1B Visa ceiling	65,000	115,000	115,000
H-1B Admissions	240,947	302,326	355,605
	2001	**2002**	**2003**
Employment ceiling	140,000	140,000	140,000
Immigrants (including families)	179,195	174,968	82,137
Waiting list	142,632		
H-1B Visa ceiling	195,000	195,000	195,000
H-1B Admissions	384,191	370,490	360,498

Employment-based immigration can exceed the 140,000 ceiling if visas were not fully used in previous years.
In fiscal year 2005, the additional 20,000 H-2B visas are available for employers hiring foreign graduates of US universities with MA degrees or more.
H-1B admissions double count individuals; 1997 H-1B admissions are estimated; the INS has no data.

Complaints about the H-1B program center on displacement of US workers and complaints against intermediaries. The trade off embodied in the H-1B program in 1990 was that employers would face few barriers to hiring H-1Bs, but there would be a cap of 65,000 H-1B visas a year. The assumption was that US workers with college degrees would complain loudly against abuses, so the H-1B program did not include provisions that, for example, prohibited employers from displacing US workers in order to hire H-1Bs. Some did just that, as when American

International Group in September 1994 laid off 130 US programmers and outsourced the work they did to Syntel, an Indian-American firm; the laid-off US programmers protested that they had to train the workers who replaced them in India and the US. Only H-1B-dependent employers, those with 15 percent or more H-1B workers, must certify that they did not lay off US workers to hire H-1B workers.

The second major complaint involves the intermediaries who recruit workers for US jobs. These so-called body brokers aim to maximize their revenues, which are obtained from migrants and employers, and often involve charging migrants fees, bringing them to the US, and then sending them to employers and profiting from the difference between what an employer pays and what the migrant receives. In one case of a broker maximizing migrant-paid fees, Atlanta-based Deep Sai Consulting Inc in November 1999 was charged with harboring illegal migrants after it brought 43 Indian programmers to the US for jobs that did not materialize in what prosecutors charged was "white-collar alien smuggling." In another case, an Indian H-1B arrived in November 2000 to work for Indian-owned ChristAm, which never found the H-1B worker a US job, paid him no wages, and went out of business after collecting his recruitment fees.

The next largest group of foreign professionals are so-called Nafta professionals. Chapter 16 of Nafta created almost freedom of movement for Canadian, Mexican, and US workers with a college degree or more by allowing Nafta employers to hire workers from other Nafta countries easily if they have a college degree or more. [12] Employers in the three Nafta countries can offer an unlimited number of jobs requiring college degrees to Nafta nationals with college degrees; unlike the H-1B program, there is no requirement that a Nafta employer pay at least the prevailing wage.

These written job offers, plus proof of the requisite education, suffice to have indefinitely renewable TN-visas issued at ports of entry. The number of Canadian professionals entering the US with Nafta-TN visas almost tripled since 1995, from about 25,000 entries a year to 70,000 entries, but the number of Mexican entries remains low, generally less than 2,000 a year.

---

[12] Under US immigration law, three of the four groups of trade-related migrants under Nafta's Chapter 16 enter with other visas, e.g. business visitors use B-1 visas, treaty traders and investors use E-1 and E-2 visas, and intra-company transferees use L-1 visas. Canadians also enter the US to work with H-visas, and an average 20,000 Canadians a year immigrate to the US.

Table 4 US admissions of Nafta professionals, 1994-2002

	Canadians	Mexicans	Total
1994	25,104	16	25,120
1995	25,598	63	25,661
1996	28,237	229	28,466
1997	48,430	436	48,866
1998	60,742	785	61,527
1999	60,755	1,242	61,997
2000	89,864	2,354	92,218
2001	70,229	1,806	72,035
2002	71,082	1,732	72,814
2003	58,177	1,269	59,446

Source: Roger Kramer, Developments in International Migration to the US, 2003, Calendar year data

Foreign professionals can also enter the US with L-1 visas for up to seven years if they are mangers or have specialized knowledge of the company's products or processes, were employed at least one year abroad, and are transferred by multinationals from a foreign to a US branch,[13] and they may adjust to immigrant status while in the US on an L-1 visa. There is no ceiling on the number of L-1 visas that can be issued, and in fiscal year 2004, some 57,245 L-1 visas were issued, about the same as in previous years, including a third to Indians.

A well-publicized incident in 2001 led to a change that requires L-1 visa holders in the US to be supervised by the multinational that brought them to the US. The L-1 change was motivated by events concerning Siemens in Florida. Siemens subcontracted its computer work to India-based Tata Consultancy Services in 2002, and required the US workers displaced by this outsourcing to train the newly arrived Tata workers in the US on L-1 visas as a condition of receiving severance pay. The US workers complained,[14] and the major change under the 2004 Reform Act is that any instructions must flow from Siemens to Tata

---

[13] It might be noted that the multinational can be a non-profit, religious, or charitable organization.

[14] There was disagreement within the US government over what Siemens did was lawful. The US Bureau of Citizenship and Immigration Services said Siemens actions were unlawful: "If an L-1 comes into the United States to work, they're coming to work for their specific company that petitioned for them, not for another company that they're being contracted out to." However, the US Department of State, which issues the L-1 visas, said "The fact that someone is on the site of (a client) does not make them ineligible for an L-1 as long as … the company they actually work for is truly functioning as their employer in terms of how they're paid and who has the right to fire them."

supervisors to the Tata L-1 workers, that is, Siemens may not deal directly with the Tata L-1 workers. [15]

However, employers are still free to displace US workers to make room for H-1B and L-1 workers, which is why the major US union federation, the AFL-CIO, has called for additional changes in both programs that center on substituting certification for attestation. However, the major change in the 2004 Reform Act is to require employers to pay a new US$500 anti-fraud fee when they apply for H-1B workers for the first time, and to require employers of L-1 visas to supervise them.

The final non-immigrant door is for foreign students. Some 637,954 foreigners with student visas entered the United States in fiscal year 2002, [16] led by students from India and China. Foreign students must be admitted or accepted by accredited US institutions, and then must convince consular officials that they have sufficient funds to study in the US and that they intend to return at the end of their studies. Foreign students may work on campus while studying (including for off-campus firms that provide on campus services such as food or janitorial services), up to 20 hours a week while studying and full time during breaks. [17] Foreign students can and do find US employers to sponsor them for immigrant and non-immigrant visas, and many remain in the US, including 90 percent of mainland Chinese students, although recent reports suggest that more Chinese graduates of US universities are returning to China.

The presence of foreign students became far more controversial after the September 11, 2001 terrorist attacks because some entered the US with student visas and never enrolled in the schools that admitted them. Most foreign students must now pay a US$100 fee to apply for an immigrant visa, and another US$100 to be tracked during their stay in the US under a computer-based program called the Student and Exchange Visitor Information System (SEVIS). The institutions where they are enrolled update their information in this web-based tracking system.

Foreign graduate students are closest to some definitions of global talent, and their number shrank in the US in Fall 2004 for the first time

---

[15] A similar issue arose when Polish workers in 2003 installed equipment in an expanding Mercedes auto assembly plant in Alabama on B-1 business visitor visas. The Polish workers reported that most of their US$1,100 a month wages were deposited in Poland while they were in the US for three to six months, and their presence set off a debate over whether Mercedes violated the intent of the business visitor program.

[16] The OECD, using different definitions, reported 586,000 foreign university students in the US in 2002, compared with 270,000 in Britain and 227,000 in Germany.

[17] After a year of US study, a foreign student can work off campus if there is "a severe economic hardship caused by unforeseen circumstances beyond the student's control."

in 30 years. [18] One reason is the post 9/11 Visa Mantis program, intended to prevent the transfer of sensitive technology, which requires a security review and annual visa renewal of foreign students who want to study in any of about 200 scientific fields (the list is not public). Within the US, academic leaders have complained vigorously that refusing to issue student visas to a third of the foreign students who have been admitted to US universities, and then monitoring them while they are in the US, will deny the US economy and society access to global talent at a time when other industrial countries are becoming more welcoming to foreign students.

There are several other US non-immigrant programs that could be used to admit global talent. The E-1 visa is for foreigners who are coming to the US to engage in trade with their countries of origin, while the E-2 visa is for foreigners who have invested in a US business and are coming to manage it; both can be renewed indefinitely. The H-2 programs admit foreign workers to fill temporary farm (A) and nonfarm (B) jobs. Most of the workers admitted with H-2 visas do not have much education, there have been instances of college-educated workers using especially the H-2B program to find a US employer to sponsor her for a H-1B or immigrant visa.

Similarly, the J-1 exchange-visitor visa allows foreigners to come to the US for "work and a cultural experience." The goal is to create good feelings about the United States abroad, and the program is administered by the US Department of State (DOS). US-based institutions create work-and-learn programs that are approved by DOS, and these programs recruit foreigners to come to the US as teachers, researchers, working holidaymakers, au pairs, and graduates of foreign medical schools seeking additional US training. US sponsors of J-1 visa programs must show that they can send Americans abroad under reciprocal arrangements.

After being in the US on a J-1 visa, the foreigner must normally return home for two years, and this return requirement is often highlighted as a "best practice" to promote truly temporary migration. However, this two-year home country requirement can be and is waived for foreign medical graduates (foreigners who graduated from one of the 1,600 medical schools outside the US and Canada that graduate 350,000 doctors a year). If J-1 doctors are employed in medically underserved areas for several years, they can get an immigrant visa if a US institution

---

[18] Sam Dillon, "U.S. Slips in Attracting the World's Best Students," New York Times, December 21, 2004.

issues a letter asserting that the foreign doctor's continued presence is necessary to avoid hardship to US patients. This happens frequently: foreign medical graduates are 25 percent of US doctors, and a third of hospital-based, full-time physicians.

Unauthorized migrants

The back door refers to unauthorized, illegal, or irregular migrants. No one knows exactly how many unauthorized foreigners are in the United States: about 1.1 million a year are apprehended, and almost all are Mexicans caught just inside the US border. US government estimates of unauthorized foreigners have been increased several times in the 1990s, and the best independent estimates of the number of unauthorized foreigners are 20 percent higher than the government estimates.

Table 5   Unauthorized foreigners in the US: 1980-2000

Year	Millions	Annual average change
1980	3	
1986	4	167,000
1989	2.5	−500,000
1992	3.9	467,000
1995	5	367,000
2000	8.5	700,000

Source: Jeff Passel, Urban Institute
About 2.7 million unauthorized foreigners were legalized in 1987-88.

Most of those apprehended are Mexicans who are returned "voluntarily" to Mexico, which means they are fingerprinted, photographed and taken to the border by bus, but are not usually prosecuted if they are apprehended again in the US. Even those who are formally removed or deported are primarily Mexican—80 percent of 149,000 persons in 2002.[19] The dominance of Mexicans among those apprehended and removed suggests that there are few professionals among the unauthorized, but legalization in 1987-88 as well as press accounts suggest that there are at least "thousands" of college-educated foreigners who are illegally in the US for at least some period of time, such as after their

---

[19] Formal removal means that an immigration judge orders an individual deported, and if that individual is caught again in the US, she can be prosecuted.

student or work visas expire. Many find ways to legalize their status, through work or marriage.

Conclusions

The United States sees itself as a nation of immigrants that is open to newcomers who benefit by immigrating while conferring benefits on the US economy and society. Most political leaders thus assert that the best way to attract global talent is to maintain an open and free society that maximizes freedom and opportunity and minimizes taxes.

However, in response to economists' recommendations to accept more highly skilled immigrants as well as requests from particular (groups of) employers, the US more than doubled the number of economic immigrants in 1990, from 54,000 to 140,000 (including family members). Relatively few of these immigrants qualify as global talent, in the sense that there is no need to test the US labor market to determine if US workers are available—an average of about 11,000 a year. Most of these immigrants are admitted after a US employer sponsors them by proving, to the satisfaction of the US Department of Labor, that US workers are not available to fill the job for which the foreigner is being requested. However, in practice most employers sponsor current employees as a reward for faithful service, and most foreigners quit their jobs as soon as they obtain immigrant visas.

There are far more non-immigrants admitted to fill vacant US jobs, and US employers must satisfy a wide range of criteria to have visas issued to the foreigners they want to employ. The largest program issues H-1B visas to foreigners with at least college degrees coming to the US for up to six years to fill jobs requiring at least college degrees. This program more than tripled to more than 195,000 admissions a year at the height of the IT boom in 2000, but has since shrunk to about half that flow. The other large program is for foreign students, many of whom stay in the US and work after graduation, but the number of especially foreign graduate students appears to have fallen significantly since the September 11, 2001 terrorist attacks.

References

Borjas, George. 1999. Heaven's Door: Immigration Policy And The American Economy. Princeton University Press.

OECD. 2004. Internationalization and Trade in Higher Education. Opportunities and Challenges. Paris. OECD.

US Department of Labor. 1996. The Department of Labor's Foreign Labor Certification Programs: The System is Broken and Needs to be Fixed. Report. 06-96-002-03-321. http://www.oig.dol.gov/public/reports/oa/pre_1998/06-96-002-03-321s.htm

US General Accountability Office. 2004. H-1B Foreign Workers: Better Tracking Needed to Help Determine H-1B Program's Effects on U.S. Workforce. GAO-03-883.

US General Accountability Office. 2000. H-1B Foreign Workers: Better Controls Needed to Help Employers and Protect Workers. GAO-HEHS-00-157.

US General Accountability Office. 2002. Highlights of a GAO Forum: Workforce Challenges and Opportunities for 21st Century: Changing Labor Force Dynamics and the Role of Government.

Appendix

Professions covered by Nafta Chapter 16

General

Accountant
Architect
Computer Systems Analyst
Insurance Claims Adjuster
Economist
Engineer
Graphic Designer
Hotel Manager
Industrial Designer
Interior Designer
Land Surveyor
Landscape Architect
Lawyer
Librarian
Management Consultant
Mathematician/Statistician
Range Manager/Range Conservationalist
Research Assistant (in college/uni)
Scientific Technician/Technologist
Social Worker
Technical Publications Writer
Urban Planner/Geographer
Vocational Counselor

Medical-related

Dentist
Dietitian
Medical Lab. Technologist
Nutritionist
Occupational Therapist
Pharmacist
Physician (teaching or research only)
Physiotherapist/Physical Therapist
Psychologist
Recreational Therapist
Registered Nurse
Veterinarian

Teaching

College
Seminary
University

Scientists

Agriculturist/Agronomist
Animal Breeder
Animal Scientist
Apiculturist
Astronomer
Biochemist
Biologist
Chemist
Dairy Scientist
Entomologist
Epidemiologist
Geneticist
Geologist
Geochemist
Geophysicist/Oceanographer
Horticulturist
Meteorologist
Pharmacologist
Physicists
Plant Breeder
Poultry Scientist
Soil Scientist
Sylviculturist (Forestry)
Zoologist

Australian experience in skilled migration

Graeme Hugo

Introduction

In Australia, like other OECD nations, there has long been recognition that in order to be globally competitive the national economy must have ongoing access to a highly skilled labour force. Unlike several, however, there also has been a longstanding practice of accessing such talent through immigration. Whereas many other nations have only introduced skill migration programmes in the last decade, in Australia large scale, explicitly skill selective, immigration polices and programmes are more than three decades old. Indeed workforce considerations have been dominant in Australian immigration policy over the entire postwar period. Without this immigration Australia's population would be around 12 million rather than the present 20.1 million (Kippen and McDonald 2000). Of all OECD nations none has a contemporary population and workforce so influenced by migration. At the 2001 population census, some 23.1 percent of the resident population were foreign born (24.2 percent of the workforce) and a similar proportion were Australian born but had at least one parent born overseas (Khoo *et al.* 2002). In addition, however, at the same time there were 554,200 persons temporarily present in Australia of whom more than a half had the right to work (DIMIA 2002). Moreover, Australia is not only one of the world's most significant immigration nations but it is also, relatively, an important *emigration* nation with a diaspora of around one million expatriate Australians, equivalent to 4.3 percent of its resident population (Hugo, Rudd and Harris 2003) and this emigration is highly selective of the young, the skilled and the workforce generally. Hence, in Australia there is a longstanding commitment to, and reliance upon, immigration in the labour force (Wooden, *et al.* 2004) while in recent years, the increase in emigration of skilled Australians has also placed the issue of "brain drain" on the national agenda (Wood (ed.) 2004).

This paper seeks to analyse the contemporary Australian experience with respect to global competition for skilled workers. It begins by briefly examining some relevant features of the Australian labour market and demographic context. For much of the postwar period Australian migration policy has concentrated totally on the attraction of people (albeit those with particular characteristics) to settle *permanently* in Australia. Accordingly, the next section of the paper focuses on the development of Australia's immigration and settlement polices which are designed to attract and retain skilled workers and on their impact on the Australian labour market. However, the last decade has seen a paradigm shift in Australian immigration policy (Hugo 1999; 2004a). Whereas it had previously eschewed the recruitment of temporary labour in favour of permanent migration, since 1996 there has been an active attempt to bring skilled workers to Australia on a temporary basis. These initiatives are discussed and their labour market effects assessed. There is also a consideration of the recent development of policies to retain substantial numbers of these temporary workers in Australia. There can be no doubt that in purely numerical terms Australia is experiencing a "brain gain" of skilled workers (Hugo 1994; Birrell *et al.* 2001). However, there is also no doubt that the tempo of emigration of skilled Australians has accelerated in recent years and the next section of the paper assesses the scale and effects of the phenomenon. As with other sections, there is an examination of policies which have been initiated and discussed with respect to the brain drain and Australia's diaspora. A final part of the paper looks to the future and speculates about likely directions in Australian policy relating to the global competition for talent.

The Australian context

Australia is a developed market economy dominated by its services sector which accounts for around two thirds of GDP. Its agriculture and mining sectors account for only 7 percent of GDP but 57 percent of exports of goods and services. The relative size of its manufacturing sector has declined over the last three decades and now accounts for only 12 percent of GDP. The economy has undergone major structural change whereby the tertiary sector has assumed greater importance in its share of GDP and employment and there has been a loss of unskilled and semi skilled jobs through automation, computerisation and to offshore developments. There have been major attempts to increase the skill levels of the Australian workforce and Table 1 shows that the proportion of the Australian workforce with qualifications has increased substantially over the last 20 years.

Table 1   Australia: Population Aged Fifteen and Over 1981 and 2001

Qualification	1981 Census No.	%	2001 Census No.	%
University Qualification	445,122	4.6	1,918,913	14.6
Other Post School Qualification	2,192,607	22.8	3,234,300	24.6
No Qualification	6,998,347	72.6	8,000,078	60.8
Total*	9,636,076	100.0	13,153,291	100.0

* Excludes not stated

Source: ABS Censuses, 1981 and 2001

Figure 1   Australia: Percent of Males and Females Aged 15-24 in Tertiary Education, 1966 to 2002

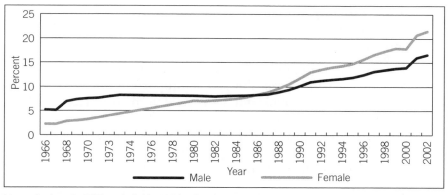

Note: Students in CAEs excluded in 1966 and 1967.

Students in Queensland CAEs excluded 1968-71.

Figures for 1985 to 1993 progressively include State-funded basic nursing students who previously would have been trained in hospitals.

Data from 1980 to 2000 refer to students enrolled at 31 March of the stated year.

In 2001 the scope used to define the data changed to include students enrolled at anytime within the 12 month period 1 September to 31 August.

Source: Calculated from National Population Inquiry 1975, DETYA 2001 and ABS 2004

There has also been a shift in the proportion of school leavers entering tertiary education (Figure 1). Nevertheless, there have been shortages in several skill areas in the labour market over this period and immigration policies have been specifically designed to fill these gaps. This has been accompanied by a debate in Australia over this period (e.g. Birrell *et al.* 2000) as to whether using immigration to fill gaps in the labour market has been a substitute for investing in the training of resident Australians. It is argued that government and private enterprises have neglected the training of Australian as a long term solution to labour market gaps and opted for the cheaper, short term answer of immigration.

Moreover, Australia's labour force like that of other OECD nations is experiencing substantial change as a result of low fertility and the consequent ageing of the population. The problem is not as severe as in most other OECD nations because Australian fertility has been relatively stable at around a total fertility rate of 1.8 and there has been a continuous flow of age selective immigration over the postwar period (Kippen and McDonald 2000). Nevertheless, the following effects of ageing on the labour force are increasingly being realized among Australian policy makers as being potential constraints on the nation's future economic prosperity...

- Notwithstanding the moderate fertility levels and immigration, the rate of growth of the Australian workforce will reduce substantially. While currently Australia's workforce is growing by around 170,000 per annum, in the 2020s it will increase by only 100,000 in the entire decade.

- The workforce itself is ageing with the median age increasing from 34.1 in 1981 to 38.4 in 2001. The proportion of the total workforce aged 40 years or older has increased from 36.3 percent in 1981 to 53.8 percent in 2001. While there is debate about the relative innovativeness, productivity, etc. of older and younger workers, there is some evidence to suggest that there are disadvantages of having a labour force dominated by older workers.

- There is considerable variation between sectors with respect to the ageing of the workforce. For example, Figure 2 overlays the age pyramid of teaching academics in Australia at the 2001 population census with that for the total workforce. Clearly the academic workforce is much more concentrated in the older ages with 51.2 percent aged 45 or over compared to 33.4 percent in the total workforce. This is due to a massive period of recruitment in the 1960s and 1970s and a stabilisation of numbers of academics in the last decade and presages a huge recruitment task in Australian academia over the next 15 years (Hugo forthcoming). This unbalanced situation is duplicated in several other niches of the labour force such as teachers and doctors.

Figure 2   Age-Sex Structures of Academic Staff and the Australian Workforce, 2001

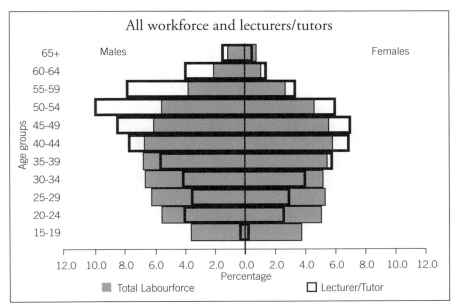

Source: ABS 2001 Census

Clearly then, growth in the need for skilled personnel in Australia is not simply a function of increasing global competition but also of the demography of the Australian workforce.

Immigration and settlement policy in Australia

Immigration has accounted directly for around a half of Australia's rapid postwar population growth as Figure 3 indicates. However, immigration policy has undergone a number of major shifts over this period. Three main eras can be recognised…

- 1947-1971 – Australia experienced substantial labour shortage in the postwar period. Immigration increased to unprecedented levels and since sufficient numbers could not be recruited from the traditional source of the United Kingdom and Ireland it extended its immigration program to include other European countries. Much of this labour was unskilled and semi skilled. It also accepted large numbers of refugees, also mainly from Europe.

- 1971-1996 – With structural change in the economy and ageing of the baby boom cohorts into the workforce, labour shortage was no

111

Figure 3   Australia: Total Population Growth Showing the Natural Increase and Net Migration Components, 1947-2004

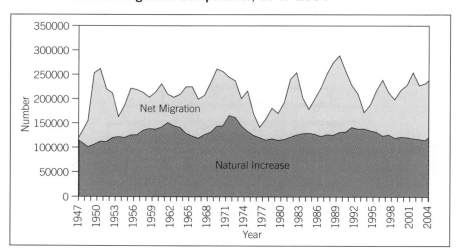

Source: ABS 1986 and ABS Australian Demographic Statistics, various issues

longer the *raison d'être* of immigration and an immigration pro-gramme based mainly on skill recruitment, family reunion and refugee/humanitarian components was developed. Also the "white Australia" policy was finally totally dismantled and significant migration from Asia followed.

- 1996-present – Australia's permanent immigration policy became more focused on skill recruitment but also new temporary migration visas were developed to attract skilled workers in particular areas.

One of the distinctive aspects of Australian immigration over the post-war period has been the fact that it has been drawn from a large range of countries and not dominated by one or two birthplace groups. Australia is one of the most multicultural of nations with 58 countries of birth having more than 10,000 persons and 112 more than 1,000. More-over, there have been fluctuations in the mix of birthplace groups enter-ing Australia. Figure 4 shows that in the early post-war decades UK-Ire-land and Other Europe were the dominant origins of immigrants but in the second half of the post-war period these origins represent only a small proportion of settlers while Asia and the Pacific provided the bulk of immigration with the Middle East and Africa also being significant. Hence, the composition of the stock of immigrants in Australia has changed. Table 2 shows the birthplace composition of migrants at the

Figure 4   Australia: Settler Arrivals by Region of Last Residence, 1947-2004

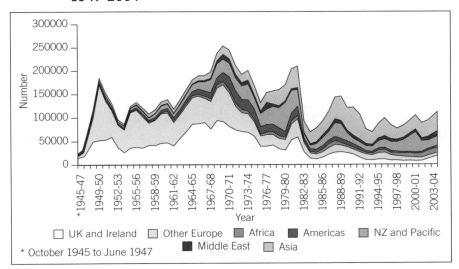

Source: DIMIA Australian Immigration Consolidated Statistics and Immigration Update, various issues; DIMIA unpublished data

1996 and 2001 censuses according to whether they had arrived in Australia in the five years preceding the census or earlier. This shows the declining significance of European origins and the increasing importance of other, especially Asian, origins.

The current Australian immigration program is highly planned with the government setting a target for each year and planning levels for each component of the migration program. The humanitarian program includes not only mandated refugees but also other humanitarian elements.

Within the non-humanitarian part of the Program there are three main components summarized in Table 3 – Family, Skill and Special Eligibility – although within each there are a number of sub-programs. Some of the smaller components, i.e. Business Skills, Employer Nominated Scheme (ENS), Distinguished Talent, Spouses and Dependent Children are demand driven and not subject to capping. Increases in demand for these visas, beyond planned levels, are compensated by reductions in other program components, i.e. Independent and Skilled-Australian Linked, Parents, Fiancés and Interdependents.

A key element in the non-humanitarian program is a points assessment system whereby applicants for settlement are allocated points according to a number of criteria. The make up of the test has varied since

113

Table 2 Origins of Foreign Born Population According to Length of Residence in Australia 1996 and 2001

| Region of Birth | 1996 Census | | | | 2001 Census | | | | Percent Change | |
| | Pre 1991 | | Post 1991 | | Pre 1996 | | Post 1996 | | 1996-2001 | |
	No.	%	No.	%	No.	%	No.	%	Longstanding	Recent
Oceania and Antarctica	285,792	8.9	78,678	13.7	310,477	9.5	118,514	19.0	8.6	50.6
Europe Former USSR	2,004,648	62.7	142,801	24.9	1,892,833	57.9	143,318	23.0	-5.6	0.4
Middle East – N. Africa	150,604	4.7	35,491	6.2	165,288	5.1	37,193	6.0	9.8	4.8
Southeast Asia	320,863	10.0	121,151	21.1	376,741	11.5	47,914	15.7	17.4	-19.2
Northeast Asia	142,265	4.4	98,821	17.2	185,096	5.7	97,526	15.7	30.1	-1.3
Southern Asia	95,568	3.0	46,100	8.0	124,081	3.8	55,163	8.9	29.8	19.7
America	114,412	3.6	31,024	5.4	123,208	3.8	30,839	5.0	7.7	-0.6
Africa (less N. Africa)	84,800	2.7	20,031	3.5	93,796	2.9	52,533	6.8	10.6	112.3
Total	3,198,952	100.0	574,097	100.0	3,271,520	100.0	623,000	100.0	2.3	8.5

Note: Excludes not stated and inadequately described.
Source: ABS 1996 and 2001 Censuses

Table 3   Program Management Structure (2001-02) Migration (non-Humanitarian) Program

Skill	Family	Special Eligibility
Skilled Independent & Skilled-Australian Sponsored*	*Parents and Preferential Family* Can be capped subject to demand in all other Family categories	Can be capped
• Points tested • Planning level adjusted subject to demand in Business Skills and ENS		
	Fiancés & Interdependents Can be capped subject to demand for spouse and dependent child places	
Business Skills, ENS & Distinguished		
Talent Demand driven	*Spouses & Dependent Children* • Demand driven	
	• Exempt from capping	
Contingency Reserve To be utilised if States and Territories, business employers and regional authorities generate additional demand, and for ICT professionals with Australian qualifications	*Contingency Reserve* Legislation defeated in Senate October 2000	

* Formerly Independent and Skilled-Australian Linked (until July 1999)
Source: DIMIA 2002

it was first introduced around thirty years ago and the criteria have included...

•   Age

•   Education

•   Occupations in demand

•   Work experience

•   English language skills

•   Skill

•   Having family support in Australia

Rizvi (2004, 17) reports that the points test in the dominant skilled category (Skilled Independent Visa) involved selection of migrants in 2003-04 as follows...

•   65 percent were aged between 18 and 30

- 87 percent achieved maximum points for English
- 96 percent achieved maximum points for skill
- 55 percent held Australian qualifications

The points test is continually being fine tuned with the points allocated to particular criteria being adjusted and the pass mark whereby entry is assured subject to medical and criminal record checks is changed.[1] In recent times there have been bonus points available to migrants who indicate they will settle in regional areas. The points test is a key instrument in the skill part of the programme, and its modification as well as other changes in the immigration selection process in the last decade have been heavily based upon the findings of research into the settlement experience of different visa categories of immigrants. A main component of this was the Longitudinal Survey of Immigrants in Australia (LSIA) which followed two groups of immigrants arriving in Australia in 1993-95 and 1999-2000 and re-interviewed them (Hugo 2004b).

Another important element in the Australian immigration program has been the proliferation of a large number of separate visa categories and sub categories. This has allowed the program to target particular groups. Figure 5 presents the breakdown of the numbers in each category for the year 2003-04. Over recent times in Australia there has been greater government intervention to shape the content of the intake of immigrants so that it can better contribute to national development goals. This has seen greater emphasis on skills in migrant selection and in the development of business migration programs involved to attract entrepreneurs with substantial sums to invest in the destination country. Hence, there has been a substantial shift toward skills/business migration and away from family migration as Figure 6 demonstrates. The proportion of immigrants in the Skill categories has increased from 29.2 percent in 1995-96 to 62.3 percent in 2003-04. In recent years, the number of skilled immigrants has successively set new records with the 71,240 arriving in 2003-04 the largest ever (Rizvi 2004, 14).

The increasing skill orientation in Australia's immigration program has borne fruit in terms of the improved labour market performance of migrants in Australia. This contrasts sharply with the experience in other traditional immigration nations like Canada (Ruddick 2003; Zhang 2003) and the United States (Martin 2004) where the labour market situation of immigrants has deteriorated in recent times.

---

[1] For example, in 2004 it was increased by 5 points to 125.

Figure 5   Categories of Immigration[a] to Australia, 2003-04

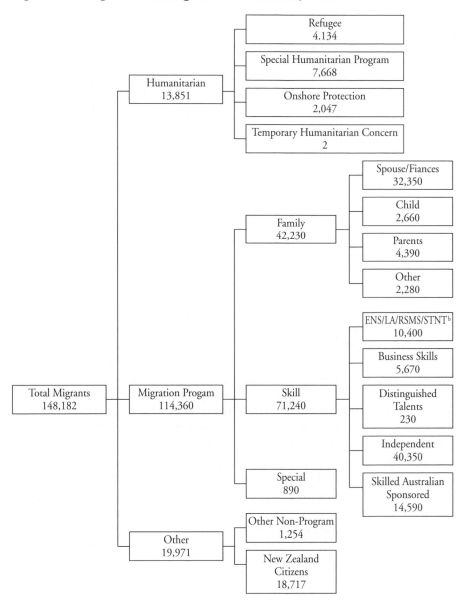

[a] Includes settler arrivals plus onshore applicants.

[b] Includes Employer Nomination Scheme, Labour Agreement, Regional Sponsored Migration Scheme and State/Territory Nominated Independent Scheme.

Source: From Rizvi 2004 and DIMIA unpublished data

Figure 6   Australia: Migration Program Outcomes by Stream

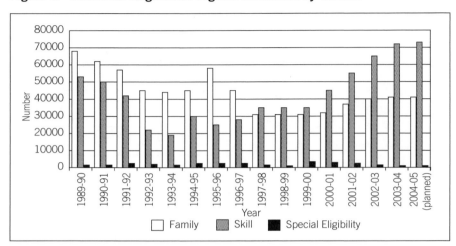

Source: DIMIA Population Flows: Immigration Aspects, various issues and Rizvi 2004, p. 14

Table 4 shows that at the 2001 census, labour force participation rates[2] were lower among longstanding immigrants (70.5 percent) compared to the Australian born and significantly lower among recent arrivals (60 percent). Despite the limitations of this measure it undoubtedly indicates significant differences between the three groups. The participation rate does not tell the degree of engagement which immigrants had with the workforce – hours worked, full time/part time, fractional, etc. but it is indicative of differences between immigrants who recently arrived and those of longstanding. Among recent immigrants there is less involvement in the workforce despite their younger age structure. This is partly due to a low level of engagement of spouses among recent immigrants and there is substantial literature indicating the problems experienced by new immigrants in Australia. Problems with language, recognition of qualifications, lack of knowledge of the labour market, lack of local contacts, etc.; have hampered the involvement of immigrants in the labour market (Wooden et al, 1994; VandenHeuvel and Wooden 1999). This is reflected in both a lower participation rate and a higher unemployment rate among recent immigrants. The fact that immigrant labour market participation is greater and unemployment is less among longer standing immigrants reflects their improvement in English language skills, upgrading work skills and increasing local knowledge and experience. It also may

---

[2] Number in the workforce as a proportion of the population aged 15-64.

Table 4 Australia: Birthplace by Period of Residence : Labour Market Variables 2001

	Australian Born	Recent Migrants	Longstanding Migrants
Employed	6,044,183	246,870	1,687,772
Unemployed	459,975	30,527	134,702
Not in Labour Force	2,210,357	184,942	762,136
Participation Rate (%)	74.6	60.0	70.5
Unemployment Rate (%)	7.1	11.0	7.4

Note: Data applies only to the population aged 15-64
Source: ABS 2001 Census, unpublished tabulations

reflect some emigration loss of immigrants who are less successful in Australian labour markets (Hugo 1994). Analysis of LSIA and ABS labour force survey data have indicated the changes made to Australia's immigration selection system and the increase of non-permanent migration has had a significant impact on the extent of immigration engagement in the labour force (Cobb-Clark 1999; Cobb-Clark and Chapman 1999; Richardson, Robertson and Ilsley 2001; Birrell, Dobson, Rapson and Smith 2001).

Table 5 Australia: Changes in Labour Force Indicators by Birthplace, 1996-2001

		Unemployment Rate	Participation Rate
Australian-born	1996	8.7	74.1
	2001	7.1	74.6
	% change	−13.7	0.5
Recent migrants	1996	20.6	56.8
	2001	14.0	60.1
	% change	−19.4	3.3
Longstanding migrants	1996	9.4	70.7
	2001	7.4	70.5
	% change	−20.6	−0.2

Note: Data applies to employed persons aged 15-64 years.
Source: 1996 and 2001 Census of Population and Housing

Table 5 presents a presents a comparison of the 1996 and 2001 census data which indicates that there has been an improvement in the labour market performance of both recent arrivals and longstanding immigrants. It should be noted however, that there was a significant

119

Figure 7   Unemployment Rates for Migrants in the Longitudinal Survey of Immigrants in Australia (LSIA)

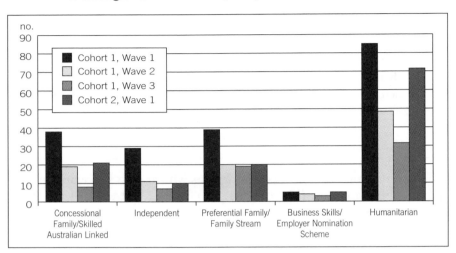

Note: Cohort 1, Waves 1-3 and Cohort 2, by Visa Category.
Source: Richardson *et al.*, 2001, p. 51

improvement in the Australian labour market between 1996 and 2001 with the level of unemployment falling from around 8.7 percent to 7.1 percent. Nevertheless, it is interesting that the level of workforce participation increased among immigrants but fell among the Australian-born due to early retirement, redundancy and increased involvement in study. There was a substantial fall in unemployment experienced by all three groups and there has been a convergence between the Australian-born and longstanding migrants rates. However the rates for recent arrivals, while lower than in 1996, are still a cause of concern. Undoubtedly though, the changes in policy and improved employment situation have improved the labour market situation of immigrants, especially recent arrivals, over the last inter-censal period.

There are systematic differences between policy category groups in their economic and social adjustment to Australia. Refugee/humanitarian settlers for example, by definition arrive with few resources and little preparation for life in a new country. They also have lower levels of English ability and lower levels of qualifications than settlers entering Australia under economic visa categories. Hence Figure 7 shows unemployment levels in the various policy categories of recent migrants interviewed in the first cohort of LSIA arriving in 1994 and interviewed soon after arrival (wave 1), two years later (wave 2) and two years later again (wave 3) as well as the first wave of the second cohort arriving in 2000.

It indicates that unemployment levels are lowest in the skill categories and very high among humanitarian migrants but also that in all categories rates decline over time. This is evident too in Table 6, which indicates that similar patterns are evident with respect to labour force participation.

The increased skilling of the immigrant intake is evident in a comparison of the occupation composition of immigrants at the 1996 and 2001 censuses. Table 7 shows that between the 1996 and 2001 censuses the number of recent migrants (those who arrived between the censuses) who were in the workforce increased by 28.9 percent. This compares to an increase of 8.6 percent in the Australian-born workforce and an increase of 3.2 percent in the workforce made up of immigrants resident in Australia for more than five years. Moreover it is clear that the increase in number of recent migrants was especially substantial in the most skilled occupations, again reflecting changes in immigration policy. The fact that there were very rapid increases in the numbers of managers and administrators (46.8 percent), professionals (36.8 percent) and associate professionals (41.9 percent) among recent migrants between the 1996 and 2001 censuses is especially indicative. At the other end of the occupational spectrum it will be noted that there was only a moderate increase in the number of recent migrants employed as labourers and related workers (14.4 percent). It is also interesting that despite the increased demand for tradespersons in the Australian economy, the numbers among the Australian-born increased by only 2.9 percent and the number of longstanding immigrants actually declined by 8 percent perhaps reflecting the ageing of migrants arriving in Australia in the 1950s and 1960s. There was also an increase of 7.9 percent of the number of recent immigrants in this occupational category which is lower than for most occupation categories.

The industries in which immigrants work, reflect the changes in Australia's economy as well as within the immigration system. Table 8 shows that there are substantial variations in the industries in which the two migrant groups and Australians work. The most striking difference relates to the fast growing area of property and business services. This was the largest group among working recent immigrants accounting for 17.2 percent of workers but for only 12.5 percent of the longstanding immigrants and 10.8 percent of the Australian-born workforce. It is interesting to note that New South Wales accounted for 48.4 percent of recent migrants working in the property and business sector. This is in spite of the fact that New South Wales had only 33.1 percent of all Australian workers and is due to the influence of Sydney. In the globalising world, one of the characteristics of cities which are most linked into global finan-

Table 6 Longitudinal Survey of Immigrants in Australia: Workforce Characteristics by Visa Category, 1993-95 (Wave 1) and 1998-1999 (Wave 3)

	Spouse	Family	Concessional Family	Marriage	Refugee/ Humanitarian	Skill	Independent	Business	Total
Per cent in Workforce									
First Wave (1993-1995)	53.1	22.1	79.2	57.8	47.5	88.4	85.8	65.4	57.9
Third Wave (1998-1999)	58.6	28.7	88.2	64.0	61.2	91.4	90.4	94.0	64.0
Per cent in Workforce Unemployed									
First Wave (1993-1995)	38.6	57.0	35.6	33.6	85.6	2.2	26.4	4.2	39.1
Third Wave (1998-1999)	17.4	33.9	10.7	12.3	37.3	2.5	3.8	0.8	15.6

Source: Longitudinal Survey of Immigrants in Australia (LSIA)

Table 7   Changes in Occupation Distribution by Birthplace, 1996-2001

	Australian Born			Recent Migrants			Longstanding Migrants		
	1996	2001	% Change	1996	2001	% Change	1996	2001	% Change
Managers & Administrators	518,306	550,244	+6.2	13,233	19,429	+46.8	135,550	140,982	+4.0
Professionals	945,871	1,075,377	+13.7	42,042	57,538	+36.8	288,378	329,027	+14.1
Associate Professionals	630,624	712,805	+13.0	17,432	24,734	+41.9	190,216	201,529	+5.9
Tradespersons & Related Workers	734,670	756,239	+2.9	22,078	23,816	+7.9	215,916	198,684	-8.0
Advanced Clerical & Service Workers	250,375	234,200	-6.5	5,459	6,019	+10.3	64,472	57,952	-10.0
Intermediate Clerical, Sales & Service Workers	932,619	1,031,584	+10.6	28,605	38,773	+35.5	234,363	251,433	+7.3
Intermediate Production & Transport Workers	464,900	474,321	+2.0	18,204	18,126	-0.4	161,327	149,963	-7.0
Elementary Clerical, Sales & Service Workers	528,374	607,507	+15.0	14,397	23,586	+63.8	115,738	128,877	+11.4
Labourers & Related Workers	462,035	496,905	+7.5	26,551	30,382	+14.4	156,555	154,431	-1.4
Total	5,469,770	5,941,183	+8.6	189,997	244,404	+28.9	1,564,511	1,614,879	3.2

Notes: Data applies only to the population aged 15-64 years. Excludes not stated.
Source: 1996 and 2001 Census of Population and Housing

Table 8   Industry by Birthplace and Year of Arrival, 2001

Industry	Australian-born No.	%	Recent Migrants No.	%	Longstanding Migrants No.	%
Agriculture, Forestry, Fishing	261,098	4.4	4,264	1.8	27,120	1.7
Mining	58,274	1.0	1,970	0.8	13,048	0.8
Manufacturing	663,377	11.2	35,635	14.8	269,011	16.7
Electricity, Gas and Water Supply	48,095	0.8	1,095	0.5	10,205	0.6
Construction	412,358	7.0	12,308	5.1	111,253	6.9
Wholesale Trade	314,563	5.3	14,922	6.2	89,449	5.6
Retail Trade	937,048	15.8	293,251	12.2	198,261	12.3
Accommodation, Cafes, Restaurants	286,238	4.8	23,154	9.6	83,012	5.2
Transport and Storage	258,071	4.4	9,285	3.9	73,623	4.6
Communication Services	104,782	1.8	5,276	2.2	34,150	2.1
Finance and Insurance	224,730	3.8	12,027	5.0	65,994	4.1
Property and Business Services	639,636	10.8	41,305	17.2	201,563	12.5
Government, Administration and Defence	290,168	4.9	4,627	1.9	65,005	4.0
Education	460,855	7.8	12,919	5.4	104,918	6.5
Health and Community Services	577,429	9.7	20,811	8.7	177,332	11.0
Cultural and Recreational Services	157,164	2.7	4,920	2.0	32,140	2.0
Personal and Other Services	231,251	3.9	6,255	2.6	51,206	3.2
Total	5,925,137	100.0	240,098	100.0	1,607,290	100.0

Notes: Data applies only to the population aged 15-64 years. Excludes 69,623 persons whose year of arrival was not stated.

Source: 2001 Census of Population and Housing

cial and trade networks is their concentration of productive services (Sassen 1991, 1995). Moreover it is characteristic of such world cities (Friedman 1986), that they have an elite of global business people that move between them frequently (Castles and Miller 1998, Sassen 1991, 1995). This also accounts for the over- representation of recent migrants in the finance and insurance area (5 percent compared to 4.1 percent of longstanding migrants and 3.8 percent of the Australian-born), in whole-sale trade and communication services.

One of the major changes in Australian immigration selection since 1996/97 is a sharpening of the skills/education/training criteria adopted. Accordingly, it is useful to examine the educational background of recent migrants and compare them to other groups. Table 9 presents a comparison of 1996 and 2001 census data on qualifications for recent migrants, longstanding migrants and the Australian-born. The first point to be made is that at both censuses, recent migrants have a substantially more skilled profile than both the Australian-born and migrants of longer standing. It will be noticed that in all areas, except vocational qualifications, there are a greater proportion of migrants than the Australian-born. This reflects the nature of the selectivity of immigrants in recent years which has been less oriented to manual skills than in the early postwar decades. There was a decrease in the proportion of each of the three populations with no qualifications between the 1996 and 2001 censuses. More than one half of recent migrants have qualifications with almost one-third having Bachelor or higher qualifications. There is no question that the changes in settler selection and the expansion of temporary resident visa programmes has contributed toward the broader skilling of Australian society.

Table 9   Highest Level of Post School Qualification by Birthplace by Year of Arrival

Highest Level of Post-school Qualification Attained	Australia-born		Recent Migrants		Longstanding Migrants	
	1996 %	2001 %	1996 %	2001 %	1996 %	2001 %
Higher degree	1.0	1.4	5.4	5.9	2.0	2.8
Postgraduate diploma	1.4	1.5	1.0	1.2	1.1	1.3
Bachelor degree	7.5	9.5	15.3	18.6	8.3	11.0
Undergraduate diploma	3.5	–	4.9	–	3.8	–
Associate diploma	2.7	5.9	3.0	9.7	2.5	6.8
Skilled vocational qualification	11.1	–	6.9	–	11.2	–
Basic vocational qualification	3.1	16.9	2.2	10.2	2.6	15.6
Level of attainment inadequately described	0.8	1.2	1.9	2.0	1.2	1.5
Level of attainment not stated	8.5	6.9	10.3	7.4	9.9	7.9
No qualifications	60.4	56.6	49.1	45.0	57.3	53.2
Total	100.0	100.0	100.0	100.0	100.0	100.0

Note: Applicable to persons aged 15 years and over.
Source: 1996 and 2001 Census of Population and Housing

125

Table 10   Persons Aged Fifteen Years and Over by Birthplace and Year of Arrival, 1996

Age left school	Australian-born %	Recent Migrants %	Longstanding Migrants %
Still at school	5.4	6.5	2.8
Never attended school	0.3	2.0	2.0
14 Years and Under	12.8	8.3	18.1
15 Years	21.8	8.4	17.3
16 Years	20.6	14.8	16.5
17 Years	21.3	16.8	15.9
18 Years	11.2	24.0	14.5
19 Years and over	2.2	13.6	7.4
Age left school not stated	4.3	5.7	5.5
Total	100.0	100.0	100.0

Note: Excludes 87,073 persons whose year of arrival was not stated.
Source: 1996 Census of Population and Housing

Table 11   Persons Aged Fifteen Years and Over by Birthplace and Year of Arrival, 2001

Highest Level of Schooling Completed	Australian-born %	Recent Migrants %	Longstanding Migrants %
Still at school	4.0	5.6	1.4
Did not go to school	0.3	2.0	2.9
Year 8 or below	8.9	3.5	12.6
Year 9 or equivalent	8.6	2.3	5.8
Year 10 or equivalent	27.1	8.8	19.3
Year 11 or equivalent	10.6	7.4	8.2
Year 12 or equivalent	36.3	65.0	43.9
Not stated	4.2	5.4	6.0
Total	100.0	100.0	100.0

Note: Excludes 175,158 persons whose year of arrival was not stated.
Source: 2001 Census of Population and Housing

Unfortunately, different coding schemes were used for the years of schooling question at the 1996 and 2001 censuses. At the 1996 census, the question asked 'How old was the person when he or she left primary or secondary school?'. The results are presented in Table 10 and it shows that 37.6 percent of recent migrants left school at age 18 or older compared to 13.4 percent of the Australian-born and 21.9 percent of long-standing migrants. This points to a much higher average level of formal education among recent migrants. It is difficult to compare with the situation in 2001, where the census question asked 'What is the highest level of primary or secondary school the person has completed?'. Table 11 shows the results. It indicates that two-thirds of recent migrants completed Year 12 or the equivalent compared to 36.3 percent of the Australian-born and 43.9 percent of other migrants. Quite clearly, the strong educational selectivity of immigration has continued.

Non-permanent migration and skill

Most assessment of the labour market impact of immigration in Australia considers only permanent residents (e.g. Richardson *et al.* 2001; Cobb-Clark and Chapman 1999). Nevertheless, as was pointed out earlier, non-permanent migration of workers into Australia has increased massively in recent years and a number of points need to be made with respect to its effects on the labour market…

- Temporary migration is more related to the labour market than permanent migration in that most visa categories involve worker movement. Hence, the overall participation of temporary migrants in the workforce is greater than for permanent settlers.

- Approval of temporary migration is a very quick process, while settlement takes much longer. It is apparent that some workers, who would have before 1996 sought to immigrate to Australia now, initially at least, seek temporary residence via a temporary visa.

- Whereas the numbers of permanent migrants to Australia is governed closely by government and the numbers in each category are capped, temporary work migration is demand driven in that sponsors nominate temporary positions.

- Temporary work migration is very much skill related and restricted to the top three ASCO[3] categories (which are the highest skill groups) and there is a minimum wage that a migrant worker can be paid.

- The median age of temporary migrants in 2003 was 27 years, which makes them younger than both the Australian total population (and workforce) and permanent immigrants.

---

[3] The Australian Standard Classification of Occupations.

The overall numerical impact on the labour market is reflected in the fact that the Department of Immigration, Multicultural and Ethnic Affairs (2004) estimated that at 30th June 2003, 584,862 people were in Australia on temporary entry visas of which only 32 percent were visitors. Most of the remainder had the right to work. This would be equivalent to around 4 percent of the national workforce at this time.

It is necessary to examine the different categories of temporary migrants with the right to work to examine their impact on the labour market. Of course there are also people who enter the country on a non-working visa and work illegally, although in recent years DIMIA has increased its efforts to detect people working illegally in Australia. In 1999, the Australian government carried out a *Review of Illegal Workers in Australia*, and as a result, a number of measures were recommended and implemented to prevent the employment of people who do not have the right to work in Australia (Rizvi 2003, 77). The review recommended sanctions to discourage business owners, employers and recruiters from employing or referring for employment illegal workers. In 2002-03, DIMIA located 3,233 foreign citizens working illegally in Australia, and issued 1,693 illegal worker warning notices to employers (Rizvi 2003, 77). The illegal workers generally work in harvesting, tourist related industries and in the restaurant sector and not in high skill areas (Hugo 2001).

Turning to the temporary migration work categories, the "temporary business short term" (456) and "long term" (457) are especially significant having been introduced in 1996 (Khoo *et al.* 2003). The 1996 legislation represented a major change with the past and had a number of features…

- Removal of previous restrictions governing the sponsoring of business persons and specialists.
- Abolition of previous requirements that sponsors establish that there are no resident Australian workers available to do the work.
- Abolition of the requirement that there would be some training benefit to Australian workers.
- Liberalisation of rules governing the sponsorship process.
- Establishment of a pre-sponsoring arrangement whereby employers can register themselves as sponsors if they meet minimal requirements. They then are allowed to sponsor any number of the new 457 temporary entry category.
- A two stage process was introduced for the entry of 457 workers:
  - the sponsor nominates the position;
  - if there is no objection from DIMIA, the applicant can apply for a 457 visa.

The process for approval has become more streamlined over time using on-line features and some employers being given special status to facilitate bringing in workers. The whole process is targeted very much at bringing in skilled workers. There has been lobbying of government by some groups, especially those associated with primary industry groups with substantial seasonal demands for harvesting labour, to extend the scheme to unskilled, lower income groups but thus far these have been rejected (Hugo 2001).

Figure 8 shows recent trends in the major forms of temporary labour migration to Australia. Some of the most rapid growth has occurred among students, predominantly from Asia, who have the right to work up to 20 hours in term time and full time during breaks, so they have had a significant effect on the labour market. There is undoubtedly a strong connection between student migration and eventual settlement of Asian origin groups in MDCs like Australia. It may occur through students:

- overstaying their education visas;

- gaining a change of status to a resident; there are indeed policies which now make it easier for student graduates in Australia to gain resident status.

- returning to their home country on completion of their studies and subsequently immigrating officially to the country where they studied.

It is of significance that in the last year more than half of all persons granted residence in Australia in the economic migration categories had an Australian qualification.

Figure 8 also shows that there has been a significant increase in working holiday maker (WHM) temporary migration in recent years. This program was reviewed by the Australian Parliament Joint Study Committee on Migration (1997). WHMs are foreign nationals aged 18-30 from selected countries with which Australia has a reciprocal arrangement,[4] who can work under certain conditions for up to 12 months. Their numbers have increased dramatically and reached 85,200 in 2001-02, 88,758 in 2002-03 and 108,659 in 2003-04 more than doubling in the 1990s. Kinnaird (1999) reports that while the economic impact nationally of WHM migration is limited it has significant impacts in specific industries in specific areas. While Europeans dominate this

---

[4] Currently Canada, Ireland, Japan, the Repulic of Korea, Malta, Netherlands, United Kingdom, Germany, Sweden, Denmark, Norway, Hong Kong, Finland, Cyprus, Italy, France and Belgium.

Figure 8   Temporary Migration to Australia by Category, 1986 to 2004

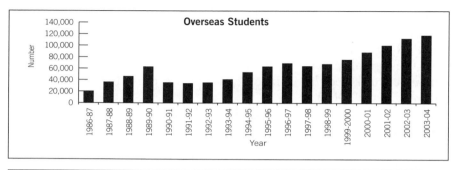

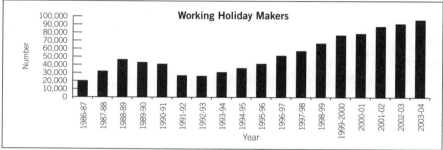

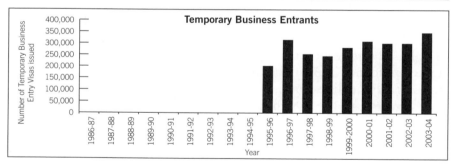

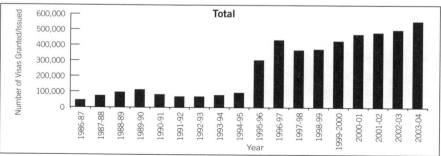

Source: DIMIA Population Flows: Immigration Aspects, various issues; Rizvi 2004

category, there are significant numbers from Japan (12,166 in 2003-04). WHM particularly work in industries which rely heavily on casual labour at peak times such as the hospitality, horticultural and tourism industries. They are a major element in the Australian harvesting workforce (Hugo 2001). A report on WHM (Harding and Webster 2002) found that...

- On average WHM stay 9 months in Australia.
- They take up the equivalent of 41,000 full year jobs although their expenditure creates another 49,000 jobs.

The estimated number of Australian young people who take advantage of the reciprocal arrangements to work in other countries is over 30,000 (DIMIA 2004, 58).

Since 1995 there has been a new visa category in Australia of Temporary Business Migrants. It can be seen that this category has gone from zero in the mid 1990s to levels of over a quarter of million business migrants per year. It comprises several groups including short term and long term (up to four years) business migrants. In 2002-03 a total of 254,180 Business Visitor visas were granted, a decrease from 254,180 in 2001-02, primarily due to the impact of SARS (Rizvi 2003,33). Among the Business Visitors, the USA accounts for 17.4 percent and the United Kingdom 8.7 percent and the main Asian groups are from China (19.4 percent), Japan (6.3 percent), India (4.8 percent) and Indonesia (3.5 percent). The Temporary Business Entry (Long Stay) sub-class 457 visa enables highly qualified/skilled persons to enter Australia for up to 4 years to take up pre-nominated positions with approved Australian sponsor-employers, mostly in professional or management positions (Rizvi 2002, p. 45). Particular mention needs to be made of the sub-class 457 of Temporary Business Entry (Long Stay), which enables temporary migrants to work for up to four years in pre nominated positions with approved Australian sponsor-employers.

Table 12 shows that the number of 457 workers increased in 2002-03 to 37,859. In the late 1990s, ICT workers were a major element in this stream but in recent years health workers especially nurses have become the fastest growing group. Table 13 shows the breakdown of occupation of 457 workers in 2001-02. It has been estimated by DIMIA that in mid 2003 there were 56,344 sub-class 457 visa holders in Australia, an increase of 2.4 percent over the previous year (Rizvi 2003, 37). It is important to stress that the stream of 457 workers is more skilled than the stream of permanent migrants as is apparent in Table 14, which compares the occupational classification of 457 visa holders and permanent migrants in economic categories in 1999/2000.

Table 12   Temporary Business Entry (Long Stay) Visa Grants, 2000-01, 2001-02 and 2002-03

Country	2000-01	2001-02	2002-03	% Change 2000-01 to 2002-03
United Kingdom	8,737	9,653	11,677	+33.6
India	3,294	3,075	3,670	+11.4
United States of America	3,005	2,640	2,846	−5.3
Japan	2,239	2,441	2,278	+1.7
South Africa, Republic of	1,995	1,887	2,210	+10.8
Irish Republic	1,441	1,626	1,648	+14.4
Korea, Republic of	1,264	1,606	1,259	−0.4
China, People's Republic of	1,341	1,104	1,165	−13.1
Canada	1,164	1,042	1,138	−2.2
France	845	909	na	−
Other countries	11,382	7,722	9,968	−12.4
Total	36,707	33,705	37,859	+3.1

Source: Rizvi, 2002 and 2003

Table 13   TBE Visa Occupations, 2000-2001

Managers, Administrators	22.5
Professionals	19.7
Associate Professionals	8.9
Trades	2.7
Doctors	1.1
Engineers	2.8
Accountants	6.3
Nurses	6.0
ICT	21.9
Other	4

Source: Rizvi 2002

In addition to the long stay (457) and short stay (456) temporary business migration categories there are a number of smaller visa categories involving temporary migration for work. These include educational visas for those entering to work in educational and research institutions (1,819 in 2001-02, 1,385 in 2002-03) and medical practitioner visas. The latter especially applies to supplying workers for regional and remote areas

Table 14   Employment Status and Occupation of Temporary Business Entrants and Settler Arrivals in the Skill Visa Categories Compared

	1999/2000	
	Temporary %	Permanent %
Occupation of employed primary applicants		
Managers/Admin.	21.5	14.3
Professionals	50.4	58.4
Para-professionals	17.4	9.2
Tradespersons	5.0	15.1
Adv. Clerical, service	0.2	0.8
Interm. Clerical, serv.	1.6	1.5
Elem. Clerical, serv.	0.8	0.1
Production, transport	0.8	0.4
Labourers, etc.	2.5	0.2
Total number employed	5,355	12,620
% employed	98.0	98.1

* Skill visa categories include Independent, Employer Nomination Scheme
Business skills and (from 1997/98) Skilled Australian-linked.

Source: Khoo et al. 2003

where difficulty is being experienced in recruiting doctors. Including dependents, there was an increase from 3,856 in 2001-02 to 5,031 in 2002-03 in this category. The Visiting Academic Visa allows for academics to visit Australian academic institutions and the numbers increased from 3,734 in 2002-03 to 3,804 in 2003-04 (Rizvi 2004, 25). Another sub-class relates to retirement and another to persons entering for cultural or sporting reasons.

Turning to students, Australia has become a significant destination of foreign students, especially those from Asia.[5] In mid 2003 there were 172,973 visaed students in Australia – a 13 percent increase over the previous year (DIMIA 2004, 59). The number of student visas granted in 2003-04 was a record 171,616 compared to 162,575 in 2002-03 (Rizvi 2004, 27). The precise proportion of foreign students who take up the option to work while in Australia is not known. One study of students from Malaysia and Singapore in Adelaide found that 23.6 percent worked on a regular basis (Tan 2003, p. 47). Little is known about the

---

[5] Foreign students are permitted up to 20 hours a week during term time and full time outside of term.

type of work that they do but Table 15 indicates the type of work undertaken by students in the Adelaide study. It shows that while some students gain employment in the skill area they are studying, most work in the low income service sector.

Table 15   Jobs Held by a Sample of Asian Students in Adelaide

University work	8
Finance	2
Administration	5
Hospitality	17
Delivery	2
Cleaning	1
Manufacturing	1
Retailing	1
Vineyard	1

Source: Tan 2003

The impacts of temporary worker migration on the Australian workforce have not been studied in detail but can be summarised as follows.

- It would seem that they occupy the equivalent of around 300,000 full time jobs in the workforce.

- They are more skilled than the resident workforce.

- There are high levels of change of status into permanent residence among temporary resident workers (Hugo 2003a).

Hence, the increased impact of international migration in the accelerated skilling of Australia's workforce since the mid 1990s has had two important components.

- The increased skill focus in selection of permanent immigrants.

- The introduction of a temporary migration program which focuses on skilled workers.

Emigration and the Australian diaspora

There is a tendency for Australia to be categorised as a purely immigration country but, in fact, it is also a country of significant emigration. Table 16 shows that over recent years departures on a permanent or long-term basis have been substantial. In 2001-02 permanent departures num-

Table 16   Australia: Settlers and Long-Term Migration, 1987-2004

Year	1987-88	1988-89	1989-90	1990-91	1991-92	1992-93	1993-94	1994-95	1995-96	1996-97	1997-98	1998-99	1999-2000	2000-01	2001-02	2002-03	2003-04
Permanent Migration																	
Arrivals	143,480	145,316	121,227	121,688	107,391	76,330	69,768	87,428	99,139	85,752	77,327	84,143	92,272	107,360	88,900	93,920	111,590
Departures	20,470	21,647	27,857	31,130	29,122	27,905	27,280	26,948	28,670	29,857	31,985	35,181	41,078	46,530	48,241	50,460	59,078
Net	123,010	123,669	93,370	90,558	78,269	48,425	42,488	60,480	70,469	55,895	45,342	48,962	51,194	60,830	40,659	43,460	52,512
Long-Term Migration																	
Arrivals	98,780	104,590	110,695	114,711	126,781	127,436	137,600	151,095	163,578	175,249	188,114	187,802	212,849	241,210	264,471	279,890	289,727
Departures	78,570	90,991	100,199	110,512	115,162	113,190	112,707	118,533	124,386	136,748	154,294	140,281	156,768	166,400	171,446	169,100	177,618
Net	20,210	13,599	10,496	4,199	11,619	14,246	24,893	32,562	39,192	38,501	33,820	47,521	56,081	74,810	93,025	110,790	112,109
Total Permanent and Long-Term Net Gain	143,220	137,242	103,866	94,757	89,888	62,671	67,381	93,042	109,661	94,396	79,162	96,483	107,275	135,640	133,684	154,250	164,621
% Net Migration from Long-Term Movement	14.1	9.9	10.1	4.4	12.9	22.7	36.9	35.0	35.7	40.8	42.7	49.3	52.3	55.2	69.6	71.8	68.1

Source: DIMIA *Immigration Update*, various issues and unpublished data

bered 48,241 compared with an average of 30,539 over the previous 14 years. This represented a 17.4 percent increase over 1999-2000 and a 61.6 percent increase over 5 years earlier. In 2002-03 there was a further 4.6 percent increase in outflow, which reached 50,463 persons and in 2003-04 it increased to 59,078. shows the numbers of permanent departures is at record levels. It also indicates that there has been a substantial increase in the ratio of permanent emigration to permanent immigration. Over the post-war period there has been a close relationship between immigration and emigration trends with the later tending to follow the former with a small time lag. This is because, as Table 17 indicates, former settlers have been a major part of emigration over the years. Moreover, the return migration effect has been understated in the data since a number of the Australia-born are the children born in Australia to overseas-born returnees. However the most striking trend in Table 17 is the fact that the Australian-born component of emigrants has been increasing at a rapid rate over the last two decades, doubling between 1999-98 and 2001-02 and increasing by another 20 percent in the last two years. This trend is associated with the globalisation of labour markets which has resulted in more high skilled Australian workers moving overseas to seek higher wages and advance their careers.

Table 17   Australia: Permanent Movement, Financial Years, 1968-2004

Financial Year	Settler Arrivals	Former Settlers* No.	Former Settlers* % of Departures	Permanent Departures Australia-Born** No.	Permanent Departures Australia-Born** % of Departures	Total	Departures as % of Arrivals
1968-69	175,657	23,537	74.3	8,141	25.7	31,678	18.0
1969-70	185,099	26,082	72.3	10,000	27.7	36,082	19.5
1970-71	170,011	28,244	71.8	11,072	28.2	39,316	23.1
1971-72	132,719	32,280	72.8	12,439	27.8	44,719	33.7
1972-73	107,401	31,961	71.2	12,945	28.8	44,906	41.8
1973-74	112,712	26,741	67.8	12,699	32.2	39,413	35.0
1974-75	89,147	20,184	64.0	11,361	36.0	31,545	35.4
1975-76	52,748	17,150	62.5	10,277	37.5	27,427	52.0
1976-77	70,916	15,447	62.8	9,141	37.2	24,588	34.7
1977-78	73,171	13,972	60.5	9,124	39.5	23,096	31.6
1978-79	67,192	13,797	54.3	11,632	45.7	25,429	37.8
1979-80	80,748	12,044	54.7	9,973	45.3	22,017	27.3
1980-81	110,689	10,888	55.8	8,608	44.2	19,496	17.6
1981-82	118,030	11,940	57.2	8,940	42.8	20,890	17.7
1982-83	93,010	15,390	62.0	9,440	38.0	24,830	26.7

Table 17   (Cont.)

Financial Year	Settler Arrivals	Former Settlers* No.	Former Settlers* % of Departures	Permanent Departures Australia-Born** No.	Permanent Departures Australia-Born** % of Departures	Total	Departures as % of Arrivals
1983-84	68,810	14,270	58.7	10,040	41.3	24,300	35.3
1984-85	77,510	11,040	54.2	9,340	45.8	20,380	26.3
1985-86	92,590	9,560	52.8	8,540	47.2	18,100	19.5
1986-87	113,540	10,800	54.2	9,130	45.8	19,930	17.6
1987-88	143,470	10,716	52.3	9,755	47.7	20,471	14.3
1988-89	145,320	15,087	69.7	6,560	30.3	21,647	14.9
1989-90	121,230	19,458	69.8	8,399	30.2	27,857	23.0
1990-91	121,688	21,640	69.5	9,490	30.5	31,130	25.6
1991-92	107,391	19,944	68.5	9,178	31.5	29,122	27.1
1992-93	76,330	18,102	64.9	9,803	35.1	27,905	36.6
1993-94	69,768	17,353	63.6	9,927	36.4	27,280	39.1
1994-95	87,428	16,856	62.6	10,092	37.4	26,948	30.8
1995-96	99,139	17,665	61.6	11,005	38.4	28,670	28.9
1996-97	85,752	18,159	60.8	11,698	39.2	29,857	34.8
1997-98	77,327	19,214	60.1	12,771	39.9	31,985	41.4
1998-99	84,143	17,931	50.1	17,250	49.0	35,181	41.8
1999-2000	92,272	20,844	50.7	20,234	49.3	41,078	44.5
2000-01	107,360	23,440	50.4	23,081	49.6	46,521	43.3
2001-02	88,900	24,095	49.9	24,146	50.1	48.241	54.3
2002-03	93,920	24,885	49.3	25,578	50.7	50,463	53.7
2003-04	111,590	29,977	50.7	29,101	49.3	59,078	52.9

* Data 1988-89 to 2003-04 constitute permanent overseas-born departures due to a change in definition by DIMA. Data prior to this constitute former settler departures.

** Data prior to 1988-89 constitute permanent departures other than former settlers.

Sources: DIMIA *Australian Immigration Consolidated Statistics* and *Immigration Update*, various issues

Turning to long-term departures, Table 18 indicates that this reached unprecedented levels in 2001-02 of 171,446. This was well above the 14 year average of 123,128 and 9.4 percent more than two years earlier. Clearly, there has been a significant growth of movement out of Australia in recent years (Hugo, Rudd and Harris 2001). There was a small fall to 169,100 in 2002-03 and in 2003-04 reflecting the impact of the insecurity created by September 11th and the Bali bombings and the SARS outbreak.

In considering this out-movement it is important to distinguish between that of Australian residents and people who have come from other nations. With respect to permanent emigration, Table 17 distinguishes between former settlers and the Australia-born. The out-standing feature of the table is the increasing share of the Australia-born in the

Table 18 Australia: Long-Term Movement, 1959-60 to 2002-03

	Arrivals			Departures			Net Overseas Movement		
	Australian Residents	Overseas Visitors	Total	Australian Residents	Overseas Visitors	Total	Australian Residents	Overseas Visitors	Total
1959-60	16,049	11,748	27,797	24,730	7,838	32,568	-8,681	3,910	-4,771
1960-61	16,870	13,320	30,190	28,542	11,823	40,365	-11,672	1,497	-10,175
1961-62	19,301	13,423	32,724	33,370	12,591	45,961	-14,069	832	-13,237
1962-63	21,376	13,971	35,347	34,324	13,219	47,543	-12,948	752	-12,196
1963-64	23,066	14,170	37,236	39,931	12,325	52,256	-16,865	1,845	-15,020
1964-65	24,065	16,484	40,549	42,702	13,640	56,342	-18,637	2,844	-15,793
1965-66	27,279	18,461	45,740	51,785	11,808	63,593	-24,506	6,653	-17,853
1966-67	31,161	20,078	51,239	53,750	12,707	66,457	-22,589	7,371	-15,218
1967-68	37,032	23,341	60,373	51,847	12,516	64,363	-14,815	10,825	-3,990
1968-69	37,376	24,442	61,818	53,296	13,817	67,113	-15,920	10,625	-5,295
1969-70	38,711	29,842	68,553	63,454	17,414	80,868	-24,743	12,428	-12,315
1970-71	43,554	31,225	74,779	66,463	19,928	86,391	-22,909	11,297	-11,612
1971-72	51,356	27,713	79,069	68,069	23,328	91,397	-16,713	4,385	-12,328
1972-73	58,292	26,733	85,025	67,379	23,579	90,958	-9,087	3,154	-5,933
1973-74	64,297	27,212	91,509	60,636	21,246	81,882	3,661	5,966	9,627
1974-75	60,239	23,615	83,854	72,397	24,386	96,783	-12,158	-771	-12,929
1975-76	60,224	21,687	81,911	64,475	21,528	86,003	-4,251	159	-4,092
1976-77	59,193	26,133	85,326	68,792	19,724	88,516	-9,599	6,409	-3,190
1977-78	57,311	28,043	85,354	60,099	19,194	79,293	-2,788	8,849	6,061
1978-79	60,947	34,064	95,011	57,255	21,216	78,471	3,692	12,848	16,540
1979-80	59,963	29,586	89,549	52,114	19,228	71,342	7,849	10,358	18,207

1980-81	59,871	34,220	94,091	47,848	18,778	66,626	12,023	15,442	27,465
1981-82	57,860	34,760	92,620	46,500	20,310	66,810	11,360	14,450	25,810
1982-83	48,990	30,740	79,730	47,020	25,440	72,460	1,970	5,300	7,270
1983-84	49,190	27,280	76,470	49,490	24,950	74,440	–300	2,330	2,030
1984-85	53,770	31,980	85,750	51,710	23,160	74,870	2,060	8,820	10,880
1985-86	56,560	37,250	93,810	49,690	24,670	74,360	6,870	12,580	19,450
1986-87	53,597	67,325	120,922	48,854	26,538	75,392	4,743	40,787	45,530
1987-88	54,804	43,978	98,782	50,499	28,054	78,553	4,305	15,924	20,229
1988-89	53,798	50,766	104,564	57,733	33,258	90,991	–3,935	17,508	13,573
1989-90	53,967	56,728	110,695	62,300	37,899	100,199	–8,333	18,829	10,496
1990-91	59,062	55,649	114,711	66,883	43,629	110,512	–7,821	12,020	4,199
1991-92	62,920	63,861	126,781	67,191	47,971	115,162	–4,271	15,890	11,619
1992-93	69,594	57,842	127,436	65,446	47,744	113,190	4,148	10,098	14,246
1993-94	75,600	62,000	137,600	64,786	47,921	112,707	10,814	14,079	24,893
1994-95	79,063	72,032	151,095	68,377	50,156	118,533	10,686	21,876	32,562
1995-96	79,206	84,372	163,578	70,253	54,133	124,386	8,953	30,239	39,192
1996-97	80,170	95,079	175,249	73,777	62,971	136,748	6,393	32,108	38,501
1997-98	84,358	103,756	188,114	79,422	74,872	154,294	4,936	28,884	33,820
1998-99	67,910	119,892	187,802	82,861	57,420	140,281	–14,951	62,472	47,521
1999-2000	79,651	133,198	212,849	84,918	71,850	156,768	–5,267	61,348	56,081
2000-01	82,900	158,310	241,210	92,960	73,440	166,400	–10,060	84,870	74,810
2001-02	88,598	175,873	264,471	92,071	79,375	171,446	–3,473	96,498	93,025
2002-03	95,790	184,100	279,890	86,200	82,900	169,100	9,590	101,200	110,790
2003-04	98,400	191,327	289,727	84,336	93,282	177,618	14,064	112,109	126,173

Source: DIMIA Australian Immigration Consolidated Statistics and Immigration Update, various issues

Figure 9 Permanent Departures of Australia-Born and Overseas-Born Persons from Australia, 1959-60 to 2002-03

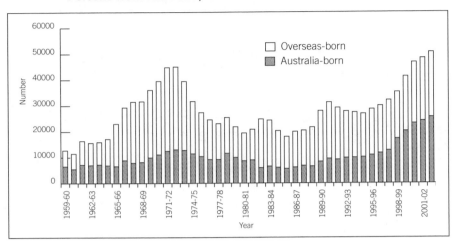

Source: DIMIA, *Australian Immigration Consolidated Statistics* and *Immigration Update*, various issues; DIMIA unpublished data.

permanent departures. In fact, 2001-02 was the first postwar year that Australia-born permanent departures outnumbered former settlers leaving the nation. It is apparent from Figure 9 that there has been an upward trend in the numbers of Australia-born permanent departures in the 1990s and this is indicative of a greater tendency for Australia-born adults deciding to move overseas on a permanent basis. If we look at the pattern of long-term out- movement of Australian residents, a similar pattern emerges. Figure 10 shows that the number of Australian residents who are departing overseas for a period of more than a year but with intentions to return has increased substantially in recent years. Between 1998-99 and 2001-02 there was an increase in the number of long-term departures from Australia from 140,281 to 171,446 persons (22.2 percent). It will be noted however, that there was a small decline to 169,100 persons (1.4 percent) perhaps reflecting some impact of the SARS epidemic and the shifting global security situation. There were net losses by long term migration among Australian residents between 1998 and 2002 but a gain in 2002-03 and 2003-04 perhaps indicating the return of some of the large numbers leaving in the late 1990s and the deteriorating global security situation.

Settler loss has been an important feature of the post-war Australian migration scene with more than a fifth of all post-war settlers subsequently emigrating from Australia, most of them returning to their home

Figure 10 Australian Resident Long Term Departures from Australia, 1959-60 to 2002-03

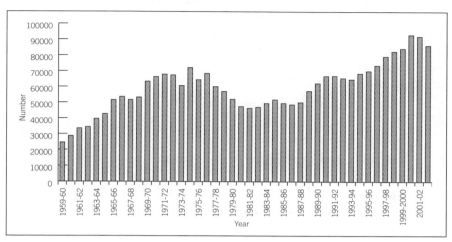

Source: DIMIA *Australian Immigration Consolidated Statistics* and *Immigration Update*, various issues; DIMIA unpublished data

nation. In the context of the present paper it is important to point out that settler loss is more selective of skilled migrants than is settler intake (Hugo, Rudd and Harris 2001). There has been concern about this settler loss among policy makers (Hugo 1994) but it has a number of components including a group of migrants who never intended to settle permanently in Australia as well as people who are influenced by family changes, are not able to adjust to life in Australia, etc. The pattern of settler loss while it varies between birthplace groups (e.g. it is high among New Zealanders but low among Vietnamese) has tended to remain a relatively consistent feature of the post-war migration scene in Australia and the fluctuations in its numbers are very much related to earlier levels of immigration. With an increase in the skill profile in immigration we can expect an increase in settler loss since skilled migrants have a greater chance of remigrating than family migrants. The recent upswing in settler loss – increasing by 38.8 percent between 1998-9 and 2002-03 – would tend to support this. This is especially the case since the level of immigration was comparatively low in the mid 1990s and trends in settler loss in the past have tended to mirror immigration trends offset by around five years (Hugo 1994).

Nevertheless, there has been a consistent increase in the level of out-movement of Australian residents. This has begun to attract policy attention since the profile of departures of residents tends to be younger and more educated than the population of the nation as a whole and the spectra of 'brain drain' has arisen (Hugo, Rudd and Harris, 2003). There has been an increasing tempo of emigration of Australia-born professionals due to Australia's increasing incorporation into international labour markets migration systems. There are a number of possible (and in several cases, probable) positive developments for the Australian economy which could accrue from this movement:

- Many expatriate workers eventually return to Australia.
- Most remit substantial sums of foreign exchange to Australia-based families, investments and bank accounts.
- The skills and experience of the Australian workers involved is enhanced.
- The linkages which this is establishing between Australian companies and their overseas counterparts and markets will further assist in embedding Australia's economy internationally.
- It may be creating opportunities for Australian companies to supply goods and services to other countries because the Australian expatriate workers will be most familiar with Australian-based suppliers.

An increasing percentage of the outflow of Australians is to Asia and we may be seeing some integration of particular labour markets between Australia and some Asian countries. This has many significant implications for Australia in a number of areas and the emigration associated with it needs closer investigation. On the one hand, there are the issues of skilled labour shortage in several Asian nations which will have implications for emigration of one kind or another from Australia. On the other, in other nations there are surpluses of educated workers in some fields, due largely to mismatches in the output of the education systems and the specialised demands for employment in the economies of those nations. The latter forces will put pressures on immigration to Australia and other destination countries. These apparent contradictory forces in Asia are a function of the diversity of the region and the enormous differences between Asian countries with respect to labour surpluses and shortages. However, they are also related to emerging demands for particular skills in the rapidly growing economies of the region, which cannot be supplied immediately by their national education systems. Moreover, in many countries human resource development policies are mismatched with, and lagging behind, the rapidly changing labour market situation. This is producing a complex situation where, between and even within individual Asian countries, there are strong tendencies toward producing both immigration and emigration on significant levels.

Table 19   National Diasporas in Relation to Resident National Populations

USA:	7 million – 2.5 percent of national population
Australia:	900,000 – 4.3 percent of national population
New Zealand:	850,000 – 21.9 percent of national population
Philippines:	7.5 million – 9.0 percent of national population
India:	20 million – 1.9 percent of national population
Pakistan:	4 million – 2.8 percent of national population
China:	30 to 40 million – 2.9 percent of national population
Japan:	873,641 – 0.7 percent of national population
Mexico:	19 million – 19 percent of national population

Source: US Census Bureau, 2002a and b; Southern Cross, 2002; Bedford, 2001; Ministry of External Affairs, India, http://indiandiaspora.nic.in; Naseem, 1998; Sahoo, 2002; Iguchi, 2004; Gutièrrez, 1999; Dimzon, 2005

It is estimated that the size of the Australian diaspora is around 900,000 persons and Table 19 indicates that this is equivalent to over 4 percent of the national population. Australia's diaspora is not only large in relation to the national resident population, it is highly selective in terms of education, income and age. A recent article in *Business Review Weekly* (James 2004, p. 66) showed how Australians are strongly over-represented among chief executives of major global companies and organisations. Australian expatriates are forming more networks not only for business purposes but also to lobby for causes and issues which effect them like voting, taxation, superannuation, citizenship, etc. Despite the size and highly selective nature of its national diaspora, Australia has not developed a policy or set of programs toward its expatriates although this is called for in a recent Senate report (Senate Legal and Constitutional References Committee 2005). Nationally, there is a debate about the issue of "brain-drain". Some commentators point out that Australia most definitely experiences a "brain gain" in that it records substantial net migration gains in all high skill occupational categories and in terms of people with high levels of qualifications (e.g. Birrell, *et al.* 2001). Others consider that it is not a simple "numbers game" and that Australia is experiencing a net loss of the "brightest and the best" especially among our top home grown scientists, innovators and business people (Wood (ed.) 2004). The reality is that we do not have sufficient information to test the latter proposition.

In 2003 the Australian Senate's Legal and Constitutional References Committee announced the setting up of an *Inquiry Into Australian Expatriates* with the terms of reference indicated in Table 20 and it reported in 2005. This report addresses in a substantial way the issue of Australia's diaspora and suggests a number of policies with respect to it. The formation of the Senate Inquiry was in response to lobbying from such active expatriate networks as Southern Cross and Young Australian Professionals in America which have been highly effective in mobilizing modern information technology to organize large numbers of Australian expatriates across many nations. Figure 11 shows the approximate distribution of Australian expatriates across the globe.

Table 20   Terms of Reference of the Australian Senate's Legal and Constitutional References Committee Inquiry Into Australian Expatriates

- The extent of the diaspora
- Factors driving Australians to live overseas
- Costs, benefits, opportunities
- Needs and concerns of overseas Australians
- Policies/Programs in other countries to respond to needs
- Ways they can be better used to promote Australia's economic, social and cultural interests

A recent report (Hugo, Rudd and Harris 2003) argued that Australia would benefit from developing a diaspora policy. It is argued that rather than argue as to whether Australia is experiencing a "brain drain" or a "brain gain" it needs to be recognized that as a small and peripheral (in the global economy) nation, Australia has a lot to gain from experiencing a "Brain Circulation" in which Australian skilled people go overseas and in which Australia receives skilled people from other countries. It argues that Australia, in order to achieve this, needs an international migration policy which embraces not only immigration but also emigration and especially circulation.

While there is not yet any governmental policy, which comprehensively addresses these issues, there are strong indications that the government is beginning to move in this area. The peak body of Australian scientists (the Federation of Australian Scientific and Technological Societies – FASTS) has been vocal about Australia's need to train more, and retain, highly skilled workers in the Science, Engineering and Technology areas (Andrews 2004; Australian Council of Deans of Science 2001; DITR and DEST 2003). An investigation into mathematical sciences (Thomas 2000; 2002) found that it was in decline and is a matter of concern since so many areas of science and technology are dependent

Figure 11   Australian Citizens Living Abroad, 31 December 2001

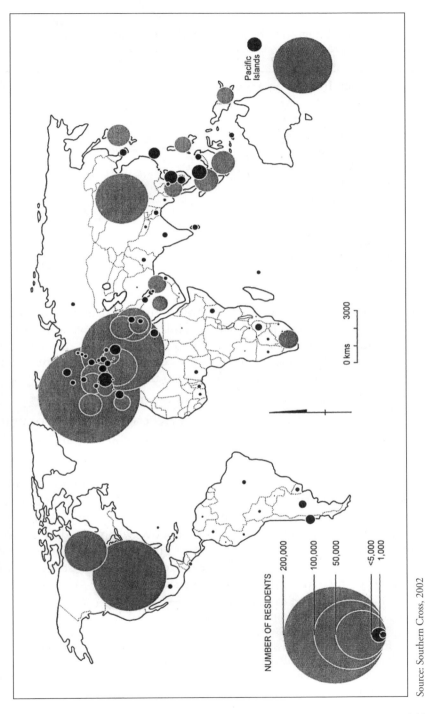

Source: Southern Cross, 2002

Table 21 Survey of Australians Overseas, 2001: Reasons Given for Emigration by Academic Respondents (N=167)

Reason	Percent of Responses
Job Transfer/Exchange	15.0
Better Employment Opportunities	55.7
Partner's Employment	8.4
Career Advancement	29.9
Marriage	20.4
Separation/Divorce	1.8
Education/Study	27.5
Lifestyle	14.4
Higher Income	26.9
Professional Development	43.1

Source: Emigration Survey 2001

on advanced level mathematics (e.g. biostatistics, advanced computing, security systems, financial services). While there are several reasons for the decline, one particular area identified related to brain drain. Thomas (2002, 1) found from an analysis of data collected from the mathematics and statistics departments of Australian universities that:

- there is a continuing brain drain of experienced researchers
- a trickle of experienced migrant researchers into Australia continues
- the balance between inflow and outflow is unfavourable
- researchers from overseas are showing less of a tendency to stay.

In a survey of over 2,000 Australian expatriates living in foreign countries (Hugo, Rudd and Harris 2003), some 167 were employed as academics (122 males and 45 females). The reasons given for going overseas are shown in Table 21 and indicate the overwhelming dominance of employment related reasons for moving. The following comments from respondents indicate that several have moved because they see their career prospects being better in overseas universities …

"I see myself as part of a 'brain drain' of academic achievers who have left Australia for the UK or USA because of the gradual decay/active destruction of Australian universities. Salaries, teaching conditions and research funding are all of massive concern – as is job security. I hope the results from this survey send a clear message that many of us who have left would like to return eventually but fear it is difficult or impossible to do at the present."

It is apparent that many are earning more in their current location than they would in Australia with almost a half earning more than A$100,000 per year. However, many also mentioned the greater access to research funding and superior conditions for research. This is evident in the following...

> "I feel very displaced by the current trend of declining university funding. There are simply no opportunities in university geology in Australia. ARC funding is unreasonably difficult to acquire. I have successfully acquired NSF funding in the USA."

Respondents were asked if they "still considered Australia home" and 67.7 percent of academics compared to 79.3 of total respondents replied that this was the case. Hence, there is still a strong identification with Australia (Hugo forthcoming). Some 34.1 percent of respondents indicated that they have plans to return to Australia. Although this is less than was the case for all expatriate respondents (50.7 percent) it does indicate that there is a substantial number of Australian academics overseas who are prepared to return. Moreover, only 24.3 percent had definitely decided not to return and 41.3 percent are undecided. The reasons given by respondents for returning are overwhelmingly non-economic and non-work related, family and lifestyle.

Partly due to lobbying by groups like FASTS resulted in the Australian government initiating the Backing Australia's Ability program (http://backingaus.innovation.gov.au/docs/BAA03-04.pdf). This consists of a package of A$8.3 billion over the 2001-02 to 2010-11 period. The three objectives are...

- to generate new ideas
- the commercialisation of ideas
- the development of retention of skills.

In the present context the latter is of particular significance and include...

- the provision of 2000 extra university places targeted at science and technology
- doubling of the number of postdoctoral fellowships of the Australian Research Council
- introduction of measures to foster science, technology and mathematics education in schools
- a science lectureship initiative
- the introduction of Federation Fellowships (25 each year), which are "highly prestigious awards designed to build world class research

in Australia. By providing an internationally competitive salary…
encourage researchers to stay in, or return to, Australia to conduct
research of significant national economic, environmental and social
benefit" (Australian Government 2004).

Clearly then the issue of retention of skill is now established in the
government agenda. Moreover, for the first time there have been government initiated explicit efforts to attract back highly talented Australian
researchers from abroad.

Conclusion

In the new global economy a nation's competitiveness is influenced
strongly by its capacity to access labour which is skilled, innovative and
entrepreneurial. People with these characteristics now operate within
global labour markets whereby they can sell their labour to the highest
bidder regardless of the country in which the bidder is located. Whereas
in the past a nation's reservoir of talented individuals was overwhelmingly
home grown, they can now enhance the pool of talent by attracting foreigners with this human capital. Australia's position in this global market
is a complex one. On the one hand it has more experience than most
nations in attracting skilled immigrants. Over recent decades national
immigration policy has been developed and fine tuned, institutions have
matured, a cadre of skilled immigration professionals has developed in
government and a culture of migration among employers and the community generally has grown so that the nation is a very effective competitor for skilled potential immigrants. Australia now has a suite of effective permanent and temporary migration policies, programs and visa
categories for the recruitment of highly skilled people and it is highly successful in using immigration to enhance the nation's pool of talent.

On the other hand, Australia, while a developed and mature economy, occupies a peripheral position in the global economy. Hence, home
grown talent can be attracted to other nations which offer higher salaries,
better conditions, the chance to work in head office, etc. While Australia
has developed a complex, flexible and effective set of polices to attract talented individuals to Australia it has done very little to *retain* or *attract
back* talented Australians. Indeed there is a strong body of opinion in
Australia that such retention is not a concern because of the net migration gain being recorded in the various skill categories (Birrell *et al.* 2001).
However in recent times it has been suggested that there may be a need
to develop policies with respect to the Australian diaspora because…

- It may be that while there is a quantitative net gain of talent, there may be differentials in the quality human capital gained and lost. Is Australia losing the "brightest and the best"?

- Why shouldn't retention polices be developed as well as immigration so that the nation's talent pool is enhanced by both? Moreover, once talented migrants arrive in Australia they also need to be retained.

- In addition, it is increasingly being realised that there may also be benefits to Australia from accessing talented Australians living overseas. Such programs as the following…

  - Using the diaspora as bridgeheads for Australian business.
  - Networking business people, scientists and researchers with Australian equivalents to ensure the speedy transfer of knowledge to Australia.
  - Encouraging investment by expatriates in Australia.
  - Encouraging the eventual return of expatriates.

The 2003 Senate Committee of Enquiry into Expatriates suggested a number of initiatives to engage expatriates (Senate Legal and Constitutional References Committee 2005). There is a growing tempo of concern in the Australian SET (Science, Engineering and Technology) community that the nation's skill base in the enabling sciences is under particular pressure (DITR and DEST 2003). They argue that an extra 75,000 additional scientists, preferably with PhDs in the enabling sciences will be required by 2010.

One issue, which has gained little attention in contemporary Australia, is the impact of talent recruitment on the nations of origin, which are increasingly Asian (Hugo 2005). Previously Australia insisted that foreign students return to their home nation for at least two years after graduation. Now there are extra points available for some foreign students to apply for permanent residency after graduation. There is concern in some quarters. For example, one group of Australian doctors is lobbying to prevent the recruitment of doctors from countries which have a shortage of doctors (Australian Institute of Health and Welfare 2003). However, as yet there has been little attempt in Australia to develop policies which explicitly facilitate migration as a development tool in countries of origin (Hugo 2003b; 2005).

Australia's future economic development will be strongly influenced by its ability to access talented, highly skilled and well trained workers. The extent to which it will be able to do so will be strongly shaped by its policies with respect to education and training. However, in a globalising world it will also depend on national policies with respect to migration of skilled workers. This can be characterised as the "Four R's" ...

Recruitment: Australia needs to build on its sustained record of recruiting high skilled persons. There needs to be a public debate about the impact of this on less developed nations and also associated polices considered which recompense the origin areas but also facilitate the immigrants having maximum developmental benefits on their home country (Hugo 2003b).

Retention: There are opportunities for small numbers among the "brightest and the best" Australians to work productively and effectively in Australia so that they do not feel that it is absolutely essential for them to leave the country permanently to achieve their potential.

Return: There is much to gain from young Australians leaving Australia and acquiring experience, knowledge and connections in foreign nations. However, if a substantial proportion can return, the country can gain a double dividend – not just retaining their talents but having those talents enhanced by the period away.

Re-engagement: It is apparent that many Australians resident overseas on a permanent or long term basis still feel a strong sense of belonging to Australia and a deep concern for its wellbeing. There does appear to be a range of ways in which the expatriate community can be incorporated more into Australia. On a cultural level, it is important that expatriates who still consider themselves Australian are included more in the mainstream of Australian life. On an economic level, there are a myriad of ways in which the expertise, experience and contacts of the diaspora can be harnessed to benefit Australia in a rapidly globalising economy, social and political context (Hugo, Rudd and Harris 2003).

References

Andrews, P., 2004. Building Brain-Based Industries? First, find the Brains, in F. Wood (ed.) *'Beyond Brain Drain' Mobility, Competitiveness and Scientific Excellence*, University of New England, Armidale.

Australian Bureau of Statistics (ABS). *Australian Demographic Statistics*, various issues, Catalogue No. 3101.0, ABS, Canberra.

Australian Bureau of Statistics (ABS), 1986. *Australian Demographic Trends*, Catalogue No. 3102.0, ABS, Canberra.

Australian Bureau of Statistics (ABS), 2004. *Year Book Australia 2004*, Catalogue No. 1301.0, ABS, Canberra.

Australian Council of Deans of Science, 2001. Science at the Crossroads, Australian Council of Deans of Sicence, Canberra.

Australian Government, 2004. *Backing Australia's Ability : The Australian Government's Innovation Report 2003-04*, AGPS, Canberra.

Australian Institute of Health and Welfare, 2003. *Health and Community Services Labour Force 2001*, National Health Labour Force Series No. 27, AIHW, Canberra.

Bedford, R., 2001. Reflections on the Spatial Odesseys of New Zealanders. Briefing Paper No. 2, New Directions Seminar, April.

Birrell, B., Dobson, I.R., Kinnaird, B. and Smith, T.E., 2000. Universities and the IT Crisis Revisited, *People and Place*, 8, 3, pp. 74-82.

Birrell, B., Dobson, I.R., Rapson, V. and Smith, T.F., 2001. *Skilled Labour: Gains and Losses*, DIMIA, Canberra.

Castles, S. and Miller, M., 1998. *The Age of Migration: International Population Movements in the Modern World (Second Edition)*, Macmillan, London.

Cobb-Clark, D.A., 1999. Do Selection Criteria Make A Difference? Visa Category and the Labour Force Status of Australian Immigrants, *Discussion Paper No. 397*, Centre for Economic Policy Research, The Australian National University.

Cobb-Clark, D. and Chapman, B., 1999. The Changing Pattern of Immigrants Labour Market Experiences, *Discussion Paper No. 396*, Centre for Economic Policy Research, The Australian National University.

Department of Education, Training and Youth Affairs (DETYA), 2001. *Students: Selected Higher Education Statistics*, Canberra: AGPS.

Department of Industry, Tourism and Resources, (DITR) and Department of Education, Science and Training (DEST), 2003. Mapping Australian Science and Innovation, Australian Government, Canberra.

Department of Immigration and Multicultural and Indigenous Affairs (DIMIA). *Australian Immigration: Consolidated Statistics*, various issues, AGPS, Canberra.

Department of Immigration and Multicultural and Indigenous Affairs (DIMIA). *Population Flows: Immigration Aspects, various issues*. Canberra: AGPS.

Department of Immigration and Multicultural and Indigenous Affairs (DIMIA). *Immigration Update*, various issues, AGPS, Canberra.

Department of Immigration and Multicultural and Indigenous Affairs (DIMIA), 2002. *Population Flows: Immigration Aspects*, various issues, AGPS, Canberra.

Department of Immigration and Multicultural and Indigenous Affairs (DIMIA), 2004. *Population Flows: Immigration Aspects,* 2002-03 Edition, AGPS, Canberra.

Dimzon, C.S., 2005. Philippine Migration, Remittances and Development in the Philippines. Paper presented at Workshop on International Migration and Labour Market in Asia organised by the Japan Institute for Labour Policy and Training, Japan Institute of Labour, Tokyo, 20-21 January.

Friedmann, J., 1986. The World City Hypothesis, *Development and Change,* 17 pp. 69-83.

Government of South Australia, 2004. *Prosperity Through People: A Population Policy for South Australia,* Government of South Australia, Adelaide.

Gutièrrez, C.G., 1999. Fostering identities : Mexico's relations with its diaspora, *The Journal of American History* 86 2: 545-567.

Harding, G. and Webster, E., 2002. *The Working Holiday Maker Scheme and the Australian Labour Market,* Melbourne Institute of Applied Economic and Social Research, University of Melbourne, DIMIA, Canberra.

Hugo, G.J., 1994. *The Economic Implications of Emigration from Australia,* Australian Government Publishing Service, Canberra.

Hugo, G.J., 1999. A New Paradigm of International Migration in Australia, *New Zealand Population Review,* 25, 1-2, pp. 1-39.

Hugo, G.J., 2001. International Migration and Agricultural Labour in Australia. Paper presented at Changing Face Workshop, Imperial Valley, California, 16-18 January.

Hugo, G.J., 2003a. Temporary Migration to Australia: Trends and Implications. Paper prepared for Annual Conference of New Zealand Geographical Society, Auckland, New Zealand, July.

Hugo, G.J., 2003b. Migration and Development : A Perspective from Asia, *IOM Migration Research Series,* 14.

Hugo, G.J., 2004a. A New Paradigm of International Migration : Implications for Migration Policy and Planning in Australia, Information and Research Services, Parliamentary Library, Canberra.

Hugo, G.J., 2004b. The Longitudinal Survey of Immigrants to Australia (LSIA), IRSS Workshop on Longitudinal Surveys and Cross Cultural Survey Design, Home Office, London.

Hugo, G.J., 2005. Diaspora and Emigration in Developed Countries, Report for IOM, January.

Hugo, G.J., forthcoming. Some Emerging Demographic Issues on Australia's Teaching Academic Workforce, Special Issue of *Higher Education Policy* on Knowledge Flow and Capacity Development.

Hugo, G.J., Rudd, D. and Harris, K., 2001. *Emigration from Australia: Economic Implications.* CEDA Information Paper No. 77, CEDA, Melbourne.

Hugo, G.J., Rudd, D. and Harris, K., 2003. *Australia's Diaspora: It's Size, Nature and Policy Implications,* CEDA Information Paper No. 80, CEDA, Melbourne.

Iguchi, Y., 2004. International migration and labor market in Japan – growing intra-regional trade, investment and migration. Paper presented at workshop on International Migration and Labour Market in Asia organised by the Japan Institute for Labour Policy and Training; Tokyo, 5-6 February.

James, D. 2004. Faces in a Global Gallery, *Business Review Weekly*, 19 February, p. 66.

Joint Standing Committee on Migration (JSCM), 1997. *Working Holiday Makers: More than Tourists*, AGPS, Canberra.

Khoo, S.E., McDonald, P., Giorgas, D. and Birrell, B., 2002. *Second Generation Australians*, Centre for Population Research and the Department of Immigration and Multicultural and Indigenous Affairs, Canberra, Australia.

Khoo, S., Voight, C., Hugo, G. and McDonald, P., 2003. Temporary Skilled Migration to Australia: the 457 Visa Sub-Class, *People and Place*, 11, 4, pp. 27-40.

Kinnaird, B., 1999. Working Holiday Makers: More Than Tourists – Implications of the Report of the Joint Standing Committee on Migration. *People and Place*, 7(1): 39-52.

Kippen, R. and McDonald, P., 2000. Australia's Population in 2000: The Way We Are and the Ways We Might Have Been, *People and Place*, vol.8, no. 3, pp. 10-17.

Martin, P., 2004. Regional Patterns of International Migration: North America Present and Future. Paper presented at Tenth Workshop on International Migration and Labour Markets in Asia organised by the Japan Institute of Labour, Tokyo, 5-6 February.

Naseem, S.M., 1998. The diaspora view of the economy, *Dawn*, 30 December.

National Population Inquiry (NPI), 1975. *Population and Australia: A Demographic Analysis and Projection*, two volumes. Canberra: AGPS.

Richardson, S., Robertson, F. and Ilsley, D., 2001. *The Labour Force Experience of New Migrants*, AGPS, Canberra.

Rizvi, A., 2002. SOPEMI 2003: Australia. Report by Australia's Correspondent to SOPEMI, November.

Rizvi, A., 2003. SOPEMI 2004: Australia. Report by Australia's Correspondent to the OECD.

Rizvi, A., 2004. SOPEMI 2005: Australia. Report by Australia's Correspondent to the OECD.

Ruddick, E., 2003. Immigrant Economic Performance – A New Paradigm in a Changing Labour Market, *Canadian Issues*, April.

Sahoo, S., 2002. 'Can India Catch up with China? From a Diasporic Perspective', *India-China Mirror* (Quarterly), Vol.VII, Issue. III, July – September.

Sassen, S., 1991. *The Global City (Second Edition)*, Princeton University Press, New York.

Sassen, S., 1995. Die Immigration in der Welwirtschaft, *Journal for Entwicklungspolitik*, x, 3, pp.261-84.

Senate Legal and Constitutional References Committee, 2005. *They still call Australia home: Inquiry into Australian expatriates*, Department of the Senate, Parliament House, Canberra.

Southern Cross, 2002. *Estimates of Australian Citizens Living Overseas as at 31 December 2001*, http://www.southern-cross-group.org/archives/Statistics/Numbers_of_Australians_Overseas_in_2001_by_Region_Feb_2002.pdf.

Tan, G.T., 2003. The Motivations and Future Intentions of Singaporean and Malaysian Students in Adelaide. Unpublished B.A. Hons. Thesis, Department of Geographical and Environmental Studies, The University of Adelaide, November.

153

Thomas, J., 2000. *Mathematical Sciences in Australia: Looking for a Future*, FASTS Occasional Paper Series, No. 3, October.

Thomas, J., 2002. Mathematical Sciences in Australia: Still Looking for a Future, FASTS Occasional Paper Series, May.

US Census Bureau, 2002a. Team 7 Final Report – Emigration of Native Born. 5 October.

US Census Bureau, 2002b. Conference on an Enumeration of Americans Overseas in the 2010 Census, 26 and 27 November 2001. US Department of Commerce, Economics and Statistics Administration, US Census Bureau.

VandenHeuvel, A. and Wooden, M., 1999. *New Settlers Have Their Say – How immigrants fare over the early years of settlement*, Commonwealth of Australia, Canberra.

Wood, F. (ed.), 2004. *'Beyond Brain Drain' Mobility, Competitiveness and Scientific Excellence*, University of New England, Armidale.

Wooden, M., Holton, R., Hugo, G.J. and Sloan, J., 1994. *Australian Immigration: A Survey of the Issues*, Second Edition, Australian Government Publishing Service, Canberra.

Zhang, X., 2003. *The Wealth Position of Immigrant Families in Canada*, Statistics Canada, No. 197, November.

Foreign talent and development in Singapore

Pang Eng Fong

Foreign Talent is *"a matter of life and death for us in the long term. ... If we do not top up our talent pool from the outside, in 10 years' time, many of the high-valued jobs we do now will migrate to China and elsewhere, for lack of sufficient talent here."*

(Goh Chok Tong[1])

"If we do not attract, welcome and make foreign talent feel comfortable in Singapore, we will not be a global city and if we are not a global city, it doesn't count for much. ... There are four million people in Singapore; one million of which are foreigners. You get rid of this one million and many will not find jobs."

(Lee Kuan Yew[2])

"Has the competition really disappeared, or has the talent just gone to another country, where they will compete more strongly against us? If we do not top up our own talent with people from abroad, will multinational corporations still come here, to recruit from a smaller talent pool? Or will we become a backwater, just one of many cities in Asia?" Citizens are *"the Government's priority and obligation ... the ones we depend on to stand up for the country at all times, and to defend it in a crisis. They elected the Government, and the Government's first duty is to serve them. ...So we treat PRs (permanent residents) well. But we treat citizens well-plus."*

(Lee Hsien Loong[3])

---

[1] 1997 National Day Rally Speech.

[2] Speech to Nanyang Technology University (NTU) students (reported in Chong 2003).

[3] 2004 Speech to NTU students (reported in Low 2004).

Introduction

Recognizing the contribution foreign talent can make to their countries, many developed countries have instituted programs to encourage their inflow (McLaughlan and Salt 2002; Anderson 2003; Pang 2004). But none probably has been as assiduous or organized as Singapore in courting them. Skilled foreigners or foreign talent as they are often referred to in Singapore are "a matter of life and death" for Singapore in the long term, said Prime Minister Goh Chok Tong (now Senior Minister) in his 1997 National Day Rally speech. Without foreigners, jobs for locals would disappear and Singapore would not become a truly global city, warned Minister Mentor Lee Kuan Yew (the first Prime Minister and formerly Senior Minister) in an exchange with university students in 2003. Recognizing their contributions, Singapore treats PRs (permanent residents) "well", noted Prime Minister Lee Hsien Loong (who took over from Goh in August 2004) in an address to university students in 2004.[4] He added that Singapore treats its citizens "well-plus".

This paper looks at Singapore's foreign talent policy and how it has evolved in practice in recent years. It is not a statistical study as post-1980 time-series and fine-grained data on skilled foreigners in Singapore are not publicly available.[5]

Trends in foreign worker inflows

A country built by immigrants and their descendants, Singapore has always welcomed foreigners. Before its post-independent economy reached full employment in the early 1970s, the annual flow of foreign workers, both skilled and unskilled, into Singapore was small (Pang and Lim 1982). The flow surged from the late 1970s. In 1980 – the only census year for which detailed data on non-citizen workers are available – about 80,000 or 7% of the workforce of 1.1 million were non-Singaporeans. By 1990, the number had risen to 248,000 or 19% of the workforce. By 2000, it had reached 612,000 persons or 29% of the workforce, thanks to the joint effect of nearly a decade of rapid economic growth and demographic changes which resulted in fewer Singaporeans entering

---

[4] "Singapore prides itself on being a very cosmopolitan city-state, welcoming people from all over the world to our shores. And we aspire to be a plug-and-play destination for professionals from anywhere in the world and their families," said Ng Eng Hen, Acting Minister for Manpower and Minister of State for Education at the Global Workforce Summit in Singapore, 2 March 2004.

[5] Statistics on the educational, occupational and industry characteristics of non-resident workers are available only for 1980. Comparable statistics are not found in census reports for 1990 and 2000 or in labor force and employment data released by the Statistics Department.

the labor force. Between 1990 and 2000, the non-resident workforce increased by 9.4% a year, seven times faster than the rate for the resident workforce.

Slower growth after September 11, 2001 and the SARS outbreak broke this upward trend and the number fell to about 600,000 in 2003. Even so, Singapore's dependence on foreign workers remains exceptionally high in comparison with most developed countries. Rising unemployment in 2003/4 did not change the government's view on the indispensable role played by foreign workers, skilled as well as unskilled, in Singapore's economy.

Most non-resident workers are work permit holders, performing unskilled or service jobs in sectors that cannot attract enough local workers. In 1980 18.5% of the non-resident workers could be considered "foreign talent" as they held administrative, managerial, professional or technical jobs. If we assume that a similar fraction (one in five) of the 600,000 foreign workers in 2003 are highly skilled or "talented", then Singapore has around 120,000 foreign workers who could be labeled foreign talent. [6] Of these around 90,000 hold employment passes (which are issued to skilled foreigners with degrees, professional qualifications or specialist skills and who are paid monthly salaries of more than S$2500 and are also not permanent residents).

The changing citizen composition of the workforce since 1970 is reflected in changes in Singapore's population. In 1970 non-residents formed only 3% of the population of 2 million. Three decades later, the non-resident share of the population had risen to 19%. The non-resident population peaked in 2001 at 812,000 and fell by 65,000 to 748,000 two years later as growth slowed (Heng and Png 2004). With renewed economic growth since 2004, the number has risen but is probably still below the 2001 peak. The growing proportion of non-residents in Singapore's total population did not happen by chance but is the outcome of a deliberate policy and its effective execution.

Foreign talent policy

Although highly-skilled foreigners have been very much part of Singapore's population for a long time, high-powered policy focus on them as indispensable to the city-state's competitiveness and future is recent, dating only from the late 1970s. Two factors explain this focus

---

[6] There is no standard definition of a skilled person. Most countries use a variety of criteria to determine whether a person is skilled or not (Auriel and Sexton 2002).

and the urgency with which the issue is viewed by Singapore's leaders. The first is demographic – Singapore's core population growth rate has fallen to less than 2% a year. Even with greater investments in education and training, the indigenous skilled pool is insufficient to meet the projected demand for skills arising from the economy's shift towards higher value-added activities. Unless addressed, this imbalance could harm the economy's competitive edge and derail its shift to a higher-value track.

The second factor is the conviction of the top Singapore leadership that foreign talent, properly identified and absorbed, would add vigor and dynamism to the population.

Foreign talent is needed to fill more than current domestic skill gaps. It is vital to inspire changes and raise standards in other areas, especially education. For this reason, Singapore has been extraordinarily open in accepting promising foreign students into its schools and highly-subsidized higher institutions of learning. Some 35,000 foreign students are in Singapore's education system (Nirmala and Soh 2004). One in five students in the three government-funded universities – the National University of Singapore, Nanyang Technological University and Singapore Management University – is a non-citizen. These non-citizen students pay fees significantly lower than what they would pay in Europe or North America. After graduation, many stay on to work in Singapore, augmenting the island's pool of educated manpower.

Evolution of foreign worker policy

Singapore's hunt for foreign talent is an integral part of its policy on foreign labor, a policy that has evolved over three decades into a highly selective tool to achieve economic, social and political goals. This policy, whose basic thrust remains unchanged, is restrictive with respect to unskilled foreign labor and liberal with respect to highly skilled foreign labor.

Singapore has developed a host of price and non-price mechanisms to regulate the flow of unskilled foreigners. Foreign workers are considered unskilled if they are paid a monthly salary of less than S$2,500. Such workers are given work permits, which do not allow them to bring dependents. Employers may recruit them only from certain countries and only for particular sectors. There are ceilings on the proportion of foreign workers they can have in their company. They must pay levies which vary with the sector and the skill of the worker. For example, the levy rate is set lower for workers with acceptable trade qualifications to encourage employers to train and upgrade unskilled workers. The levies and dependency ceilings are adjusted to reflect new circumstances and objectives. There are stiff penalties for hiring workers without work permits. Employers found guilty of hiring illegal workers may be jailed for up to two years and/or fined up to S$6000. Mandatory caning is imposed if an employer hires more than five illegal workers. The illegal worker is fined up to S$5000 and/or jailed for a year.

In sharp contrast to its restrictive policy on unskilled foreign workers, Singapore allows employers much greater flexibility to import foreign workers with skills they cannot find in Singapore. Singapore ranks third among countries with the least restrictive immigration laws in the import of talent (IMD 2004). A 2005 survey of multinational corporations by PricewaterhouseCoopers found that Singapore's talent management policies are among the friendliest in the world (Straits Times 2005). Only 3% of these corporations reported having problems with Singapore's immigration policies (in contrast to 46% for the United States and 24% for China). To hire foreign talent, employers need only satisfy certain criteria relating to qualifications, skills and salary minima set by the Ministry of Manpower. There are several types of employment passes, each with their own requirements and benefits. Foreigners with approved qualifications or experience can apply for a "P" employment pass if their basic monthly salary is more than S$3,500.[7] Employment passes are valid for varying durations and may be renewed. An EntrePass Scheme was launched in 2003 to facilitate the entry of entrepreneurs and innovators who plan to start business ventures in Singapore. The Scheme recognized that entrepreneurs and innovators may not possess the educational qualifications required under the employment pass scheme.

In July 2004 a new "S" work pass was introduced to meet the needs of industries for middle-level skill manpower. Applicants for the "S" pass must satisfy a points test which takes into account four main criteria – salary, education qualifications, work experience and job type. Employers will have to pay a monthly levy for "S" pass holders, which changes with market conditions. The number of "S" pass holders in each company is capped at 5% of the company's local and work permit workforce. Unlike work permit holders, "S" pass holders earning a S$2,500 basic monthly salary or more can bring their dependents with them (see Appendix for details).

Government policy encourages pass-holders with the appropriate cultural and social characteristics to apply for permanent residence and

---

[7] There is another type of employment pass. "Q1" passes are granted to foreigners whose basic monthly salary is more than S$2,500 and who possess acceptable degrees, professional qualifications or specialist skills.

eventually citizenship. Hui and Hashmi (2004) estimate that 230,000 persons, mostly employment pass holders and their immediate family were granted permanent residence in the 1990s. In 2000, there were 112,000 foreigners working in Singapore as professionals, managers or technical workers. Past trends suggest that many will apply for permanent residence and be eventually granted Singapore citizenship.

Indeed, the changing profile of foreign talent will reinforce these trends. Before the 1990s, a significant proportion of expatriates were from developed countries, people on employment passes who were in Singapore on job assignments with expatriate compensation packages. In recent years more of the people granted employment passes are from the region, especially China and India (Seneviratne 2004). More than half are on local contracts – close to 60% according to a survey (Thompson 2004) – and do not enjoy the perks (housing, support for children's education, home leave, etc) usually enjoyed by expatriates from developed countries or by those working for multinationals. A growing network of recent immigrants from their own home countries has made Singapore an increasingly attractive place for them to seek work and settle permanently. Singapore ranked first among 29 economies with a population of under 20 million in attracting top flight talent (IMD 2003).

A number of related factors explain the ability of Singapore to attract more than its share of internationally mobile talent. Perhaps the most important one is the unwavering commitment of its leadership to the policy. Foreigners and foreign firms are left in no doubt about this commitment. Even in the worst of economic times, Singapore leaders have stressed that employers would be allowed to act in their own best interests even if it means retrenching Singaporeans before foreigners.

The second is policy implementation. Rules on employment pass applications are clear and explicit. Applications are processed quickly, within days rather than weeks. A director of a well-known consulting company said recently:

> "Bain & Company has never had a request for an employment pass turned down. This is incredibly important to us because we need to have a reasonably free flow of people between our office here and clients and satellite offices throughout the region. Of course, our firm and our people pay a significant amount of income tax and contribute in other ways to the local community. It is virtually impossible to use other South-east Asian countries as hubs in this manner because numerous laws prevent Asian expatriates residing in these countries." (Business Times, 13 December 2004).

The establishment in the late 1990s of a new agency called Contact Singapore, whose primary role is to attract talent to Singapore, also played a part. Contact Singapore has offices in Australia, China, Europe, India, and North America. These offices provide both foreigners and overseas Singaporeans with information on jobs and life in Singapore. They help match foreign talent who are looking for jobs with employers in Singapore who are seeking skilled people. Contact Singapore not only helps attract skilled foreigners to Singapore, it facilitates the return of trained and experienced Singaporeans who are studying or working abroad. Figures on the number of Singaporeans who migrate or give up their Singapore citizenship are not known. But the number is probably small compared to the many thousands who are granted permanent residence or who become citizens every year.

Another factor is the cost of living in Singapore and its quality of life. According to a cost-of-living survey of over one hundred cities by Mercer in 2003, Singapore is less costly for expatriates than Hong Kong or Beijing. The survey compared the cost of more than 200 items in each city including housing, food, clothing and household goods, transport and entertainment (Mercer Human Resource Consulting 2003). The city-state itself is seen as a safe and secure place to live and bring up children.

Tax incentives also help. According to the Inland Revenue Authority of Singapore (IRAS), non-resident workers are taxed only on income derived from or accrued in Singapore. They do not have to pay taxes on foreign income received in Singapore. Also, they are exempted from income tax if they work in Singapore for 60 days or less in a calendar year.

Contributions of foreign workers

Singapore's experience with both skilled and unskilled foreign labor has been highly positive. Foreign workers have contributed significantly to the island's economic growth. Using a growth accounting model and unpublished data, Tan et al (2002) estimated that 41% of Singapore's GDP growth in the 1990s came from the inflow of foreign workers, skilled as well as unskilled. They calculated that 37% of the GDP growth was due to skilled foreign manpower, that is, workers holding employment passes. Their results imply that skilled foreign workers, although only a quarter as numerous as work permit holders, contributed an astonishing nine times more to Singapore's GDP growth than unskilled foreigners.

Another study (Chia, Thangavelu and Toh 2004) reinforced the huge importance of foreign talent to Singapore. It finds that foreign workers and local labor in Singapore are complements, not substitutes. Using unpublished data, it estimates that since the mid-1980s a 1%

change in the number of employment pass holders is associated with a 1.9% change in skilled local employment and 0.2% change in unskilled local employment. The influx of skilled foreigners therefore has a significantly greater positive impact on skilled jobs than on unskilled jobs for Singaporeans. This differential impact holds also for work permit holders. Unskilled foreign labor "supports" the employment of more skilled local workers than unskilled local workers. In brief, skilled Singaporeans have benefited more than unskilled Singaporeans from the influx of foreign workers.

Foreign labor in Singapore has had other positive, though unquantifiable, effects. It has relieved cost pressures in many sectors and so improved their competitiveness. It has enabled more local women to enter and remain in the workforce. It has stimulated the creation of new enterprises, spurred innovation, transferred skills and technology to nationals, and quickened the internationalization of Singapore firms (Chia, Thangavelu and Toh 2004). Immigration policy is integrally linked to economic policy as well as population policy.

Sending countries, especially neighboring ones that are large exporters of unskilled foreign workers, have benefited as well. Exporting labor to Singapore has eased employment pressures and resulted in a steady flow of remittances. Returning workers have enlarged their supply of people with international experience and skills. Some have used money earned from their stay abroad to establish small enterprises.

The interests of Singapore and those of labor-sending neighbors are, however, not always identical. Relations with them can become tense as they did in the late 1980s when Singapore repatriated large numbers of illegal workers after its economy contracted sharply. Like all labor-importing countries, Singapore has to be sensitive to the impact foreign labor has not only on its own economy and society but also on those of labor-sending countries.

Issues arising from the influx of foreign talent

Most Singaporeans agree with the political leadership that foreign talent is critical to Singapore's prosperity and future. A Gallup poll of them in 1997 found that 70% of them supported the policy. This endorsement, though, does not mean they have no reservations about the influx of skilled foreigners or that there are no problems in integrating them into Singapore's multiethnic and increasingly cosmopolitan society. Half the Singaporeans interviewed feared the loss of jobs as a result of the influx of foreign talent. Their anxieties are correlated with the state of the economy. Before 1997 when there was full employment, few Singapore-ans were particularly worried. After 1997, with growth slackening and becoming more volatile, concerns about job competition from the rising number of foreigners have grown. These concerns reflect in part the emergence of a new phenomenon in Singapore, namely, the unemploy-ment of older white-collar workers, some laid off by the relocation of production to neighboring countries, others by corporate restructuring and mergers. With the return of strong economic and employment expansion in 2004, these concerns have eased. Nevertheless, job and wage competition from foreigners will remain a controversial issue, one not likely to be settled by statistical analysis or the release of more government data.

Perceptions differ also on other issues. According to a 2001 survey (reported in Nirmala and Soh 2004) by researchers from the National University of Singapore, most Singaporeans thought foreigners were in Singapore for the economic benefits with no intention of staying perma-nently. But half the employment pass holders interviewed said they intended to become permanent residents. The survey also reported that more than half of the foreigners said they mixed frequently with Singa-poreans and had Singaporean friends. Most reported they felt welcomed by their Singaporean colleagues. Few Singaporeans interviewed said they interacted much with skilled foreigners or count them among their close friends. Four in ten thought foreign talent would out-perform them in the workplace. That foreign talent and locals do not share the same per-ceptions is not surprising. It is natural for foreigners to want to feel wel-comed. It is equally unsurprising that locals should be concerned about the social and economic impact of having more strangers in their midst. The practical challenge is to find ways to increase interactions between foreigners and locals and so reduce misperception on both sides.

Conclusions

Singapore has derived substantial benefits from its exceptionally large dependence on imported labor, both skilled and unskilled. As a nat-ural resource-poor and low-fertility nation, it has long recognized that this dependence must be properly managed if it is to contribute to Sin-gapore's stability and long-term prosperity. That it has been largely suc-cessful in this policy objective is due to several factors. As a high-income, English-speaking and meritocratic society that welcomes unequivocally foreign talent, the island-state offers opportunities for economic advance-ment for foreign workers from within the region as well as from other

163

parts of the world. Political stability and policy continuity have encouraged immigrant workers with the right background and skills to work and settle permanently.

In Singapore, as in other countries keen to get their share of mobile talented people, attracting talent is not just a matter of weighing economic benefits against economic costs. Allowing foreigners into the country – whether as immigrants or as temporary workers to alleviate shortages – is a political decision that is often the result of heated debate. Countries differ in their approach. Singapore, like Australia, has been much more pro-active than Germany and Japan. Reflecting a stronger national consensus on skilled immigration, Singapore, like Australia, has been effective in implementing policies to bring in foreign talent. Also like Australia, Singapore has set up overseas offices to promote successfully their programs to attract skilled people.

One important and critical factor in Singapore's success in attracting talent is that English is the main language of government and business. English is the first or second language of highly-educated people in the world. Countries like Australia or the United States where English is the official language have had greater success with the talent-attracting programs than countries like Germany or Japan.

Another factor that has reinforced Singapore's attractiveness to mobile talent is its multiethnic and increasingly cosmopolitan society. The island offers lifestyle possibilities that appeal to educated people who are not looking only to maximize their incomes but for a secure place where they can feel comfortable quickly and bring up their families.

A country's ability to attract talent can change due to developments that are not related to a country's policy commitment or program design. Tougher admission visa rules such as those implemented for security reasons by the US after September 11, 2001 can change foreign perceptions and reduce a country's attractiveness as a place to study or settle in.

Another development that could alter the flow of global talent is business process outsourcing. The outsourcing of skilled jobs in the IT sector from the high-cost countries including Singapore to places like India could dampen the demand for foreign talent. The impact of outsourcing on skill flows is a subject that Singapore (and also other high-income countries) must build into their programs to attract and integrate global talent.

Finally, economics will continue to clash with politics in the global competition for talent. Singapore, like other countries competing for talent, must balance the economic benefits of importing foreign talent with the political costs of integrating it into their societies. It is an easier balance to achieve when policy and program design are clear and well-aligned, as it appears to be the case for Singapore, and when the economy is expanding and creating new job opportunities for both locals and foreigners.

Appendix Table 1

Comparison of Rules and Regulations of Work Permits, S-Passes and Employment Passes

Type of Permit	Type of Workers	Duration	Sector	Levy (Monthly)	Maximum Dependency Ratio (Foreign: Local)	Nationalies Prohibited	Security Bond	Comments
Work Permit – Unskilled	unskilled foreigner with a monthly basic salary of up to S$2,500	up to 2 yrs, renewable annually for a total of up to 4 years.	Service	S$240(< 30% depend.); S$500 (betw. 30% and 40% depend).	3:7	NTS	S$5,000 is required for each NTS/NAS/PRC worker	–
			Manufacturing	S$240 (< 40% depend.); S$310 (betw. 40% and 50% depend); S$500 (betw. 50% and 60% depend)	1:1	NTS		–
			Process	295	3:1			–
			Town Council Conservancy	–	3:7	–		–
			Grass-Cutting		3:7	–		–
			Marine	295	3:1	–		–
			Construction	470	4:1	–		–

Appendix Table 1 (Cont'd)

Type of Permit	Type of Workers	Duration	Sector	Levy (Monthly)	Maximum Dependency Ratio (Foreign: Local)	Nationalies Prohibited	Security Bond	Comments
Work Permit – Skilled	skilled or an unskilled foreigner with a monthly basic salary of up to S$2,500	up to 3 years, renewable for a total of up to 10 years.	Service	S$80(< 30% depend.); S$500 (betw. 30% and 40% depend).	3:7	NTS	S$5,000 is required for each NTS/NAS/PRC worker	–
			Manufacturing	S$80 (< 40% depend.); S$80 (betw. 40% and 50% depend);S$500 (betw. 50% and 60% depend)	1:1	NTS		–
			Process	80	3:1			–
			Town Council Conservancy	–	3:7			–
			Grass-Cutting	–	3:7			–
			Marine	80	3:1			–
			Construction	80	4:1			–

Appendix Table 1 (Cont'd)

Type of Permit	Type of Workers	Duration	Sector	Levy (Monthly)	Maximum Dependency Ratio (Foreign: Local)	Nationalies Prohibited	Security Bond	Comments
S Pass	skilled manpower at the middle level who is offered a monthly basic salary of at least $1,800	2 years in the first instance and 3 years upon renewal	NA	50	1:19	NA	NA	S pass holders earning more than $2,500 will also be eligible for a Dependant Pass (DP).
Employment Pass – P Pass	A P1 Pass will be issued if the applicant's monthly basic salary is more than S$7,000. A P2 Pass will be issued if the applicant's monthly basic salary is more than S$3,500 and up to S$7,000	2 years in the first instance and 3 years upon renewal	NA	NA	NA	NA	NA	Can Apply for DP. Eligible for permanent residence after months. Long-Term Social Visit Passes
Employment Pass – Q1 Pass	monthly basic salary is more than S$2,500 and possess acceptable degrees, professional qualifications or specialist skills	2 years in the first instance and 3 years upon renewal	NA	NA	NA	NA	NA	Can Apply for DP. Eligible for permanent residence after months.

*A skilled foreign worker is one who possesses at least a SPM qualification or its equivalent, or a NTC-3 (Practical) Trade Certificate [Also known as ITE's Skills Evaluation Certificate (Level 1) from July 2002] that is relevant to his/her occupation. Non-Traditional Source (NTS) countries include Thailand, India, Sri Lanka, Bangladesh, Myanmar, the Philippines and Pakistan.

Source: Ministry of Manpower, http://www.mom.gov.sg/InformationOnWorkPermit/, accessed 11 Aug 2005

References

Anderson, S., 2003. "The Global Battle for Talent and People", *American Immigration Policy Focus*, 2 (2) (Sept):1-23.

Auriol, L. and J. Sexton, 2002. "Human Resources in Science and Technology: Measurement Issues and International Mobility". In OECD (2002).

Business Times 2004. "Views from the Top", 13 December.

Chia, B, S. M. Thangavelu and M. H. Toh, 2004. "The Complementary Role of Foreign Labour in Singapore," *Economic Survey of Singapore*, First Quarter 2004: 53-64.

Chong V., 2003. "Foreign Talent Policy Here to Stay: Lee Kuan Yew" *The Business Times*, 19 February.

Economic Development Board, 2004. "In the News", Volume 7, Issue 37, 14 Sep 2004

http://www.sedb.com/edbcorp/sg/en_uk/indrx/in_the_news/publications/singaporenpw_-_2004/volume_7_issue_37.html, accessed 11 August 2005.

Economic Development Board, 2002. "Media Report – Enterprise Services", pg 68, March 2002, http://www.sedb.com/etc/medialib/downloads/about_edb.Par.0070.File.tmp/page68_services.pdf, accessed 11 August, 2005.

Heng T. C and M. T. Png, 2004. "Singapore's Demographic Trends in 2003", *Statistics Singapore Newsletter: 12-16*, September.

Hui, W T and Hashmi A R.,

2004. "Foreign Labor and Economic Growth Policy Options for Singapore", paper presented at the Center for Labor Market Research Seminar Series, University of Western Australia, 26 May.

Institute of Management Development (IMD), 2003. *World Competitiveness Yearbook 2003*.

Institute of Management Development (IMD), 2004. *World Competitiveness Yearbook 2004*.

Low, E., 2004. "Foreign talent better in than out," *Straits Times*, 6 April.

McLaughlan, G and J Salt, 2002. *Migration Policies towards Highly Skilled Foreign Workers*. Report prepared for the UK Home Office, March.

Mercer Human Resource Consulting, 2003. "Cost of living survey 2003", June.

Ministry of Manpower, Singapore, 2004.

Labor Market, Third Quarter 2004 Report, 16 December, www.mom.gov.sg, accessed 20 December, 2004.

Ministry of Manpower, Singapore, 2004. Information on Work Permits

www.mom.gov.sg, accessed 4 August, 2004.

Ng E. H., 2004. "Opening Address", *Global Workforce Summit*, 2 March, Singapore.

Nirmala M and W. L. Soh, 2004. "Foreign talent: A new class act," *Straits Times*, 24 April.

OECD, 2002. *International Mobility of the Highly Skilled*, Paris.

Pang, E. F., 2004. "Attracting Global Talent: The Experience of Six High-Income Countries". mimeo.

Pang, E. F. and L. Lim, 1982. "Foreign Labor and Economic Development in Singapore". *International Migration Review* 16(3): 548-576.

Seneviratne K., 2004. "Low-cost Professionals Pour into Singapore", Inter-Press Service 17 December.

Straits Times, 2003. "S'pore a top draw for talent, cuts labor cost", 23 May.

Straits Times, 2005. "Immigration laws here among world's friendliest", 18 August.

Tan, K. Y et al, 2002. "Has Foreign Talent Contributed to Singapore's Economic Growth? An Empirical Assessment". Ministry of Trade and Industry, Singapore.

T Y, Mui, 2004. "Country Report –Singapore", *Institute of Policy Studies.*

Thompson M., 2004. "Home Truths," *Straits Times,* 20 September.

Current migration of IT engineers to Japan: Beyond immigration control and cultural barriers

Chieko Kamibayashi

Introduction

This paper deals with foreign workers in Japan, especially IT engineers, and includes a discussion of the recent policy change toward the active recruitment of highly skilled human resources from Asian countries. In spite of the government's policy, foreign IT engineers in Japan are still small in number, due to the historical context of Japanese society and cultural barriers such as Japanese language, business practices, and employment practices. Japanese IT-related firms give special training to foreign workers and are careful in screening trainable human resources. They are now at the stage of strategizing how to employ foreign workers and keep them employed.

Since the 17th century, not only Japanese firms, but also Japanese society as a whole has faced the question of migration. Japan was a country of emigration until the middle of the 1980s when the bubble economy created a labor shortage. For a long time, the aim of immigration control policy has been to prevent foreigners from becoming permanent residents.

Most Japanese never dreamed of a day when they might depend on a labor force from outside Japan. For example, from 1868 to 1941 the number of emigrants totaled 1 million, mostly headed for Hawaii, the mainland US, Manchuria and Brazil. Post-war emigration resumed in 1952, the year of the San Francisco Peace Treaty, with the tide headed for the US and Brazil, and less for Argentina. The total number reached 260,000. On the other hand, our history of immigration is only 10 to 15 years long. The entry into force of "The New Immigration Control and Refugee Recognition Law" in 1990 was a turning point for Japanese migration policy and, in a way, designed to cope with the increase of illegal foreign workers. The labor shortage in Japanese firms, small and medium-sized firms especially, moved the government to accept a foreign labor force with the conciliation of public opinion.

During the last 15 years, the Japanese government's immigration policy attracted much attention from the business world, even from global companies. Thanks to discussions among the government, the business world, and policy makers, the structure of immigration policy has become clear. While unskilled workers remain an object of exclusion and illegal workers have become subject to strict law enforcement, immigrants with the potential to contribute valuable skills and technology to society are positively welcomed. In a word, the government tries to make a clear demarcation between foreign workers with working visa status and illegal workers, the former encouraged, the latter discouraged. Encouragement of any kind indicates a major turning point in the history of Japanese immigration policy.

Current foreign IT engineers in Japan

The Japanese government is not exceptional in giving priority to the promotion of information (communication) technology. This is the same as in other technology-oriented nations. The competition on this already highly competitive world market has amplified because the technology in this field changes so fast. The recent increase of foreign IT engineers in Japan is due to the fact that the product market is becoming increasingly more global, and to a lesser extent, to a more global labor market. However, the number of foreign engineers in Japan is still small compared with other countries that try to attract IT workers from other parts of the world.

Japanese immigration control system and foreign workers in Japan

According to the statistics by the Japanese immigration control bureau in 2002, the number of foreign workers is 760,000, including 220,000 illegal workers. Its share in the total labor force is 1%. Data from the census of 2000 indicates that the share of resident foreigners in the total Japanese population is also 1.01%. The figure had been 0.6% from 1950 to 1985, and then it increased from 0.72% in 1990 up to 1.01% in 2000. Both in the labor force and in the population, the ratio of foreigners is still quite small, compared with that of the US or EU countries. That may indicate that the present immigration control system is extremely comprehensive and tight.

Table 1 Registered workers with visa status for the purpose of employment

	2000	2001	2002	2003
Total	154,748	168,783	179,63	185,556
Engineer	16,531	19,439	20,717	20,807
ratio	10.7%	11.5%	11.5%	11.2%
Specialist in humanities/ international services	34,739	40,861	44,496	44,943
Intra-company transferee	8,657	9,913	10,923	10,605
Entertainment	53,847	55,461	58,359	64,642
Others	40,974	43,109	45,144	44,559

Source: Immigration Bureau, Ministry of Justice.

The number of registered foreign workers who hold visa status with special and/or technical skills was 185,556 in 2003 (see Table 1). The number has doubled since 1995. Those who possess this special and/or technical visa are the only ones legally entitled to be employed in Japanese firms. In other words, a special and/or technical visa is equivalent to a work permit certificate. Residual categories of foreign workers are either foreigners of Japanese descent, mostly Brazilians, and foreign students. Thus, a door has opened to the Japanese labor market only for skilled labor, and that is and will continue to be the basic principal for immigration policy. Although the number of foreign workers of Japanese descent is almost 230,000, those workers are free from work limitations such as location, wage, and job content.

There are 14 visa statuses for the purpose of employment in the special and/or technical skill category. Entertainment visa holders are the largest among them, followed by specialists in the humanities/international services, mostly translators. Engineers are the third in this visa category, with 20,000 or 11.2% of the total with work permits. The maximum period of stay for those in employment is three years, except for entertainers with permits of one year only. The government extended the period of residence for those with working visas from one year to three years in 1999. This change represents one of the measures intended to deregulate the present immigration control.

Registered foreign engineers

There are 20,807 foreign engineers permitted to reside in Japan. The estimated number of engineers in electrical/electronics and computer-related fields was 950,000, according to the census of 2000. Most

Table 2   Number of foreign residents with visa "engineers" by nationality in 2003

Total	20,807	100.0%
China	11,079	53.2%
Korea	3,019	14.5%
India	2,001	9.6%
Philippines	789	3.8%
US	568	2.7%

Source: Immigration Bureau, Ministry of Justice.

foreign engineers are computer-related, as shown in Figure 1. The share of foreign engineers in the engineers' labor market in Japan is a little more than 1%, a figure greater than the percentage of the foreign workers in the total Japanese labor market, but still very small. Both the manufacturing sector and blue-collar occupations are areas where the share of foreign workers exceeds that of Japanese workers. Those foreign workers are mostly Japanese-Brazilians and Japanese-Peruvians with "special" visa status, which enables them to work on production sites. In the field of engineering, especially in the field of information technology, the day when foreign engineers play an active role is yet to come.

Table 2 shows the nationality of foreign engineers in Japan at present. More than half of the foreign engineers come from China. The second most represented nation is Korea, followed by India. Engineers from these three Asian countries occupy almost 80% of the total foreign engineers.

Influx of foreign engineers to Japan

The trend in the influx of foreign engineers to Japan resembles that of registered foreign engineers. The numbers are increasing. In 2003, the total number was 2,643, and the share of the newly entered visa holders with special and/or technical visas (visas for the purpose of employment) was only 1.7%. While the share of entertainers is as high as 40%, the percentage is less for those who possess high skills such as professors, engineers and intra-company transferees. The engineers' nationalities are again Chinese, Korean, and Indian.

Figure 1 shows the sectors for those foreign engineers. The computer-related industry, consisting of mostly software engineers (SE) and programmers, employs 58% of the foreign engineers.

Table 3   Influx of foreign workers with visa status for the purpose of employment

		China	Korea	India	US
Total	155,831				
Engineers	2,643	1,016	472	312	252
Specialists in the humanities/ international services	6,886	429	244		1,833
Intra-company transferees	3,421	715	426	203	533
Entertainers	64,642	3,848	804	–	374

Source: Immigration Bureau, Ministry of Justice.

Figure 1   Newly entered foreign engineers in the hiring sector in 2003

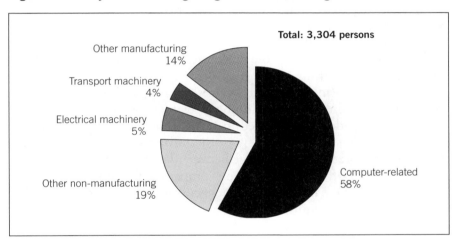

Total: 3,304 persons

Other manufacturing 14%

Transport machinery 4%

Electrical machinery 5%

Other non-manufacturing 19%

Computer-related 58%

Source: http://www.moj.go.jp/PRESS/040827-2 (in Japanese).

Based on the influx data and registration data of foreign engineers, foreigners are mostly IT workers who are in short supply in the world labor market. In the case of Japan, half of them come from the neighboring country China. However, from Chinese IT workers viewpoints, their destination is not Japan but the US. The *White Paper on International Economy and Trade, Year 2003* by the Ministry of Economy, Trade and Industry (METI) states that "Although acceptance of foreign workers with special and/or technical skills has been increasing in recent years, the number is clearly low, for example, in comparison to the number of H-1B visas issued by the US. In addition, looking at the current state where there are many H-1B visa holders from Asia, especially China,

Table 4 **Permission to change visa status from college student
to new visa status**

		China	Korea	Others
Total	3,778	2,258	721	799
Engineer	849	496	161	192
Specialists in the humanities/ international services	2,378	1,547	410	421
Others	551	215	150	186

Source: Ministry of Justice, http://www.moj.go.jp/PESS/040827(in Japanese).

reveals that many highly skilled Chinese human resources are headed to
the US instead of the geographically closer Japan." [1] Presumably, this quo-
tation describes quite well the present position of the Japanese government vis-à-vis highly skilled foreign workers.

Another source of foreign engineers is foreign students who graduated Japanese universities. Table 4 indicates the number of persons who
changed visa status from college students to either engineer or specialists
in the humanities/international services. Again, college students from
China are the main source for finding foreign engineers.

College graduates employed in firms in Japan serve as a bilingual
"bridge SE." This concept is new to the information service industry.
Their role is more to act as a bridge between Japanese firms and offshore
local affiliates or offshore outsourcing companies because of their knowledge of the Japanese language, Japanese customs, and the networks they
have in their home countries.

Skill shortage in the IT labor market and the government's promotion measures for foreign IT engineers

Shortage of IT engineers

The shortage of IT engineers is a worldwide phenomenon, due to
the spread of the internet. In Japan, the government set up an "IT strategy center" in 2000 to promote information technology. This national
strategy looks like a good business chance for IT related industries. The
restructuring of the banking business requires the skills of IT engineers

---

[1] METI (2003) p.227-228.

Table 5   Foreign IT engineers by jobs compared with total regular employees

	Foreign engineers	Total regular employees
Consultation	2.1%	4.8 %
Project management	7.4	11.1
Architect	18.1	20.1
Development/Programming	62.1	39.5
Operation/Support	2.3	10.8
Others	8.0	13.7

Source: Fuji Sogo Kenkyusho (2002), p.8.

more than ever, without mentioning the demand for IT engineers for the implementation of IT systems at the levels of small and medium-sized firms and for the development of e-commerce.

Estimations of the skill shortage vary according to the estimation bodies. The study group on information communication software, set up in the Ministry of Internal Affairs and Communication (MIC), published a report in 2003 warning that 420,000 highly skilled engineers are necessary in IT fields, and that, in particular, 120,000 network security engineers are in short supply.

The Ministry of Economy, Industry and Trade (MEIT), and the Japanese Information Service Association (JISA) conducted a joint survey titled "Urgent Survey on IT Engineers" in 2001. The survey's intention was to ascertain the needs of the information service industry, to which software producers belong. The result was interesting because the ensuing report said that there was no shortage of IT engineers and that only certain jobs, namely IT consultants, project managers, and highly specialized engineers were lacking in the labor market. The changing aspects of IT investment from hardware to systematic usage of packaged software or system integration have created a vacancy for those high quality jobs. [2] This shortage imbalance among IT engineers poses a difficult question for foreign IT engineers. The job content of those jobs in the upper stream process requires not only technical skills but also Japanese language ability and a good knowledge of business practices.

At present, foreign national IT engineers take jobs more as programmers than as managers. Table 5 shows the job distribution among foreign engineers compared with that of the total regular employees of

---

[2] Employment Security Bureau, Ministry of Health, Labor & Welfare (MHLW) (2003) *Study report on employment management of foreign workers in special and/or technical fields- IT engineers,* (in Japanese) MHLW, p.21-22

the surveyed firms. If we take into account the fact that those foreign engineers have only short terms of service in Japan, there is a possibility for them to take jobs in higher grades.

The shortage of IT engineers, with the government announcing an IT strategy as a national goal, prompted the government to take some measures for accepting more foreign engineers. The next section explains some of these efforts.

Deregulation of immigration control

Japanese immigration has no quota system and anyone who satisfies certain requirements is entitled to work in Japan. Requirements for engineers are either that they are college graduates with a natural science major, or they possess work experience as engineers for more than ten years. These requirements are quite strict given that technical school graduates cannot get work permission until a certain age.

Therefore, a system of mutual accreditation of qualification was introduced. Without an examination of one's academic background or work experience at the time of visa application, those who want to work as engineers clear landing requirements based on qualifications in their home countries. Table 6 shows those countries that already have mutual accreditation with Japan. But until August 2004, only 29 engineers, both from Korea and from China, were allowed to enter Japan under this mutual accreditation system. [3] To set up a new system is one thing, to operate it is another. The system may take years to come to fruition.

Another deregulation of immigration control was the introduction of "the certificate of eligibility for visa status" in 1990. With this certificate issued by immigration control offices in Japan, those who apply for special and/or technical visas are able to pass entry examinations quicker than under the former system. Employers are supposed to take the responsibility for the application and mail the certificate to a pre-employed person before s/he enters Japan. Usually this application process, from the first application to the last permission for a visa status, took a few months.

The government knew this application process posed a big concern for firms employing foreign immigrants. Those firms regarded the visa application system as a prohibitively complicated process, increasing the cost of hiring foreign engineers. Therefore, in 2002, the cabinet decided to shorten the examination process to within two weeks, on condition

---

[3] http://www.moj.go.jp/PRESS/040827-2 (in Japanese).

Table 6 Countries that are implementing mutual accreditation of IT qualifications with Japan

Date of conclusion	Country	Examining body	Eligible qualification	Relaxing of residence requirements
Feb.2001	India	DOEAC Society	Level A, B and C of the IT technician examination(DOEACC)	Yes
Aug.2001	Singapore	Singapore Computer Society	Certified IT Project Manager(CITPM)	Yes
Dec.2001	Korea	Human Resources Development Service of Korea	Engineer Information Processing	Yes
			Industrial Engineer Information Processing	Yes
			Information terminal operator	No
Jan.2002	China	Center for IT Education	System Analyst	Yes
			Software Engineer	Yes
			Programmer	Yes
Apr.2002	Philippines	JITSE-Philippines Foundation	Basic IT technicians	Yes
Jun.2002	Thailand	National Electronics & Computer Technology Center(NECTEC)	Network System Professional	No
			Database System Professional	No
			Fundamental IT Professional	No
Jul.2002	Vietnam	Hoa Lac Hi-tech Park Management Board, Vietnam IT Examination & Training Support Center	Basic IT technicians	Yes
Nov. 2002	Myanmar	Myanmar Computer Federation (MCF)	Software design technicians	No

that the employers' business dealings are not antisocial, are stable and continuous.

The last deregulation measure is the introduction of the APEC Business Travel Card (ABTC). This applies to business travelers, not to immigrants. Under this system, traveling card-holders can enter APEC areas without having to go through a long examination process for entry.

In short, Japan has long considered itself as a country of emigration, and the recent deregulation of immigration control is a first step toward accepting foreign human resources.

Introduction of IT Skill Standard (ITSS)

The IT skill standard represents a skill map of IT engineers. The Ministry of Economy, Industry and Trade (MEIT) actively promotes ITSS for the sake of the IT service industry. There have already been similar attempts elsewhere, namely the United States' NWCET (National Workforce Center for Emerging Technology) and the United Kingdom's SFIA (Skills Framework for the Information Age). Japan's ITSS follows those cases. Presently, the ITSS divides IT engineers' jobs into 11 categories, each with seven skill levels. The intention of the ITSS is to secure fair trade in the IT industry and to guarantee product quality, as well as to enhance the immigration of IT engineers by assessing their abilities.

The project only began a few years ago, and still is in a trial period. As with the case of any standardization, concerning products or human skills, the question remains of how to measure higher-level occupational ability.

Jobs of foreign IT engineers in Japan: Bridge SE

Jobs of foreign IT engineers

There are three main reasons for Japanese IT-related firms to recruit foreign engineers. The first one is to obtain highly-skilled engineers who are scarce in the domestic labor market. The second is to employ engineers who function as a bridge between the head office in Japan and local branch or joint-venture firms overseas. The third is to reduce employment costs.

To secure high-tech engineers is the main reason for many firms in the information service industry. The demand for this kind of engineers is increasing rapidly while the education and training of high-tech engineers takes a certain number of years. The introduction of foreign-born engineers offers a quicker response to labor shortages than training human resources from the beginning. A case in point is the introduction to the US labor market of high-tech engineers on H1-B visas. However, in the case of Japan, foreign engineers may have difficulties developing their technical abilities and rising to high-tech engineer positions due to their limited Japanese language abilities.

A few engineers or researchers are free from the language barrier because of their contributions to the cutting-edge of technology. In order to retain such engineers, a firm does not ask them to learn the Japanese language. Instead Japanese engineers work with them as bridge SE. Some conglomerate electrical firms locate R & D centers in several places in the US and Europe in order to attract brains from around the world, knowing that those brains usually do not choose Japan as a place for their career destination.

However, in general, even for high-tech engineers, as long as they work in Japan, knowledge of the Japanese language is a requisite. Usually language training is either the employers' responsibility or the responsibility of employment agencies. In some cases, foreign engineers learn Japanese by themselves at night school. Without language ability, their job placements are limited to downstream jobs, or jobs of technically lower levels. As shown in table 5, foreign IT engineers concentrate on lower grade IT jobs, mainly for short-term services without a language requirement.

Secondly, it does not require much persuading to employ foreign engineers for the purpose of labor cost reduction. It is true, some firms employ foreign engineers for this reason, but their wage level should be as high as that of equivalent Japanese engineers at the time of their entry to Japan. If Japanese firms seek a cost reduction in their products, they should use offshore outsourcing, and not introduce foreign engineers. Now Japanese firms are trying hard to develop offshore outsourcing mainly in China, India, and Korea. They need human resources who are skilled both in technology and in language. These people are called "bridge SE".

Bridge SE

Currently, foreign bridge SE play an important role in Japan. They help with the operation of offshore-outsourced companies or offshore local affiliates of Japanese companies in their home countries. A recent trend among Japanese IT firms is to outsource their business overseas. In 2000, the number of offshore local affiliates of Japanese companies in

East Asia reached 6,919, compared to 4,482 in 1995.[4] These numbers include all industries, but the IT industry is no exception from the overall upward trend. More outsourcing creates an even greater need for bridge SE.

Bridge SEs bring several advantages to the firms that employ them. They are accustomed to the customs and culture of the two countries and are themselves IT engineers. They are employed based on their own merits, not to deal with the shortage of Japanese engineers. If they are college graduates, they are among the brightest and most capable, because very few graduate from college in their home countries. Their pay is much higher in Japan than in their home countries. Both from the points of view of talent and wage incentive, bridge SEs make good human resources. Moreover, the number of college graduates with a natural science major is limited in Japan. There are good reasons for Japanese IT companies to hire foreign engineers if they learn the Japanese language and are familiar with Japanese customs, including business customs.

According to a survey titled "Report on the acceptance of foreign IT engineers" sponsored by the Ministry of Health, Labor and Welfare (MHLW), and conducted by Fuji Sogokennkyusho (Soken) in 2002, 20% of the surveyed IT firms employ foreign engineers, directly or indirectly as a form of agency engineers. The average number of foreign engineers in a firm is 4.1. 53% of those firms that organize offshore local affiliates employ foreign engineers. Therefore, larger firms employ more foreign engineers than smaller firms. Almost 70% of the firms that presently have offshore affiliated firms intend to keep hiring or have recently hired foreign engineers.[5] As long as IT firms intend to hire foreign engineers in the future, the number in Japan is sure to increase in the near future.

Problems of foreign IT engineers in the workplace

Lack of communication

The prospect of a further increase of foreign engineers in Japan is clear, yet Japanese IT firms have not accumulated know how about their employment. They saw several problems when employing foreign engineers. According to Fuji Soken's report, 63.3 % of the firms identified a lack of communication with Japanese co-workers as an obstacle to hiring

---

[4] METI(2003) p.136.

[5] Fuji Sogo Kenkyusho(2002), p.38-51.

foreign IT engineers. This percentage is up to 70% in firms that once hired foreigners but hire them no longer. Other factors, such as the process of immigration control (the long period before the certificate of eligibility is issued) or the evaluation of technical skills, are behind the lack of communication. Immigration factors, which the government works to improve, are less important than communication factors. An act of communication is rooted in culture; to fill a communication gap requires more effort than to set up a new system of immigration control.

Communication ability is something that seriously concerns Japanese firms. Another survey regarding firms that employ foreign workers shows that Japanese firms put priority on communication ability when they hire new graduates from high school or colleges. In the workplace, most tasks are performed by a group, not by an individual, which may also be true in companies in other parts of the world, but Japanese companies definitely place more importance on group responsibility and on group leaders' responsibility. Communication with co-workers is quite important. For example, workers need to perform clearly defined miscellaneous jobs along with a project. Although these tasks might be unrewarding, is it necessary that they be completed.

Table 7 Problems with hiring foreign IT engineers

| | (MA) total number: 744 firms % | | | |
| | Total | Foreign engineer as an employee | | |
		at present	in the past	none
Process of immigration control	34.8	49.7	34.0	30.5
Evaluation of technical skills	34.0	26.2	35.8	36.0
Communication with Japanese co-workers	63.3	53.7	70.8	65.0
Period of service	41.9	32.2	52.8	42.8
Adaptation to work process in Japanese firms	43.0	36.2	53.8	43.0
Allocation of work	30.5	26.8	30.2	31.9

Source: Fuji Sogo Kenkyusho (2002), p.54

For foreign engineers, language ability is one factor for the lack of communication. As is often the case with foreign language, the same words, or the same sentences can be interpreted differently depending on the context. For example, the words "I will think it over" in Japanese usually mean, "I won't accept your proposal." Even Japanese people who are not familiar with Japanese business custom may mistake the real intention. Today, at some language schools for foreign engineers, they teach not only Japanese language in general, but also give lessons in Japanese for talking with native speakers of Japanese.

Miscommunication is not only limited to language problems. Business practices are different. Specification at the time of the contract is usually too simple in IT firms in Japan, and everyday specification changes occur. If foreign engineers pursue their careers in Japan, developing an ability to read between the lines on a specification sheet is indispensable.

To communicate with people is certainly a cultural behavior. Technology in general, especially IT technology, is universal. The same software can be applied to different countries with little customization. Yet workers who are engaged in IT work are subject to the cultural influences they grew up with.

Conclusion

A deregulation of immigration control and certain other measures are gradually being implemented in Japan, but only since the last few years. Social security issues have been added to the agenda. Pension accumulation systems through social security agreements will be promoted in the near future to facilitate foreign immigration. Presently, Japan has concluded agreements only with Germany in 2000 and with the UK in 2001. These institutional changes will continue in the future.

Despite system changes, whether concerning immigration control or social security, barriers for immigrants remain high, especially cultural barriers. While IT engineers often work in English, those who work with Japanese IT firms need Japanese language ability and knowledge of Japanese customs. As long as Japanese customers ask IT firms for specific kinds of products in Japanese and for products that conform to their organization and business practices, knowledge of Japanese is necessary for upper grade engineers.

Japan is far behind in accepting foreign IT engineers; however, the number is gradually increasing and will continue to increase in future. Japanese IT firms are now in the process of trial and error. Since cultural barriers have protected Japanese engineers from global competition, there is no desire to bring down these barriers. Those Japanese engineers who are not content with this enclosure go overseas as emigrants, but they are too few in number to collect reliable data on them.

Since public opinion on foreign workers in Japan is changing in favor of their acceptance, with strong law enforcement directed toward illegal workers, one can expect that five years from now the migration of IT engineers will have increased in number and the job content and level of positions available to foreigners will have changed.

References

Employment Security Bureau, Ministry of Health, Labor & Welfare (MHLW), 2003. *Study report on employment management of foreign workers in special and/or technical fields- IT engineers,* (in Japanese) MHLW.

Fuji Sogo Kenkyusho, 2002. *Report on acceptance of foreign IT engineers,* (in Japanese) Fuji Sogo Kenkyusho.

Immigration Control Bureau, Ministry of Justice (MOJ) (ed.), 2004. *Immigration Control 2004,* (in Japanese), Ainet.

Kamibayashi, Chieko, 2002. "Acceptance of Foreign IT Engineers and Information Industry," (in Japanese), in Komai, H. (ed.) *The agenda of immigration policy under globalization,* Akashi Shote.

Kurata, Yoshiki, 2004. "On Employment of Foreign-National IT Engineers in Japan," (in Japanese) Discussion Paper No.217, Hitotsubashi University.

METI, 2003. *White Paper on International Trade 2003,* http://www.meti.go.jp/english/report/index.html.

MIC (Ministry of Internal Affairs & Communications), 2004. *Information & Communications in Japan,* (in Japanese). http://www.johotsusintokei.soumu.go.jp/whitepaper/ja/h16/pdf/index.html

OECD, 2004. *OECD Information Technology Outlook,* OECD.

Rengo Soken, 2003. *Report by Domestic Specialists on International Mobility of Human Resource,* (in Japanese), Rengo Soken.

Sato, Shinobu, 2004. "Foreign IT Engineers in Japan," (in Japanese), *Kagawa University Economic Journal,* vol.77, no.2.

Learning to compete:
China's efforts to encourage
a "reverse brain drain"

David Zweig

Introduction [1]

A unique quality of China's efforts to encourage people trained overseas to return and work in China is the fact that so many levels of government and organizations actively promote returnees. While the national government sets broad guidelines for policy, and moulds the overall socio-economic and political climate, many institutions have actively engaged in generating a return wave. Also over the past 20 years, these different levels of government and organizations have changed the way they view and recruit returnees largely due to their divergent interests. Early on, city governments learned to compete among themselves over returnees. However, the central government had to go through a serious learning process, where it recognized that the best way to improve science and technology in China was by letting people go abroad freely, and then compete for them in the international marketplace by creating a domestic environment that could attract them back. And while leaders of academic, scientific and business institutions initially may have harboured serious concerns about returnees, because their knowledge threatened those who did not go overseas, China's internationalized economic, scientific and educational system has led most institutions to value, if not overvalue, the contributions that returnees can make.

[1] Funding for this research came from the Research Grants Council of Hong Kong, and a Direct Allocation Grant from the Hong Kong University of Science and Technology. This paper is part of a larger study carried out in collaboration with Professor Stanley Rosen of USC and Professor Chen Changgui of Zhongshan University. Research assistance was provided by Dr. Chung Siu Fung, HKUST. An updated version of this paper will appear in article form in the *International Labour Review*, Vol. 145 (2006), No. 1.

China's recent success in drawing back people who studied overseas shows that individual calculations, too, have changed. For years, the return rate for those who received degrees overseas was very low. And while serious questions remain about the quality of the current crop of returnees—an issue we address in this paper—their number has risen dramatically since 1999. China is following the path of South Korea and Taiwan, where a thriving economy and liberalized polity turned a brain drain into a brain gain. Yet China's return flow has picked up despite an authoritarian regime and low per capita income.

Hence the question: why this return flow? To answer this query, the paper describes the efforts of the different levels of government and domestic institutions to create a reverse brain drain. It then assesses whether government policy is key in encouraging people to return. Most studies argue that governments have limited impact on the return tide. Preferential policies for returnees can, in fact, increase the numbers going abroad, since preferred benefits are available only to returnees. However, rewarding returnees does increase their quality if not their numbers.

Before proceeding, we should show that there has been a reverse tide in the past eight years. During the mid- to late-1990s, the average annual increase in the number of returnees was approximately 13 percent, and since 2000, the rate of increase jumped. Figure 1 shows the dramatic increase in the number of returnees. Still, returnees as a percent of people going overseas have not increased, as liberalization of the policy on going overseas on one's own money *(zi fei liu xue)* has led to a massive increase in the number of people going abroad.

Figure 1   Number of returned students, 1978-2004

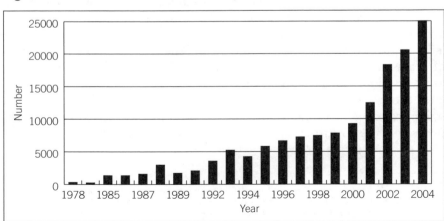

Source: *China Statistical Yearbook*, 2004, p. 781.

National level policies: Changing the environment for returnees

Central policies towards returnees have been complex and have shifted over time. Differing government sectors have espoused different views, based largely on their institutional interests. Also, domestic political evolution led to policy adjustments on overseas education. For example, following student demonstrations against the central government in late-1986 and early-1987, the party tightened regulations on overseas studies. This pressure persisted through 1987 when Deng Xiaoping criticized the large number of students going to the United States. This speech became Central Document No. 11 (1987) and triggered the State Education Commission's own Document No. 749, which proposed to cut the flow of students going to the U.S. from 68 to 20 percent of the total and pressure students in the U.S. to return. [2] In 1988, the State Education Commission (SEDC) forced lecturers in universities (many with MAs) to shift from "private" to "public" passports, making them eligible for more restrictive U.S. J-1 student visas, rather than highly flexible F-1 visas. [3]

A year later, a serious debate ensued about the whether China should continue to send students overseas. [4] During a central meeting about overseas study, then Party General Secretary Zhao Ziyang, took a long-term perspective, describing China's brain drain as "storing brain power overseas." Similarly, the State Science and Technology Commission supported sending more people abroad, despite the brain drain, arguing that only those who stayed abroad would really learn the positive quality of American scientific research and be capable of contributing to China's scientific advancement. However, the Education Commission, more conservative and concerned about "face", felt that the lack of returnees called for a tightening of the outflow. Today's "reverse brain drain" has proven the former viewpoint to be prescient.

The Tiananmen crackdown of 1989 reinforced this tendency to restrict the flow and led the state to view most overseas students as threats to the Communist Party and created an inhospitable environment for those who contemplated returning. With internal documents at that time imbued with the language of class struggle, echoing the Cultural

---

[2] Interview with a former official in the Ministry of Education, Cambridge, MA, 1989.

[3] Interview with a Wuhan education official.

[4] Lecture by Xu Lin, Fairbank Center, Harvard University, December 1989.

Revolution, it is no surprise that most surveys of overseas scholars found that very few were willing to even consider returning to China.[5]

But when students selected the "exit" option and refused to come home, some Chinese leaders listened. Deng Xiaoping called on overseas students to return to help the motherland. "We hope that all people who have gone overseas to study will come back. It doesn't matter what their previous political attitude was, they can all come back, and after they return things will be well arranged. This policy cannot be changed."[6] Deng also said that "if people want to make a contribution, it is better to return". Deng reportedly tried to improve the climate for returnees in 1991, but strong opposition prevented him from instituting a new policy.[7]

In March 2002, the Ministry of Personnel responded to Deng's initiative and announced a strategy to entice returnees under the slogan of "improving services for returned students". The policy included:

1. job introduction centres for returned students in Shenzhen, Shanghai, and Fujian (although five cities had already established their own centres);

2. preferential policies, including: (a) giving returnees more living space and more higher professional titles; (b) letting family members move to new cities where returnees found jobs; (c) permitting students who had signed two- or three-year contracts with their research centres to either remain or switch jobs once their agreements expired;

3. establishing a national association of returned students;

4. increasing support for scientific research.[8]

In August 1992, Li Tieying, chair of the State Education Commission, publicly raised a new 12-character slogan that defined the changed perspective on returnees. The slogan, "support overseas study, encourage people to return, and give people the freedom to come and go" *(zhichi liuxue, guli hui guo, lai qu ziyou)*, became official policy at the Fourth

[5] Xiaoping Zhang, *Residential Preferences: A Brain Drain Study on Chinese Students in the United States* (Ph.D. dissertation, Graduate School of Education, Harvard University, 1992).

[6] Jiao Guozheng, "*Pengbo fazhan de chuguo liuxue gongzuo*" (Flourishing development of the work of sending out overseas students), Zhongguo gaodeng jiaoyu (Higher education in China, Beijing) 12 (1998): 6-8, in *Higher Education in China*, Research Materials from People's University, 2 (1999): 72-74.

[7] Paul Englesberg, "Reversing China's Brain Drain: The Study Abroad Policy, 1978-1993", in *Great Policies: Strategic Innovations in Asia and the Pacific Basin*, eds. John D. Montgomery and Dennis A. Rondinelli (Westport, CT.: Praeger, 1995), p. 117.

[8] "China to Improve Service for Returned Students," *Xinhua General News Service*, 13 March 1992, on Nexis. Later reports indicated that "Returning Students Find Jobs at Home", *China Daily*, 22 May 1993.

Plenum of the 14th Party Congress in November 1993.[9] This policy, as well as a series of related innovations, demonstrated a new spirit of flexibility towards returnees. In fact, in a form of self-criticism, a conference on the "Work of Sending Personnel to Study Abroad," convened in April 1993, admitted that policies since 1989 had been "too political."[10]

Allowing returnees to work in units and cities other than the one from which they had left created a new talent market, which enervated inter-city competition for returnees, as cities could now attract overseas scholars who had not previously worked in their city. This policy change allowed Chinese who had left from cities or units, which they did not like, to move to any city or unit that would employ them.

In 1996, the Foreign Affairs Bureau of the Ministry of Education (MOE) began to encourage people who remained overseas to return to China for short visits and "serve the country" *(wei guo fuwu)* from abroad. Under the *"chunhui jihua"*, or "spring light program," the government funded short trips for lecturing or research collaboration. Some scholars may have taken such trips to see if conditions in China warranted returning. President Jiang Zemin reinforced this perspective in 1997, when at the 15th Party Congress of the Chinese Communist Party, he called for people to return and serve the country from overseas.

In 1998, the central government increased investment in higher education and encouraged universities to use those funds to attract overseas talent. In May that year, Jiang Zemin's speech on the occasion of the 100th anniversary of Peking University *(Beida)*, called for China to establish world-class universities, and called on Beida to lead the way. Under the "985 Plan," named after the date of his talk, the government invested billions of RMB in nine universities to make them world-class universities and poured an enormous amount of funds into Qinghua and Beijing Universities.

Other national policies indirectly improved the domestic environment for returning to China. A key reform occurred when the 1999 National People's Congress declared the private sector part of the national economy, and not a mere supplement to the state-led sector. At that time, few mainlanders living overseas had any interest in working in state-owned industries, preferring instead employment in foreign invested

---

[9] See "The decision on several questions on establishing a socialist market economy" *(Guanyu jianli shihuizhuyi shichang jingji tizhi rugan wenti de jueding)*. Interview with an official in the Ministry of Education, 2004.

[10] "SEC Holds Work Conference, Decides to Relax Policies for Overseas Study", *Xinwen ziyou daobao* [Press freedom guardian] 16 April 1993, p. 1.

firms or setting up their own firms. Now those who wanted to return to China and establish a company could feel relatively confident that the state would not shut them down. [11]

Entry to the World Trade Organization enhanced domestic demand for returnees. Possessing the very qualities that China needs to compete in the global economy, such as Western business knowledge and knowledge of international law, overseas students became a valuable commodity in the domestic economy. WTO accession brought many multinational corporations to China, which needed mainlanders with Western experience and training; not surprisingly, many mainlanders were keen to return to China on expatriate terms.

A significant change in the worldview of China's leaders created more flexible policies. [12] In particular, Jiang Zemin recognized that there is a global market for talent and that China must compete within that market, even for its own people. According to Jiang, "Competition in scientific research is competition for talents." [13] Under globalization, China can no longer lock up its own people; if its intellectuals and business people are to learn from the world, China must let them go out into the world. But they then become international commodities over which China must compete with other countries. Thus under globalization, reforms become even more critical. Premier Zhu Rongji concurred when, at the end of 2001, at the 6th Session of the Worldwide Chinese Businessmen's Association, he remarked that henceforth China would stress the infusion of human talent and technical skills, rather attracting foreign capital. This was an important response to the policy of "building national strength through science and education" *(ke jiao xing guo)* and an important step towards the current policy of "strengthening the country through human talent" *(rencai qiang guo)*.

In October 2002, the central government adopted its most flexible position when it recognized that since most people will not return, nonreturnees must participate in China's development. This turned a failure in overseas education policy—the "brain drain"—into a positive attribute, as those who remain overseas could still serve the goal of national self-strengthening. In a document coauthored by numerous ministries, people overseas were encouraged to participate in projects in China in a

---

[11] David Sheff, *China dawn: the story of a technology and business revolution* (New York: Harper Business, 2002).

[12] Thomas Moore, "China and Globalization," in Sam Kim, ed., East Asia and Globalization (Lanhamn, MD: Rowan and Littlefield, 2000).

[13] Comments by Jiang were made during an interview with editors from Science Magazine. See "Many Chinese students don't go back home," *Singapore Straits Times,* 19 June 2000.

Figure 2   Structure of organizations in the Ministry of Education that facilitate returnees

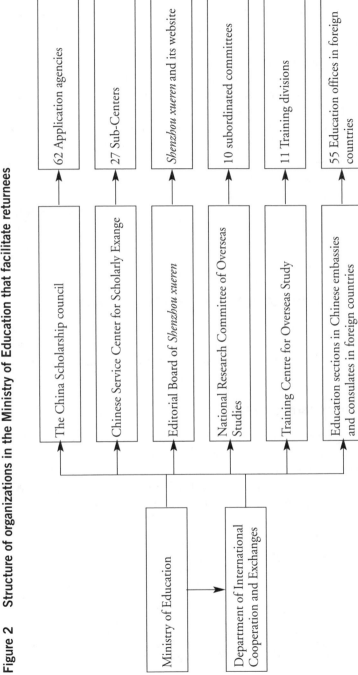

variety of ways. [14] In adopting this perspective, China joins many developing countries, which have turned to the "diaspora model" through which they encourage their citizens who have settled abroad to help their motherland. [15]

In 2003, President Secretary Hu Jintao and Vice President, Zeng Qinghong, gave a series of speeches, known as the "three talks" *(san pian jiang hua)*, which have reconfirmed the support of the central leadership for overseas study. These speeches confirmed that the role of returnees is "irreplaceable" *(buke daitide)* and of "outstanding historic role" *(dute de lishi zuoyong)*. While returnees need to see concrete benefits—salaries and working conditions—if they are to be enticed back, an improved climate, created by a central government that now values human talent, is critical to their individual decisions to return.

Today, the Ministry of Education has a plethora of organizations, which are engaged in encouraging more returnees or in assisting those who have returned to settle down in China more comfortably. Figure 2 shows the list of organizations.

Central policies to encourage more returnees

The list of specific programs or policies introduced by the Ministry of Education, the Chinese Academy of Sciences, and other related ministries, is too long to present here. Instead, I will create a taxonomy of policy directions and discuss the more important policies in some detail.

Mobilizing official forces overseas

To encourage returnees, the state mobilized officials in embassies and consulates to organize overseas scholars into various organizations. In the 38 countries where overseas students are most concentrated, the government established 52 educational bureaus in embassies and consulates, which helped form over 2000 Overseas Students Associations and

---

[14] The ministries included the Ministry of Personnel, Education, Science and Technology, Public Security and Finance. See "A Number of Opinions on Encouraging Overseas Students to Provide China with Many Different Forms of Service," Renshibu, jiaoyubu, kejibu, gonganbu, caizhengbu guanyu yinfa "Guanyu guli haiwai liuxue renyuan yi duozhong xingshi wei guo fuwu di rogan yijian" de tongzhi," 14 May 2001 (Renfa, No. 49, 2001), in *Chinese Education and Society*, vol. 36, no. 2 (March/April 2003): 6-11.

[15] See Jean-Baptiste Meyer, et. al., "Turning Brain Drain into Brain Gain: The Colombian Experience of the Diaspora Option," *Science, Technology and Society* 2 : 2 (1997): 285, and David Zweig and Chung Siu Fung, "Redefining China's Brain Drain: 'Wei Guo Fuwu' and the 'Diaspora Option'," Paper prepared for the *40th Anniversary Reunion Conference: The State of Contemporary China*, The Universities Service Centre for China Studies, The Chinese University of Hong Kong, Hong Kong, January 5-7, 2004.

over 300 professional associations for overseas scholars. [16] Science officers organize overseas scholars to attend the Science and Technology Convention for Overseas Scholars held annually in Guangzhou in December.

Service Centers for Overseas Study under the MOE, which have been set up in most cities, send out recruitment delegations, part of the state's efforts to strengthen the reverse flow. Articles in Chinese community newspapers announce the impending arrival of such delegations, describing extremely high salaries that companies in the delegation are offering to returnees. However, the salaries or housing benefits often do not materialize when the scholar returns to China—particularly if they are moving to a university or research lab. Also, while the delegations collect many resumes, they rarely send acknowledge letters, leading many overseas scholars to see such trips as junkets for local officials. In some cases, even after overseas scholars visit China for job interviews, no job ever materializes, generating a great deal of cynicism about such overseas delegations. [17]

In 2002, the Office for Work on Overseas Study and Returnees (*Liuxue huiguo gongzuo bangongshe*) was established, unifying resources expended on, and efforts to attract, returnees. It then immediately began encouraging exceptional overseas scholars to return and serve the country. [18]

Financial policies

Numerous state programs give overseas students and scholars financial support if they return. In 1987, the former Education Commission established the "Financial Support for Outstanding Young Professors Program" (youxiu qingnian jiaoshi zizhu jihua), which by the end of 2003 had awarded 2,218 returning professors with a total of 144 million RMB. Other programs, and the year of initiation, include the "Seed Fund for Returned Overseas Scholars" (1990), "Cross Century Outstanding Personnel Training Program" (1991), the "National Science Fund for Distinguished Young Scholars" (1994), [19] and "The One Hundred, One Thousand, and Ten Thousands Program" (1995). [20] Also, as discussed

---

[16] Interview in Beijing with MOE official, 2004.

[17] "*Wo wei shenme xuanzi liu zai meiguo—yu guo nei zhaoping daibiaotuan jiechu de qian qian hou hou*"(Why did I choose to stay in America—before and after meeting with a recruitment team from the mainland). Source: Online: Wenxue cheng, huiguo fazhan, 12 August 2002.

[18] Shenzhou xueren, "*Chuguo liuxue gongzuo da shiji, 1978-2003*", (Major events in overseas study work), at www.chisa.edu.cn/newschisa/web/0/2003-06-20/news_2276.asp.

[19] Under this program, funding given to people overseas must be used within China.

[20] For a detailed discussion of these projects see Cong Cao, "China's Efforts at Turning 'Brain Drain' into 'Brain Gain,' *East Asian Institute Background Brief*, No. 216, November 2004.

above, the state increased funding for universities and the Chinese Academy of Sciences.

Improving the flow of information

To encourage people to return, the government improved information flows on conditions in China and between units in China and scholars overseas. In 1987, the Education Commission established *"Shenzhou xueren"* magazine and its electronic board, an important bridge between overseas scholars and domestic organizations. Over the past few years, the MOE has expanded the yearly Overseas Chinese Scholars meeting in Guangzhou, which introduces domestic governments and companies to overseas scientists who present recent projects. The 7th annual meeting was held in December 2004.

The Ministry of Education (MOE) established several research organizations to direct policy. In October 1991, it established the All-China Research Association on Overseas Study *(Quan guo chuguo liuxue gongzuo yanjiu hui)*, with Beijing and Qinghua universities as the leading bodies of the association. It holds annual meetings to analyze trends and suggest guidelines for work on overseas study and publishes a research magazine and yearly reports.

Easing the process of returning

Government policies now make returning less painful. In 1989, the Education Commission established 33 Overseas Study Service Centres *(Zhongguo liuxue fuwu zhongxin)* in 27 provinces and cities, to help returnees find jobs. The Investment Affairs Department at these centres helps overseas mainlanders invest in China or bring back technology. The state encourages cities to create schools for the children of returnees, whose weak Chinese language skills leaves them unable to compete with classmates whose parents had never gone overseas.

The Ministry of Personnel and the MOE established "post-doctoral stations," as holding stations for overseas Ph.D.s who could not find jobs in China. As of 2002, there were 970 mobile post-doc stations *(boshi hou liudong zhan)* and 400 post-doc enterprise workstations *(qiye boshi hou gongzuo zhan)*, employing over 7,000 post-docs. In 2002, the Minister of Personnel announced plans to double the number of stations and increase the number of post-docs to between 12,000 and 15,000.[21]

---

[21] *Zhongguo jiaoyu bao* [China Education News], 10 July 2002, p. 1, at www.jyb.com.cn.

The state simplified residency requirements and entry visas for overseas scholars who had taken foreign citizenship. The Foreign Ministry first gave these returnees longer-term visas. Shanghai was the first locality to experiment with permanent residence status for overseas scholars, which has since become national policy. Yet these people are ineligible for most preferential policies unless they renounce their citizenship. One returnee in Beijing was furious about this, because as a foreign passport holder, he could not apply for the "Hundred Talents Programme." Yet when people question his patriotism, because he insists on keeping his Canadian citizenship, he reminds them that he chose to return despite a comfortable life in Vancouver. [22]

Bringing people back for short term visits to "serve the country"

The government now encourages people to return for short periods of time to engage in cooperative projects or give lectures. Through these visits, overseas scholars get a taste of how China has changed. The state hopes that such visits will encourage people to return permanently, but even if they only bring back new information or technology, or transfer information to other overseas scholars or graduate students about conditions in China, the state benefits.

The government began to encourage overseas scholars to return for visits in 1992, and between 1992 and 1995, the MOE helped over 1200 people "serve the country" in some form. [23] In 1997, after a visit by mainland students in Germany, the "spring light project" *(chun hui jihua)* was established, offering funds for short-term visits. [24] Apparently, the program pays only for one-way tickets, under the assumption that scholars with overseas positions can use their own research grants to pay for the return airfare. [25] The first year, 600 scholars came on the program, and in 1998 funding was increased. In November 2000, a new program encouraged people to return during summer vacation and paid them as much as five times their overseas salaries. Between 1996 and May 2003, the MOE brought over 7,000 individuals and 50 groups of mainlanders back

---

[22] Interview in Beijing, November 2004. Also, because he held foreign citizenship, he was not allowed to rejoin the Communist Party.

[23] Editorial Board, "Kuokuan bao guo zhi lu," *Shenzhou xueren dianziban* (China Scholars Abroad Electronic Board), http://www.chisa.edu.cn/service/chunhui13.htm.

[24] See Zi Hui, "The Ministry of Education Set up a Project Under the "Light of Spring" Program for Overseas Student Talent to Come Back and Work in China During their Sabbatical Leaves," *Chinese Education and Society*, vol. 36, no. 2 (March/April 2003): 40-43.

[25] Interview with Chinese consular official, Toronto, 2003.

to "serve the country," [26] and in 2002 alone, the MOE awarded 14 projects under this program to seven universities for a total of 670,000 RMB. [27] The "spring light program" is the forerunner of the concept of "serving the nation" from abroad *(wei guo fuwu)*, rather than insisting that people "return to the country" *(hui guo fuwu)*, another indicator of China's learning process.

Local governments compete for global talent

Pressures on officials to enhance local economic development and a close link between the territorial government and local enterprises under its administration make local state leaders aggressive recruiters of overseas talent. Even in the wake of the Tiananmen crackdown, as central leaders engaged in a leftist binge, searching for class enemies at home and abroad, urban leaders looked for business opportunities to renew their stalled economies. Thus, inter-city competition emerged in the early 1990s and has continued unabated. Preferential policies, such as subsidized home purchasing, tax breaks on imported automobiles and computers, schooling for children of returnees, finding jobs for spouses, long-term residence permits, etc., are instituted by local governments in order to enhance their level of technical development. Personnel departments in these cities actively pursue overseas scholars, as do education and science and technology officials. In some cases, too many organizations engage in this arena, causing difficulties for returnees who do not know which way to turn. [28] Cities send delegations overseas to seek talent; sometimes education officials in Chinese consulates only learn of these visits when they are reported in the local Chinese language newspaper. [29]

Shenzhen instituted its own local policies only weeks after the Tiananmen crackdown. According to its August 1989 regulations, returnees could come directly to the Special Economic Zone (SEZ), legally change their residence and that of their families, keep any foreign exchange they earned in Shenzhen, even if they left the SEZ, buy a new

---

[26] "Chugu liuxue gongzuo jianjie" (A brief discussion of the work of sending people overseas), *Shenzhou xueren*, at http://www.chisa.edu.cn/newchisa/web/3/2003-05-23/news_46.asp. As of 2001, the reported number was 3000, suggesting that 4,000 had come in two and a half years. See http://www.why.com.cn/abroad_3/weiguofuwu/10_1/2.htm.

[27] This is the website of Zhejiang University. See http://www-2.zju.edu.cn/zxw.

[28] Interview in Shanghai with Ministry of Personnel, April 2002.

[29] One overseas scholar said that he would never attend a recruitment talk by officials from small cities or counties as they cannot pay large salaries and their delegations are just junkets for local officials who use the idea of attracting overseas talent to spend public money on overseas travel.

house at near cost, establish private businesses, and "enjoy precedence over ordinary people with similar conditions and qualifications in the use of scientific and technological development funds." [30]

Weihai, on the coast of Shandong province, near South Korea, also used preferential policies to promote its interests. A 1992 document, in response to a central government policy, offered returnees a bonus of 500 RMB/month, which was separate from the bonuses that individual units were encouraged to grant. Returnees were eligible for a 20% housing discount, exclusions from import taxes, including taxes on autos; schooling was to be arranged for their children and a job for their spouse. Foreign income generated while working in Weihai could be sent overseas. Also, if the technology they brought back to China generated major economic or social benefits, their home unit was encouraged to give the returnee a large bonus. [31]

Shanghai is the most successful city in recruiting returnees. To strengthen links with overseas scholars, the city's Office of Overseas Chinese Affairs *(Qiao ban)* sought relations with overseas alumni associations from Shanghai universities by offering to strengthen them. They used the networks of existing overseas scholar organizations to collect information about new organizations. In response to efforts to shrink the government's role, the Shanghai Education Bureau transferred the responsibility for helping returnees find jobs from the government to the marketplace by establishing a "human talent market" *(rencai shichang)*. They also were among the first cities to establish long-term residence visas for returnees with foreign passports.

Cities establish incubators in their development zones for returnees, called "parks for overseas scholars to establish businesses" *(liuxue huiguo renyuan chuangye yuan)*. These incubators are comfortable entry points for overseas scholars with few links in China, as officials there steer people through the maze of paperwork that otherwise might deter them from returning. Shanghai's municipal government built four Centres for Returned Scholars in the city's four development zones and by 1994, had attracted over 100 returned Ph.D.s to the Zhangjiang High Tech Zone. [32] By 1998, there were 14 such zones for overseas scholars, spread out

---

[30] Shenzhen announces detailed regulations on students returning to work in the country, *Zhongguo xinwen* she, 15 August 1989, in FBIS-CHI-89-157 (16 August 1989): 47-48.

[31] See *"Weihai shi xiyin liuxue renyuan youhui zhengce"*, October 1992 (Weihai city government's preferential policies for attracting overseas scholars), in *Liuxue huiguo gongzuo wenjian huibian* (A Collection of Articles on Work Relating to Overseas Studies and Returnees; Beijing: Ministry of Education, 2003), p. 40.

[32] "News Briefs," *China Exchange News*, 22 (Spring 1994): 14.

around the entire city. Today, Beijing, too, has 14 such zones, competing with Shanghai in this respect.

On the negative side, local governments, or the companies that are the legal owners of the incubator, are often major investors in start-up companies, which can be a problem for returnees seeking separation from the state. [33] Moreover, newly arrived returnees, more than local entrepreneurs, dislike having to work with the government. Still, more than local entrepreneurs, returnees are forced to turn to local governments for assistance as they start up their company. [34]

Institutional efforts to attract overseas talent

Universities and government-funded research units, particularly the Chinese Academy of Sciences (CAS), actively recruit returnees to their organizations. In 1978, the Ministry of Education (MOE) and CAS chose all the people who went overseas. Only after the central government decentralized control over educational exchanges in 1985 did individual universities become key players in sending people abroad. Moreover, after people graduated overseas, they had been expected to return to their home unit, so until the central government liberalized its policy, allowing returnees to switch jobs, these two organizations monopolized returnees as well.

The central government uses various programs to encourage key academic and scientific institutions to recruit overseas talent. For universities, the most important program is the Cheung Kong Scholars Programme *(Changjiang xuezhi jiangli jihua)*, funded by Hong Kong tycoon Li Ka-hsing. Between 1998 and 2004, it brought 537 scholars from overseas to become leaders in key research fields. When the central government dramatically increased its financial contributions to nine top universities, it insisted that 20 percent of those funds be allocated to improve the quality of the faculty—through importing talent from overseas.

As a result, many universities have programs to recruit overseas scholars. Shanghai Jiaotong University, one of the country's pre-eminent universities, and a beneficiary of the MOE's added donations to the top nine schools, established a new hiring system, which stressed the importance of overseas education; it also established a promotion system which

---

[33] Hu Yuanyuan, "The Perplexities of Returnees—A Report from Chengdu" in *Chinese Education and Society* (May/June 2003).

[34] See Wilfried Vanhanocker, David Zweig and Chung Siu Fung, "Transnational or Social Capital? Returned Scholars as Private Entrepreneurs," in Yanjie Bian and Anne Tsui, eds., (forthcoming).

includes overseas experience as a key criterion of promotion.[35] Similarly, Shanghai University made spending time overseas a criterion for hiring and promotion.[36]

In December 1998, the MOE and 63 Chinese universities advertised in overseas editions of *Renmin ribao* (People's Daily) and *Guangming ribao* (Guangming Daily) for 148 academics, known as "100,000-yuan professors." Universities were to give these scholars first-rate research benefits to attract overseas talent and show returnees how welcoming China could be. Press reports noted that these 148 professors would "receive the highest salaries ever given since new China was founded."[37]

This emphasis on global experience was at the heart of the Beida debate on educational reform, led in part by Beida's returnee party secretary, Min Weifeng, a Stanford Ph.D. To meet Jiang Zemin's call to turn Beida into a world-class university, he sought more and more returnees. By emphasizing the contacts that returnees can build overseas and the importance of working overseas, publishing in overseas journals, and teaching in a foreign language, Beida tried to force people educated locally to go abroad for some time.[38] But Beida's idea to fire faculty who did not gain foreign experience generated such a strong backlash that the overall reform plan at Beida has been cancelled.[39]

The Chinese Academy of Sciences aggressively pursues returnees through its "Hundred Talents Programme" *(Bairen jihua)*, and competition among CAS institutes is quite keen.[40] To get these fellowships, each institute writes a report to the Hundred Talents Program Office and the committee responsible for their speciality in CAS, outlining their overall development goals and how the fellowships will strengthen that plan. CAS then allocates a fixed number of fellowships to each institute. The institutes, then, advertise these positions in journals, such as *Science or Nature*. Candidates for the fellowship, if they are overseas, must return to China and present their research accomplishments or plans to a hiring committee at the institute, which decides whether to recommend the

---

[35] *China Educational Daily,* 4 April 2004, at http://www.jyb.com.cn/gb/2004/04/04/zy/jryw/5.htm.

[36] Interview with a Vice-President of Shanghai University, November 2004.

[37] Yang Gu, "Ph.D.s who have studied abroad vie for jobs," *Beijing qingnianbao* [Beijing Youth Daily], Janaury 10, 1999, pp. 1, 3.

[38] See Topic Group for the 'Study Concerning Beijing University Returnees Assuming Leadership Posts,' "Beijing daxue liuxue guiguo renyuan danren lingdao zhiwu wenti yanjiu" "Study on Beijing University Returnees Assuming Leadership Posts," *Chuguo liuxue gongzuo yanjiu* [Research on Overseas Studies Work] No. 3, 2002, pp. 7-22, at p. 8. in *Chinese Education.*

[39] Stanley Rosen, ed., *Chinese Education.*

[40] Interview with an official responsible for personnel at CAS, December 2004.

scholar to CAS for approval. Apparently, CAS rarely denies any request, giving each CAS institute a great deal of leeway and authority.

Winners of the grants receive two million RMB, with which they usually start a laboratory, including buying equipment and hiring technical personnel; 20 percent of the funds can go to supplement their salary. Fellowship holders become Ph.D. advisors, giving them MA and Ph.D. students who can work in their lab. Awardees receive housing subsidies; a CAS institute in Changchun built 20 enormous apartments—the size of apartments allocated to central government ministers—for the recipients of this award as a further inducement to return to China. Recipients are very competitive for other fellowships as well, as the awarding of the Hundred Talents fellowship identifies them as high quality researchers.

Recently, state-owned enterprises (SOEs) have begun aggressively recruiting returnees, particularly in firms looking overseas for markets and resources. In December 2004, the State Assets Supervision and Administration Commission (SASAC), in cooperation with the Communist Youth League, held a job fair where 48 high-level SOEs, some of whom are now Fortune 500 companies, recruited people for 228 jobs and 57 projects.[41] Returnees with foreign language skills and overseas work experience are in demand within this sector. Moreover, their salaries are becoming more competitive. Over 500 returnees attended this fair.

Do government efforts affect individual calculations?

Have state policies triggered the "reverse brain drain?" Or has the increase in returnees been largely the result of China's growing market, shrinking opportunities in the West, and increased opportunities for talented people in China? This question can be answered only by looking at what brings people back to China.

But first we assess whether returnees are superior to people who never went overseas. Did they earn "transnational capital"—skills, technology, information, networks or capital derived from time overseas— and thereby increase their value relative to the locals? Or are they simply beneficiaries of a misguided policy that expends a great amount of resources to attract mediocre talent? Second, are returnees of high quality relative to people who remain overseas? In other words, is China attracting mostly second-rate talent, while the best stay abroad? If true, then gain funding may be better spent elsewhere.

---

[41] "SOE job fair lures talent," *China Daily*, 22 December 2004, p. 9.

Evaluating the quality of returnees

Returnees seem to be of higher quality than people who have not gone abroad. Various surveys show that that, in universities, research labs, and science parks, returnees possess skills, information and research methodologies generally unavailable to people who have not gone abroad. They have stronger global networks. They receive more grants and fellowships. They publish more articles in international journals. [42] Yet, many of these returnees got overseas because they were more talented than people who stayed behind. So, a selection biases affects these findings.

Returnees in the private sector often bring back high-level technology unavailable in China, promoting China's technological development and allowing them to earn large profits in the domestic economy. A 2002 survey among 154 returnees and locals in high tech zones in six cities in China found that 48 percent of returnees had imported a foreign technology as compared to 21 percent of locals. [43] A survey in summer 2004 supported those findings: when we compared 100 returnee entrepreneurs and 100 local entrepreneurs from Shanghai, Beijing and Guangzhou, returnees were four times as likely as locals to possess the "latest international technology" (34% vs. 9%), and almost 50% as likely (46% vs. 30%) to have technology that, "while not the newest internationally, is new for China." [44] Moreover, the opportunity to benefit from that technology in China brings many people back. [45] When asked why they returned to China, 27% of returnee entrepreneurs selected— *"I have a technology that I believe will have a good prospect in China"*—as their primary reason for returning. Another 28 percent chose it as their second reason.

As to the quality of returnees relative to those who stay abroad, the dominant view is that the truly talented people stay abroad, even though some very talented people have returned. The director of a research institute under the Chinese Academy of Sciences placed most returnees in the top 50%-80% of overseas scholars, arguing that the top 20% remain overseas. As of 2003, the High Energy Physics Laboratory under

---

[42] Data supporting this view is in *inter alia* David Zweig, *Internationalizing China: Domestic Interests and Global Linkages* (Ithaca, NY: Cornell University Press, 2002), p. 190; David Zweig, Chen Changgui and Stanley Rosen, "Globalization and Transnational Human Capital: Overseas and Returnee Scholars to China," *The China Quarterly*, no. 179 (Sept. 2004): 750-1; and Stan Rosen and David Zweig, "Transnational Capital: Valuing Academics in a Globalizing China," in Cheng Li, ed. *Bridging Minds Across the Pacific: U.S.-China Educational Exchanges*, 1978-2003 (Lanham, Md.: Lexington Books, 2005).

[43] Zweig, Chen and Rosen, "Globalization and Transnational Human Capital."

[44] Wilfried Vanhonaker, David Zweig and Chung Siu Fung, "Transnational or Social Capital? Returned Scholars as Private Entrepreneurs," in Yanjie Bian and Anne Tsui, eds., forthcoming.

[45] Vanhonaker, Zweig and Chung, "Transnational or Social Capital?" op.cit.

CAS had failed to attract back anyone with a Ph.D. They had either stayed abroad or gone into business in China. This position is supported by Dr. Rao Yi, a professor at Washington University in St. Louis and an advisor to CAS, who argued that in terms of international reputation and prestige, few academic returnees are comparable to those who stay abroad.[46] He estimates that perhaps 800-1,000 life scientists of Chinese origin run independent labs in the U.S. Also, getting people to return is one thing; getting them to stay is another. A returnee to a CAS institute, with stellar publications, had received a "Hundred Talent's" fellowship, excellent housing and a fellowship for his wife. However, he was uncertain if they would stay in China. Finally, there are reports that the quality of people accepted by CAS under the Hundred Talents Program *(bairen jihua)* is decreasing.

Returnees to CAS interviewed in 2002 had not been particularly successful overseas. Table 1 lists some of our findings.

Table 1   Evaluating the quality of returnees

• Only 2/82 scientists interviewed in Changsha, Guangzhou, Wuhan and Kunming, earned over US$50,000/year on the eve of returning; another three earned US$35,000-$49,999.
• Very few had patents, despite the fact that 17 of them had earned Ph.D.s overseas.
• Among 109 academics interviewed in 2002, only eight had left behind salaries of over US$25,000/year, while 77% of them earned under US$12,500/year.

So, very few of them were leaving stable academic positions to return to China. In fact, unlike most academics who went abroad from China,[47] our academic returnees had not been looking for opportunities overseas; 91% of them reported that they had always intended to come home after fulfilling their program. Therefore, one might assume that these were not the most talented or entrepreneurial people.

Our academic returnees did have valuable skills. And while 19% of them reported that the research area that they had developed overseas was in great demand in China, 9% of locals expressed the same view; but the finding for this question was not statistically significant, suggesting that

---

[46] Cited in Cong Cao, "The Brain Drain Problem in China," *East Asian Institute Background Brief,* No. 215, November 2004, p. 11.

[47] Among 272 people who we interviewed in the U.S. in 1993, only 28% reported that when they left China they had "definitely planned to return after their studies." See Zweig and Chen, *China's Brain Drain,* 1995, p. 130.

our returnees are not more likely than people who have not gone over-seas to possess skills that are in great demand. They are also not more likely to import technology, nor to have that much better publication records. While 28% of our returnees had published articles in overseas journals, so had 22% of locals.

Still, local academics admit that returnees demonstrate more posi-tive work results than themselves. When asked to compare their own accomplishments *(gongzuo de chengguo)* with those of returnees, 2 per-cent of locals believed that returnees produced much more *(duo de duo)*, while 51% believed that they produced "somewhat more" *(duo yixie)*. Given that the local academics interviewed in these schools strongly believed that returnees got much more research funding and much better housing than the locals, we must assume that the returnees really were producing more.

The role of government policy in creating the reverse tide

Did government policy attract talented people to return? Our 1993 survey shows the issues that stopped people from returning (table 2). Political instability had been important, reflecting decades of political campaigns and the army's assault on Tiananmen Square on June 4th 1989. A political variable we created, which combined the effects of the Tiananmen crackdown on their decision to return, as well as their trust in the government's assertion that it would let people "come and go freely" *(lai qu ziyou)* which became official policy in 1993, was a statisti-cally significant explanation of people's attitude about returning in our 1993 survey. At that time, people also complained about the lack of qual-ity equipment and difficult work conditions, as well as the inability to develop their own career. However, our conclusion to that study sug-gested that if China could remain politically stable and develop its econ-omy, 20 percent of overseas scholars might return to China if conditions warranted it. [48] As we wrote in 1995, "As economic and social conditions liberalize and improve, if China's government becomes more proactive in recruiting, and if the post-Deng era proves to be relatively stable, Chinese students and scholars will return to their homeland in larger numbers than today." [49]

---

[48] See David Zweig and Chen Changgui, *China's Brain Drain to the United States: Views of Overseas Chinese Students and Scholars in the 1990s*, (Berkeley: Institute for East Asian Studies, China Research Mono-graph Series, 1995).

[49] Zweig and Chen, p. 86.

Table 2 Why a person might not return to China, 1993

Choices	Rank (1st choice)	Frequency	%	Rank (2nd choice)	Rank (3rd choice)	Combined Rank*
1) Lack of political stability	1	76	27.8	5	7	1
2) Lack of political freedom	2	31	11.4	2	6	2
3) Fear of being arrested	11	3	1.1	15	11	15
4) No chance to change jobs	6	15	5.5	6	4	6
5) No opportunity for career advancement in China	3	29	10.6	3	2	3
6) Poor work environment	4	21	7.7	1	3	4
7) Lack of modern equipment	7	14	5.1	9	3	7
8) Low living standard	5	19	7	4	8	5
9) Family does not want to return	12	2	0.7	12	12	14
10) Difficulty getting out the time	9	8	2.9	10	5	10
11) Returnees seen as failures	10	6	2.2	13	10	13
12) Fear not being able to get out a second time	9	8	2.9	7	10	9
13) Better future for children overseas	8	9	3.3	8	9	8
14) Difficulty competing with children in China	13	1	0.4	14	10	16
15) Few suitable jobs given education and training	11	3	1.1	12	6	12
16) Few exchanges with international scholars	10	6	2.2	11	2	11
Total	n/a	251**	91.9**	n/a	n/a	n/a

NOTE: * Score based on the sum of 1st, 2nd, and 3rd choices (1st choice= 5, 2nd choice=3, 3rd choice=1).

** 22 (8.1%) no response

Source: Zweig and Chen, *China's Brain Drain to the U.S.*, 1995.

Clearly, many problems have been addressed, if not quite resolved. China's political scene has remained relatively stable, as witnessed by the passing of the political torch from Deng Xiaoping to Jiang Zemin, and then to Hu Jintao. Most returnees see China as an excellent place to develop their talent. The growth of the private sector and the expansion of China's market has attracted large numbers of returnees. Interpersonal relations within work units remain a major problem; but this problem is as much cultural as it is institutional, and so remains somewhat beyond the governments reach. But more private sector firms will weaken this negative aspect of working in China. Low salaries and difficulties maintaining contact overseas also confront returnees. But people who return with a large fellowship, such as those granted under the Cheung Kong Scholars or the Hundred Talents Programme, do not face these problems. Therefore, these fellowships may have increased the quality of returnees, as the theory would predict.

In terms of creating a favourable atmosphere through various reforms, our findings show some government success. When asked why they returned, only two scientists selected "changes in the domestic environment" as their first reason for returning. However, as table 3 shows there has been some government success.

Table 3   Why scientists return: Indicators of government success

- 18 of 82 (22 percent) chose" changes in the domestic environment" as their second reason for returning;
- "the freedom to come and go": first choice of 3 percent, second choice of 10 percent, and third choice of 10 percent;
- Political stability: second choice of 7 percent; third choice of 3.4 percent;
- "changes in how the government uses people" (*yong ren zhengce*): third choice of 9 percent.

Source: Interviews with CAS Scientists, 2002 and 2004, N=86

However, asking the question differently increased the government's role. We asked people to select from a list of reasons as to "why the number of returnees has increased" (table 4). They could select more than one reason. While 58% chose China's rapid economic development, 47% selected "good government policy," and 42% believed they had a good opportunity to develop new technologies in China. Among respondents, 32% chose "hard to find good opportunities overseas," while 31% referred to a glass ceiling overseas for Chinese. Finally, 19% selected political stability in China. Clearly some of these people believe that good government policy is important, and that the government's role in increasing political stability deserves recognition.

Table 4   Why has the number of returnees increased?

•	China's rapid economic development	58%
•	good government policy	47%
•	good opportunity to develop new technology in China	42%
•	hard to find good opportunities overseas	32%
•	glass ceiling overseas for Chinese	31%
•	political stability in China	19%

Source: Interviews with CAS scientists, 2002 and 2004, N=86.

Yet people thought the government could do more. When asked what the government should do to increase the return rate, people chose: developing the economy, improving policies towards intellectuals, expanding democracy, fully utilizing people who had already returned, and investing more in science and education, in that order. Table 5 shows the results of that question.

Table 5   What should the government do to encourage more returnees?*

Policy Options	1st Choice (%)	2nd Choice (%)	3rd Choice (%)
1. Develop the economy	31.2	6.5	7.8
2. Expand democracy	15.6	25.9	7.8
3. Improve policy towards intellectuals	23.9	16.7	34.0
4. Invest more in science and education	10.1	23.1	15.5
5. Liberalize policy on overseas studies	4.6	14	9.7
6. Fully use people who have returned	14.7	11.1	21.4
7. Other	0.0	2.7	3.8

Note:* People were asked to select from the above list in response to the question: "What is key to attracting more people to return to China?"
Source: Survey in 2002.

Similarly, when asked what the state should do "to allow returnees to utilize their talents fully" *(fahui tamen de zuoyong)*, 59% felt the government needed to improve its policies towards people with talent. In this case, improving government policy was much more important than "increasing research funding" (22%) or "raising salaries" (17.4%).

Still, there are many people living overseas who would not set up a company in China, let alone move back. Using data from a survey in Silicon Valley in 2001 among Chinese entrepreneurs, we can see that the relationship with the government can be problematic. Table 6 shows that government bureaucracy and regulations are the most important reason why people would not start a business in China (58 percent). China's inadequate legal system ranks second (50 percent), and political instability ranks third (38 percent). [50] These are all issues that the Chinese government can address, and in fact, since China joined the WTO, the power of approval of many government bureaus has been taken away, significantly decreasing the level of government interference in business relations. Of the key problems listed by 31 firms who had established firms in China, bureaucracy/regulation was the most common problem (16/31), matched by the immature nature of the Chinese market (16/31). Still, 6 of the 31 people who had established businesses in China cited financial incentives from the government as one of three factors influencing their decision to set up a business in China. Finally, since returnees or overseas scholars are outsiders to China, 37.0 percent of people selected "unfair competition" as one of the three reasons for not starting a company in China.

However, government policy to invest in scientific institutions has a very important indirect influence. Interviews by the author in fall 2004 show that increased funding for the Chinese Academy of Sciences has rejuvenated some institutes. Two units where we did interviews had declined due to the aging of their leading researchers. The Cultural Revolution stopped China from training a new generation of scientists, creating what some call a "talent fault," [51] and many of those trained after it, including the best or even second best, had gone abroad. Only money and opportunity will bring them back. Thus one institute, which had

---

[50] Among three reasons why Chinese help their country from overseas are positive conditions for establishing enterprises created by China's rapid economic development and political stability. Chen Changgui and Liu Chengming, *Rencai: hui gui yu shiyong* (Human talent: Its return and use) (Guangzhou: Guangdong People's Publishing House, 2003), pp. 183-184. In 1993, over 30 percent of respondents interviewed by Zweig and Chen cited political instability as a key reason for not returning to China. Zweig and Chen, *China's Brain Drain to the U.S.* Recent interviews in the U.S show that instability still affects decisions about returning. Interview by Stan Rosen in Los Angeles.

[51] See Bihui Jin, Ling Li and Ronald Rousseau, "Long-Term Influences of Interventions in the Normal Development of Science: China and the Cultural Revolution," in *Journal of the American Society for Information Science and Technology*, 55 (6): 544-550. See also Cong Cao, *China's Scientific Elite* (New York: Routledge-Curzon, 2004), pp. 47-49. According to Cao, China lost at least one million undergraduates and 100,000 graduate students to the Cultural Revolution. p. 49.

Table 6 Why people would not set up a company in China (top 3 reasons)

Government bureaucracy/regulation	57.5%
Inadequate legal system	50.0%
Political or economic uncertainty	38.3%
Unfair competition	37.0%
Immature market conditions	32.9%
Unreliable infrastructure	19.9%
Lack of access to capital	18.4%
Poor business services	16.6%
Inferior quality of life	13.0%
Poor quality of manpower	5.2%
Rising cost of labour	1.8%

Source: Data collected by Anna Lee Saxenian, funded by Public Policy Institute of California.
Note: Data was collected in May-June 2001   N=368. We reanalyzed her data set.

received funds for 18 "Hundred Talents" fellowships over two years, had attracted a large cohort of young and middle-aged Ph.D.s trained overseas. However, few of these returnees had been directors of institutes overseas; many were post-doctoral fellows, or assistant professors.

Conflict generated by preferential policies

Government efforts to promote a return wave can create problems. Granting returnees preferential policies creates bad blood between returnees (commonly called the *"hai gui pai"* or "returning sea turtles faction") and people who have not gone overseas (*"tu bie pai"* or "land turtle faction"). Articles in the press and on websites in China refer to this confrontation. The decision of units to favour "outsiders" who have studied overseas over long-term members of their unit who have not been abroad has been criticized as "giving up a son to get a son-in-law." [52] In fact, at a meeting of academicians of the Chinese Academy of Sciences, Premier Wen Jiabao reportedly warned against overemphasizing the role of returnees.

Table 7 shows the different views among returnees and locals towards government policy.

Among academics, locals more than returnees, thought that the government overemphasized returnees. Similarly, more locals than

---

[52] See *"Zhao lai nu xu, qi zou erzi"*, http://www.wenxuecity.com, 2/28/02.

Table 7   Views on returnees: Comparing locals and returnees

Among Academics	Locals	Returnees
The government overemphasized *(tai zhongshi)* returnees	10%	3%
Returnees got "much more" *(duo de duo)* research funding	19%	3%
Returnees got "much better" *(hao de duo)* housing	14%	2%
Returnees got "much faster" *(kuai de duo)* promotions	19%	2%
Among Scientists	Locals	Returnees
Very satisfied with their housing	41%	15%
The housing for returnees was much better *(hao de duo)*	18%	4%
Returnees got much more *(duo de duo)* research money	29%	18%
Returnees had been promoted much faster *(kuai de duo)*	28%	12%
The state's emphasis on returnees was too high *(tai gao)*	21%	16%

Note: N= 86.
Source: Interviews with scientists in CAS, 2002, 2004.

returnees felt that the latter got "much more" research funding; "much better" housing; and, "much faster" promotions. Among scientists, almost three times as many locals than returnees were not very satisfied with their housing, while 50 percent more locals than returnees felt that returnees got much more research money. More than twice as many locals versus returnees thought returnees were promoted much faster, 21 percent of locals versus 16 percent of returnees felt that the state's emphasis on returnees was too high.

The animosity between the two groups became clear during interviews in a university in China's southwest. Locals uniformly felt that returnees to the university were not very special, while some locals were very good. Yet the university only helped returnees buy housing, get money to settle on campus *(anzhuang fei)*, and start their research. This situation may be common in border regions, or parts of China where only overseas scholars who were originally from the locality are willing to return. Such schools cannot attract talented people from other regions. But the locals may have gone to very good schools in China—in this case several Ph.D.s were from Qinghua University and the Chinese Academy of Sciences—and therefore were not inferior to some, if not many, returnees. Yet across the board, returnees got preferential treatment.

In the two institutes in the Chinese Academy of Sciences, there was less hostility about the favouritism that returnees received. This was partly because returnees had reinvigorated the institutes. However, one local Ph.D. complained about housing—he lived in a small, two-bedroom apartment, while returnees had been subsidized to buy new large apartments. Second, the state had not promoted domestic talent, due to its concerns with returnees. And while he felt that bringing in overseas talent was sound policy, it harmed the work enthusiasm of the locally trained. "My heart is not stable," he asserted, and he believed that all locals felt like him.

Even returnees believe that promoting all of them to full professor immediately upon their return was short sighted, even though all returnees insisted on it. Many returnees, having just completed a post-doctoral fellowship under their thesis director's supervision, had yet to prove themselves capable of independent research, let alone leading others in research. According to one returnee, "we can offer little in terms of research environment, so we give them an empty title of 'professor.' This is our bargain with them, but it is not healthy, as they haven't proven themselves yet." [53] But once promoted to full professor, they are very difficult to remove, so if they do not perform, the unit is stuck with them for a lifetime. Also, with the number of positions fixed in many units, "granting this title too quickly can change the dynamic of a research institute."

Conclusion

The Chinese government, at all levels of the system, has invested a great deal of time, energy and capital to attract overseas academics and businessmen to return. New government organizations, particularly related to the Ministry of Education, the Chinese Academy of Sciences, or the State Science and Technology Commission, established numerous programs to advance this goal. These extensive efforts are due in part to China's sensitivity about "face"—when people do not return, it harms China's reputation. But more importantly, China needs talented people and government leaders know it. They recognize that they cannot prevent talented citizens from going abroad, either to study or work, so the state must find ways to compete for that talent and bring its own people back. To achieve this, the central government has endeavoured to transform the overall domestic political, administrative, and economic environment, while cities themselves compete aggressively with each other by providing myriad incentives of their own. And though problems remain, China is experiencing a significant "return wave." Political stability,

---

[53] Interview in CAS, November 2004.

improved housing, better business opportunities and a more vibrant private sector, more modern equipment and management procedures, higher salaries and special incentives all improve this environment.

Market forces, facilitated by national government reforms, are the most important factor bringing people back in the private sector, as a tremendous market awaits those who learned a valuable skill or received access to advanced technology while overseas. Overseas mainlanders know the opportunities or "rents" that await them in the domestic economy if they return. Also, China has created an environment conducive to foreign direct investment which has attracted many multinational companies (MNCs), creating excellent jobs for overseas mainlanders who return. But the Chinese Academy of Sciences seems to be succeeding as well, although there are questions about the quality of their talent.

Our findings also suggest that returnees are better than those who did not go abroad, although it was often the more talented who went overseas in the first place. Thus funds expended to bring people back are not wasted. But most returnees we interviewed had been on soft money overseas on the eve of their return; few gave up very successful careers to return. Nevertheless, extensive government efforts and new funding programs have meshed well with the growing interest of many people to return to China. The result of this synthesis—a "reverse brain drain"—could transform China's scientific, academic and business communities in the coming decade.

India's experience
with skilled migration

Rupa Chanda and Niranjana Sreenivasan

Introduction

India is one of the most important source countries for both skilled and low skilled migration. There are an estimated 20 million plus Indians living abroad, who generate about US$ 160 billion in annual income, and account for US$ 400 billion worth of output (80% of the Indian economy).[1] (Table 1) Between 1975 and 2000, remittances to the Indian economy amounted to US$ 97 billion and averaged between 1.5 to 2 percent of GDP during the 1990s.[2] According to officially reported statistics, the outflow of migrant workers from India was put at 355,000 in 1998.[3]

India is a particularly important source country for skilled migration in sectors such as information technology (IT), engineering, and health care. Indian health care workers and software professionals provide services that are in short supply in the US and the UK. Shortage of nurses and doctors in the Middle East and in several developed countries like the UK has led to contractual arrangements between Indian establishments and host country governments and establishments to facilitate the temporary entry of Indian medical and nursing personnel.

In recent years, India has also experienced increased incidence of return migration and a growing role of overseas Indians in its economy, especially in sectors such as IT and business process outsourcing (BPO). These trends have mainly been spurred by the phenomenal growth of

---

[1] India Today (October 2002).

[2] India Today (January 2003).

[3] See, Wickramasekara (August 2002), Table 1, p.15.

Table 1 Estimated size of overseas Indian population: Major countries, 2002

Region/Country	Total – Non Resident Indians and Persons of Indian Origin
USA	1,678,765
Malaysia	1,665,000
Saudi Arabia	1,500,000
UK	1,200,000
South Africa	1,000,000
UAE	950,000
Canada	851,000
Mauritius	715,756
Trinidad and Tobago	500,600
Fiji	336,829
Kuwait	295,000
Australia	190,000

Source: Report of the High Level Committee of Indian Diaspora (2002).

these sectors in India in the past five to ten years, including the presence of important multinationals, and growing employment opportunities.

There have been many studies on the impact of skilled migration from India. While the earlier studies dating to the 1960s and 1970s focused on a simplified cost-benefit matrix, namely, brain drain and loss of public subsidies in higher education on the cost side and remittances and financial savings of migrants on the benefit side, recent studies have taken a more nuanced approach. The focus has shifted to understanding the impact of skilled migration through brain circulation, in terms of contributions such as skill and technology transfer, foreign direct investment and startup capital, Diaspora networks, trade, and return migration. These studies and surveys show that while there has been loss of human capital and public investment, the Indian economy has also reaped many benefits. These include upgrading of skills, increased productivity, technology transfer, alleviation of underemployment and unemployment, externalities such as the formation of social and economic networks, cross border investment flows, setting up of new firms and subsidiaries of multinational companies (MNCs), and inducement of incentives for higher and technical education. As one eminent Indian has noted, "Brain drain is better than a brain in the drain." In the past few years, the Indian government has begun to appreciate these benefits and has introduced various initiatives to facilitate the participation of the overseas Indian Diaspora in the Indian economy through trade, investment, and technology transfer and to a more limited extent attract back skilled migrants through various financial and tax-based incentives.

This paper provides an overview of the Indian experience with skilled migration, both permanent and temporary. The following section highlights the general nature of India's skilled migration outflows, followed by a detailed discussion of the nature of outflows in the IT and healthcare sectors. It also briefly discusses the implications of the growing BPO sector for skilled migration flows from India. The next section highlights recent trends in skilled migrant inflows into India. The discussion focuses on the role of the IT and BPO sectors in driving such inflows, mainly in the form of return migration and very recently in the form of inflows of foreign professionals working in these sectors. The paper further discusses research and survey findings to highlight the impact of skilled migration inflows and outflows on their source sectors in India and on the overall Indian economy, through channels such as Diaspora presence, networks, trade, and investment. It focuses in particular on the IT, health, and BPO sectors. The last section concludes by outlining the Indian government's overall approach to managing skilled migration to and from the country and provides details on recent initiatives by the Indian government to benefit from such migration and to retain or attract talent.

Nature of skilled migration from India

Existing migration statistics, notwithstanding their many limitations, highlight four important facts about migration from India. The first characteristic is that the bulk of migration from India is low skilled in nature, in occupations such as transport operations, construction, repair and maintenance, and domestic help. The second fact is that there are three main destination markets for Indian migrants. These include (1) countries in the Gulf and Middle East, chiefly Saudi Arabia, Kuwait, and UAE; (2) the English speaking industrialized countries, in particular, the UK, the US, Canada, and Australia; and increasingly (3) South East Asia, chiefly Singapore and Malaysia. The third fact is that the skill and occupational profile of Indian migrants varies according to the destination market. Migration to the industrialized countries is mainly in higher skilled and professional occupations, such as medicine, information technology, engineering, and teaching. Migration to the Middle East is dominated by the lower skilled occupational categories, in particular construction work, transport operations, and domestic services, although

217

Table 2   The distribution of annual labour outflows from India by destination, 1999-2003

Number	Country	1999	2000	2001	2002	2003
1.	UAE	79,269	55,099	53,673	95,034	143,804
2.	Saudi Arabia	27,160	58,722	78,048	99,453	121,431
3.	Kuwait	19,149	31,082	39,751	4,859	54,434
4.	Oman	16,101	15,155	30,985	41,209	36,816
5.	Malaysia	62	4,615	6,131	10,512	26,898
6.	Bahrain	14,905	15,909	16,382	20,807	24,778
7.	Singapore	19,468	18,399	27,886	24,399	23,438
8.	Qatar	–	–	13,829	12,596	14,251
9.	Libya	1,129	1,198	334	1,339	2,796
10.	Others	22,309	32,003	11,645	13,765	17,810
	Total	199,552	243,182	278,664	367,663	466,456

Source: Emigration Division, Indian Ministry of Labour, various years.

there is some movement of professionals, especially doctors, nurses, and accountants. Migration to South East Asia is again a mix of skilled and lower skilled occupations, including domestic services, plantation work, as well as doctors and information technology personnel. The fourth fact about Indian migration is that it is temporary in the case of the Middle East and South East Asia while it tends to be permanent in the case of the industrialized countries. In the latter case, even when the migration is initially temporary, migrants tend to change their immigration status once in the host country. Table 2 highlights the magnitude and geographic orientation of labour flows from India to the rest of the world.

Although the bulk of migration from India is low skilled in nature and skilled Indian migrants face constraints in the form of immigration quotas and non-recognition of qualifications, there is still a sizeable volume of skilled migration from India. Skilled and white-collar workers constitute about 20 percent of the total migrant workforce from India.[4] Indian professionals account for a significant share of overall skilled immigration and a disproportionately large share of skilled immigration in selected sectors such as IT, in major host countries like the US and the UK. Table 3 highlights the large stock of Indian knowledge workers present in various countries.

[4] D'Sami (2001), p.1.

218

Table 3   Indian emigrants to Europe, America, and Oceania (knowledge workers)

Country	Number
France	42,000
Germany	32,000
Netherlands	103,000
UK	790,000
US	815,000
Portugal	102,000
Canada	250,000
Australia	200,000
New Zealand	30,000
Indonesia	30,000

Source: D'Sami (2001), p.3.

Table 4   Net inflow of professional and managerial workers by citizenship group in the UK, 1995-99

Citizenship group	Professional and managerial	All migrant workers	Professional and managerial as % of net inflows
Old Commonwealth	56,000	73,000	77%
EU/EFTA	20,000	34,000	59%
East/Other Europe	8,000	10,000	80%
Other foreign developed countries	28,000	35,000	80%
Bangladesh/Pakistan/India/Sri Lanka	19,000	29,000	66%
Rest of the developing world	43,000	57,000	75%

Source: Findlay (2001), Table 5, p.16. Based on Migration Research Unit report (2001)

India's significance as a supplier of skilled and professional manpower is evident from host country immigration statistics on visas and work permits. According to a migration study of the UK, two-thirds of all migrants from the Indian subcontinent and working in the UK were engaged in professional and managerial occupations during the 1995-99 period (Table 4). India was the single most important country within this group. It was the leading recipient country for work permits issued by UK authorities, with 12,292 work permit approvals during the October 2000 to March 2001 period. [5] Similarly, in the case of Canada, India

---

[5] Findlay (2001).

ranked second among the top ten source countries for foreign labour in Canada, with a share of 10 to 12 percent in overall as well as skilled inflows into Canada for the years 2000, 2001, and 2002.[6]

Immigration statistics from the US similarly reveal India's leading role as a supplier of skilled manpower. Indian workers accounted for nearly 37 percent of Asian immigration to the US and around 17 percent of all immigration to the US under the professional, technical, executive, and managerial categories during the 1994-96 period. If one adds to these categories occupations such as sales and administrative support, which also require some level of skills and qualifications, then the share of Indian workers in Asian immigration and in world immigration to the US, was 57 percent and nearly 25 percent, respectively. India was the leading recipient country in all H-1 visas (designated for skilled workers in the US) during the 1990s (Tables 5 and 6). In 1999, Indian workers accounted for 47 percent of all US H-1 visas (some 55,000 out of a total of nearly 117,000 visas) issued that year. This was significantly greater than their share of 4.4 percent in 1989, and far greater than the share of the second recipient country, China, which accounted for only 5 percent of these visas in 1999.[7] Furthermore, a decomposition of the H-1 visa scheme in the US indicates that in recent years, India has been the most important source country in the specialty occupations (H1-B) category, which is based on professional education, skills, and/or equivalent experience. In 2002, Indians received close to 65,000 visas in specialty occupations (Table 9).

Occupational and sectoral composition

Although skilled migration from India has spanned a wide range of professions, including architecture, engineering, management, scientific and consulting services, computer services, and accountancy and auditing services, it has mainly been concentrated in two or three occupations and sectors. Before the 1990s and the rise of the IT industry, the bulk of skilled migration from India was in engineering, science, and healthcare. Sukhatme (1994) estimated that on average, during the 1980s, 7.3 percent of engineering graduates produced in the country left each year. These shares were estimated at 2.8 percent for medicine (only doctors) and 2.1 percent in natural sciences. Moreover, most of these migrants were from well-reputed publicly funded institutions in the country. For

---

[6] http://www.cic.gc.ca/english/pub/facts2002/immigration/immigration_5.html
[7] Commander et. al (2002).

Table 5 Total issue of USA H-1 visas and sending country shares. 1989-1999

	1989	1990	1991	1992	1993	1994	1995	1996	1997	1998	1999
India	4.4	4.6	6.9	10.7	18.0	22.9	26.3	32.0	39.3	44.0	47.2
China	1.7	1.0	1.9	1.7	2.4	2.5	3.2	3.9	4.0	4.2	5.0
Philippines	12.4	12.4	12.2	14.6	18.0	17.8	17.0	7.7	3.3	3.0	2.6
Mexico	6.0	6.4	5.4	4.8	3.1	2.3	2.5	3.2	3.5	2.5	2.1
Russia	4.6	6.3	6.6	3.2	4.5	2.5	2.0	2.1	1.7	1.5	1.4
Total LDCs	29.2	30.8	33.1	35.1	46.0	48.1	50.9	48.8	51.8	55.4	58.2
UK	13.6	12.2	14.8	13.0	9.5	8.6	8.1	9.3	8.6	6.9	5.7
Japan	7.5	6.5	8.7	5.4	5.1	4.5	3.5	4.0	3.6	3.1	2.9
France	4.7	3.9	4.1	3.3	2.1	2.0	2.1	2.4	2.3	2.3	2.3
Germany	3.7	2.8	3.2	2.9	2.4	2.2	2.5	2.5	2.6	2.5	2.1
Australia	1.8	1.4	1.9	1.9	2.0	2.1	1.8	1.9	1.8	1.8	1.4
Total Developed Countries	31.4	26.8	32.6	26.5	21.1	19.5	17.9	20.2	19.0	16.7	14.3
Others	39.4	42.4	34.3	38.4	32.9	32.4	31.2	31.1	29.3	27.9	27.4
Total no. of Visas	48820	58673	59325	51667	42206	49284	59093	60072	80608	91378	116695

Source: Commander et al (2002), based on Statistical Yearbook of the Immigration and Naturalization Service, various years.

Table 6   India's share in Asian and world immigration of workers 1994-1996

Occupation	Indian immigration	Asian immigration	World immigration	Indian as % of Asian	Indian as % of world
Overall occupational	114,528	688,327	2,440,777	13.2	4.7
Total occupational	38,395	295,516	851,507	13.0	4.5
Professional, technical	19,603	89,917	201,568	22.0	9.7
Executive, managerial	6,246	41,841	83,631	14.9	7.5
Sales	1,489	14,581	39,950	10.2	3.7
Administrative support	2,390	20,816	61,610	11.5	3.8
Production, craft and repairs	767	17,775	66,780	4.3	1.1
Operator, fabricator and labour	846	43,543	195,861	1.9	0.4
Family, forestry and fishing	3,567	20,366	42,698	17.5	8.4
Service	3,467	47,406	159,409	7.4	2.2
No occupation reported	76,133	572,811	1,589,270	13.3	4.8

Source: Khadria (1999), based on Statistical Yearbook of the Immigration and Naturalization Service, various years.

Table 7   India's brain drain in engineering, medicine and natural science and degree holders of IIT, Bombay: Estimate for 1980s

Field	Yearly average national output in the 80s	Estimate of brain drain (yearly average for 80s)	Per cent
Engineering	24,088	1,765	7.3
Medicine	21,175	590	2.8
Natural sciences	22,714	470	2.1

Degree	Number of typical annual output	Number likely to settle abroad	Estimate of brain drain
B.Tech	250	77	30.8
M.Sc.	80	20	25.0
M.Tech.	250	34	13.5
Ph.D.	60	6	9.8
Total	640	137	21.4

Source: Sukhatme (1994) in Khadria (1999)

Table 8   A comparative overview of the DST sponsored brain drain studies on migration in India

	IIT Bombay	IIT Madras	AIIMS Delhi	IIT Delhi
Year of study	1987	1989	1992	1997
Period covered	1973-77	1964-87	1956-80	1980-90
Population size	1,262	5,942	1,224	2,479
Sample size	501	429	402	460
In India	179	184	200	316
Out of India	322	245	202	144
Magnitude of brain drain	30.8%	25-28%	56.2%	23.1%

Source: Khadria (1999).

Table 9   H1-B beneficiaries in the top 5 H1-B receiving countries, 2002

Category	India	China	Canada	Philippines	United Kingdom
Computer-related	47,477	5,357	2,770	1,561	1,250
Fashion models	5	4	92	1	50
Managers and officials	1,212	388	1,204	315	908
Miscellaneous, professional, technical and managerial	690	349	379	115	283
Administrative specialization	2,689	1,660	1,342	2,186	795
Architecture, engineering and surveying	5,780	2,633	1,629	993	1,235
Art	113	76	133	65	245
Education	1,908	3,593	1,507	957	893
Entertainment and recreation	69	28	77	9	89
Law and jurisprudence	72	93	165	34	99
Life sciences	727	1,965	415	63	360
Mathematics and physical sciences	693	1,401	446	76	272
Medical and health	2,530	674	949	2,524	297
Museum, library and archival sciences	11	30	56	5	31
Religion and theology	7	2	14	6	7
Social sciences	738	413	365	257	206
Writing	77	91	133	44	83
Unknown	182	84	84	84	68
Total	64,980	18,841	11,760	9,295	7,171

Source: Statistical Yearbook of the Immigration and Naturalization Service, 2002.

instance, on average, between 20 to 30 percent of all B.Tech graduates produced in the famous Indian Institutes of Technology (IITs) migrated from the country during the 1980s and 1990s. About eighty percent of these graduates were from the engineering stream and the rest were from natural sciences. On average, over 50 percent of medical graduates from reputed medical training institutions like the All India Institute for Medical Sciences (AIIMS), migrated from the country during the 1980s.[8] Tables 7 and 8 highlight the magnitude and nature of skilled migration in the medical and engineering fields from the country.

Since the 1990s, the main source sector for skilled migration from India has been the IT sector, followed by medicine and engineering. US immigration statistics from the 1990s indicate the disproportionately high share of Indian computer professionals in all H-1 visa admissions to the US. Table 9 shows that 47,477 visas or 73 % of all H-1B visas granted to Indians were in computer related fields. Table 10 shows that Indian professionals accounted for around 60-70 percent of all H1-B visas granted in the computer-related occupational category across countries during the 2000-2002 period. The significance of the IT sector in skilled Indian migration to the US reflects the surge in demand for IT workers in the US during the late 1990s and the subsequent increases in the H-1B quota from 65,000 to 115,000 in 1999 and further to 195,000 in 2000 under the American Competitiveness and Workforce Improvement Act. Table 11 also highlights India's significance as a source country for skilled persons across many occupational categories, including medical and health related occupations.

Evidence from other countries further confirms India's importance as a supplier of IT, engineering, and health care professionals to the rest of the world. For instance, Germany, Austria, Singapore, and Japan have introduced special work permit and visa schemes in recent years to attract Indian IT professionals and meet shortages of such workers in those markets. India has the largest stock of overseas doctors among all countries and also exports nurses to several developed countries like the UK and Australia. A detailed account of the work permits issued in the UK by occupational group shows that Indians received admission in the engineering, computer science, health, teaching, management and administration, business, and finance professions. The two main source sectors were IT and healthcare, with over 60 percent of the over 12,000 work permits granted to Indians being allocated to computer professionals,

---

[8] See, Sukhatme (1994) and Khadria (1999).

Table 10 India's share in H1-B visas, Asia and world, 2000-2002

Category	2000		2001		2002	
	India % share in Asia	Indian % share in world	India % share in Asia	Indian % share in world	Indian % share in Asia	Indian % share in world
Computer-related	79.62%	68.18%	81.53%	71.39%	76.43%	63.21%
Fashion models	10.53%	0.33%	2.00%	0.11%	11.63%	0.67%
Managers and officials	32.45%	12.28%	37.16%	13.92%	31.79%	11.42%
Miscellaneous, professional, technical and managerial	27.62%	11.49%	33.63%	15.98%	30.82%	13.97%
Administrative specialization	23.69%	13.88%	28.98%	17.14%	22.26%	12.74%
Architecture, engineering and surveying	39.47%	26.01%	42.36%	27.87%	38.10%	22.94%
Art	6.09%	3.36%	8.81%	4.64%	7.62%	3.90%
Education	17.26%	8.36%	19.99%	9.45%	18.64%	9.26%
Entertainment and recreation	38.42%	17.37%	19.26%	6.74%	23.08%	8.89%
Law and jurisprudence	12.90%	4.77%	15.31%	5.02%	14.40%	5.01%
Life sciences	19.76%	11.06%	19.03%	10.52%	18.85%	10.52%
Mathematics and physical sciences	18.40%	10.03%	21.95%	12.21%	22.33%	12.73%
Medical and health	27.86%	18.00%	31.86%	20.34%	30.50%	19.58%
Museum, library and archival sciences	18.99%	8.06%	14.18%	5.65%	9.48%	3.49%
Religion and theology	10.34%	4.41%	14.71%	6.02%	15.56%	5.93%
Social sciences	29.64%	16.37%	26.01%	13.46%	25.47%	13.30%
Writing	12.12%	6.18%	15.38%	7.73%	10.24%	5.23%
Unknown	38.93%	18.88%	50.00%	23.66%	31.71%	13.22%
Total	61.64%	44.42%	65.82%	48.78%	50.91%	32.89%

Source: Statistical Yearbook of the Immigration and Naturalization Service, various years.

Table 11 Category-wise breakdown of temporary workers from Asian countries, 2002

Country/Class of Admission	China	India	Japan	Korea	Philippines	Israel
Registered nurses (H1-A)	57	228	32	25	21	13
Specialty occupations (H1-B)	15,838	81,091	13,287	8,000	5,509	5,357
Nurses, nursing relief Act, 1999(H1-C)	-	2	-	-	84	-
Services unavailable in US (Non-agricultural workers) (H2-B)	108	310	461	128	221	31
Industrial trainees (H-3)	94	96	529	25	17	24
Exchange visitors (J-1)	9,795	4,866	12,684	9,951	1,333	4,039
Intracompany transferees (L-1)	4,572	20,413	31,044	4,769	2,077	4,440
Workers of extraordinary ability/achievement (O-1)	282	523	741	227	191	510
Workers accompanying performance of O-1 workers (O-2)	117	138	40	72	73	34
Internationally recognized athletes or entertainers (P-1)	795	95	395	166	117	246
Artists/entertainers in reciprocal exchange programs (P-2)	50	41	16	40	25	32
Artists/entertainers in culturally unique programs (P-3)	509	946	367	234	61	77
International cultural exchange programs (Q-1)	77	6	303	10	2	1
Total	32,911	110,103	60,631	24,487	10,417	15,335

Note: The figures for China include People's Republic of China and Taiwan.
Source: Statistical Yearbook of the Immigration and Naturalization Service, 2002

followed by 9 percent of all work permits being granted to healthcare professionals. [9]

The following sections discuss in some detail the nature of skilled outflows in India's IT and health sectors and emerging trends in the BPO sector.

Characterizing outflows in India's IT sector [10]

The information technology sector in India has been a driving force behind skilled migration from India in recent years, facilitated by India's abundant, low cost, and high quality of personnel in this sector and notwithstanding a variety of immigration and labour market restrictions to such movement. [11] Temporary movement of service suppliers is critical for the Indian IT industry. A large part of India's software services exports involve on-site delivery of custom application, software development, and maintenance services by Indian IT professionals in overseas markets. These services are provided across a wide range of sectors, especially banking, finance, and insurance. On-site professional services contributed over US$ 5 billion in export earnings in 2003-04 or 43 percent of total export revenues of US$ 12.2 billion that year. In most years, on-site services provided by Indian programmers, coders, systems analysts, and maintenance personnel, have accounted for around 40 percent of total export revenues in the IT sector (although this share has been declining in recent years due to the rise in offshoring to India). Industry sources in India estimate that out of a supply of 132,986 newly entering IT professionals in 2001-02, about 64,350 left India to provide on-site services that year. Migration for on-site work accounted for 15 percent of the total stock of 428,636 IT professionals in 2001-02. Given the importance of the US as a market for Indian software services exports, the US has been the most important destination market for skilled migration from India in the IT sector, followed by the UK.

Surveys of IT companies in India on migration and return migration, indicate that the majority of these professionals who go overseas have backgrounds in engineering or computer applications, from universities, colleges, polytechnics, and training institutes. They include graduates, postgraduates and diploma holders. They provide a wide range of services including programming, systems design, administration, and

---

[9] These statistics are based on Findlay (December 2001).

[10] The discussion in this section is mostly based on NASSCOM (2002), unless otherwise noted.

[11] See, Chanda (April 2003) for a discussion of the factors that facilitate and constrain migration in India's IT sector.

integration, software maintenance, software development and customization, coding and testing. Most of these professionals are employed at the middle level of their respective organizations and are mostly in their twenties and thirties. There is also movement of suppliers who are in managerial, executive, and specialized positions, mainly in the case of the few Indian companies which have commercial presence overseas and multinational IT companies located in India, but such movement at the higher level is much more limited.

Migration in the IT sector is quite fluid and dynamic in nature, with considerable amount of repeat migration under time bound contracts with duration limits on visas and work permits. However, many Indian IT professionals tend to adjust their immigration and residence status once they are overseas and stay on permanently. The National Association of Software Services Companies (NASSCOM) estimates the extent of return migration to be only around 3 to 4 percent of all migrants in IT services, as shown in Table 12. A web-based survey of Indian IT professionals in the Silicon Valley found that about 32 percent of the 769 respondents from India did not intend to return from the US. This percentage was much higher at 50 percent for respondents under age thirty five. [12] Thus, there is a significant amount of permanent migration of engineers, computer application graduates, and IT specialists from the country, mainly to the US market.

Table 12   Return migrants in the Indian IT industry, 2000-2005

Category	2000-01	2001-02	2002-03	2003-04	2004-05
India new IT labour		132,986	158,099	172,977	192,194
Number of professionals living in India (onsite work)		64,350	64,350	64,350	21,450
Number of IT professionals returning to India		–	20,109	24,131	29,250
Number of IT professionals	360,000	428,636	542,495	675,233	875,248
Percentage of migrants		15.01%	11.86%	9.53%	2.45%
Percentage of return migrants			3.7%	3.57%	3.34%

Source: NASSCOM (2002).

---

[12] Saxenian (2002). Findlay (2001) shows the low incidence of return migration by professional managerial workers from South Asia as well as other developing countries from the UK. In the 1995-99 period, there were recorded outflows of only 4,900 South Asian migrant workers in the professional and managerial occupations from the UK, barely a quarter of all such workers in the UK.

Healthcare workers

Migration of Indian health care workers, including doctors, nurses, paramedics, and technicians, is a long-standing phenomenon, notwithstanding immigration and recognition related barriers to entry and practice. Indian health care providers are found in the Middle East, Africa, the US, Canada, and other major developed countries and are reputed for their quality and skills around the world. [13]

Movement of Indian health care workers to the Middle East and Gulf countries has mainly been under short-term arrangements. As of 1992, there were 33 bilateral agreements between India and six countries in the Middle East for providing doctors on short-term assignments. This number is likely to be an underestimate as it only captures the assignments by government doctors who need to clear a formal process before they can leave the country. Private short-term contractual arrangements between doctors and these countries are also present. There has also been a steady stream of Indian nurses to the Middle East and the Gulf countries on short-term assignments. According to a WHO (1979) study, there were an estimated 4,000 Indian nurses abroad, representing about 5 percent of the total stock of nurses in the country, most of it being to countries like Bahrain and Oman. [14] Thus, migration of nurses has been much lower than migration of physicians. There is some migration of Indian technicians and paramedics, mainly to the Gulf countries, but little is known about its magnitude and nature.

Movement of Indian healthcare workers to the industrialized countries and has been mostly long-term in nature. The majority of Indian physicians, who are abroad, are based in Commonwealth countries, in particular. The UK as India is a member of the Commonwealth. There are an estimated 60,000 doctors and 35,000 doctors of Indian origin in the UK and the US, respectively. [15] It is important to note that these numbers are likely to be underestimated as many Indian physicians enter the US or the UK markets from countries other than India. Estimates of the total stock of physicians that have left the country range between 11 and 15 percent. [16] Most of this movement has been permanent in nature. There has, however, been some movement under short term arrange-

---

[13] See, Chanda (September 2004) and Chanda (April 2003) for a discussion of the factors that facilitate and constrain the movement of Indian healthcare professionals.

[14] Mejia et. al (1979).

[15] The estimates of migration in India's health sector vary. The figures given here are from UNCTAD/WHO (1998) and the Commonwealth Secretariat (1996).

[16] Meija (1979).

ments to developed countries, for instance, under special US visa schemes like the H-1A for registered nurses or under bilateral agreements between institutions in India and in developed countries such as the US, the UK, Germany, Australia, New Zealand, and Canada. [17] There has also been some short-term movement of nurses and other health personnel from India to developed countries for training purposes. In the past few years, there has been a surge in demand for Indian nurses due to huge shortages in markets like the US and the UK. As a result, many nursing schools and big hospitals are training nurses for working overseas in American and British hospitals and placement agencies and even big hospitals are advertising for nurses. [18]

There has also been migration of Indian medical graduates. It is estimated that on average, over 50 percent of medical graduates from reputed medical training institutions like the All India Institute for Medical Sciences (AIIMS), migrated from the country during the 1980s, mainly to developed countries. [19] Although there are no hard statistics on the actual number of medical students leaving the country, there is evidence to indicate that this movement is considerable. For instance, over five thousand Indian medical graduates take the Educational Commission for Foreign Medical Graduates (ECFMG) exam each year and over 30 percent of these graduates pass the exam. Since the number applying for the exam is an indication of those interested in going abroad, the potential number of medical graduates leaving the country is over a thousand per year. India's most prestigious medical schools figure among the main exporters of medical students to developed countries.

Thus, if one combines the statistics for doctors migrating on short or long term assignments, for nurses, technicians, and medical graduates, the extent of movement of service suppliers in India's health sector is huge. It is therefore not surprising that according to a 1979 WHO study, India emerged as the world's largest donor of medical manpower.

The profile of health care personnel moving abroad from India has varied depending on the occupational and skill category. Within the category of physicians, most of the movement is by specialists, probably

---

[17] Even as early as the 1960s, India was one of the main source countries for doctor migration to the UK. There were about 6,000 registered civilian doctors in the UK between 1962-67, who were born in India. While some of these doctors also returned to India, the number of doctors arriving from India to the UK was double the number of those who left the UK for India, during this period. Hence, concerns about brain drain and labour market shortages for doctors, have been long standing in India. See, Gish (1971).

[18] Conservative estimates put the shortage of nurses in the US at 100,000. It is projected that by the year 2008, there will be a demand for 450,000 nurses, a large part of which can be met by India. See, Economic Times (May 5, 2004).

[19] See, Sukhatme (1994) and Khadria (1999).

reflecting the fact that the effective market demand for persons with very specialized skills is low in a country like India and the opportunities are much better in overseas markets. Within the category of medical graduates, most of the movement is from the best medical training institutions in the country. Little is known about the profile of the migrating service suppliers in the case of nurses and health technicians.

India's experience with skilled inflows: return and foreign migrants

Although much of the skilled migration from India to the developed countries has tended to be permanent in nature, increasingly, there is a reversal of such flows. Following the recent slowdown in the US economy and the bursting of the tech bubble coupled with the growing business and employment opportunities in India, return migration to India is on the rise.

Return migration

The Indian IT and BPO industries are playing an instrumental role in driving return flows to India. According to NASSCOM, between 2001 and 2004, roughly 25,000 Indian IT professionals settled abroad have returned to India. Though these numbers are small, the point to note is that they are rising. It is estimated that around six to seven thousand technology professionals returned to India in 2001 and that this number was around eight to ten thousand in 2004. These professionals are willing to take pay cuts of around 30 to 40 percent. It is estimated that between 30-40 per cent of the Indian IT expatriates who return, take up employment in offshore IT services set-ups. Furthermore, according to NASSCOM sources, reverse migration is not restricted to the IT industry but is also visible in the financial services sector. [20]

The growing interest in returning to India is indicated by the results of a recent online survey of Indian American executives in US corporations. According to the findings of this survey, 68 percent said that they were actively looking into opportunities for retuning back to India, 12 percent said they were returning to India, and an equal percentage noted that they were open to exploring such ideas. The survey found that many who

---

[20] See, Hindu Business Line, "Indian IT pros heading back on home attraction" (December 17, 2004) and Nair, "Indian IT Pros are Homeward Bound" (December 1, 2004).

came to the US in the seventies, eighties and even the nineties were planning to go back to India. [21]

The recent recession and the rise in unemployment in North America is an important reason for the increased return migration. Skilled immigrants are opting to go where the jobs are going – to the Gulf States, India, Malaysia, Hong Kong, the Philippines and China, to work in the new subsidiaries and associated operations that American and Canadian companies have or are in the process of setting up to produce the goods and services outsourced from North America. [22] In addition, improving economic conditions in India are also spurring return migration. Many overseas Indians want to return in order to contribute to and participate in India's growing and dynamic economy, such as by providing research and leadership skills in its growing outsourcing market. Overseas Indians are increasingly viewing employment opportunities in India as being comparable to those in the US, especially since offshoring activities are on the rise and leading companies like Intel and IBM are now doing cutting edge work in India. The growing global presence of many Indian companies, particularly in the IT sector, is also helping to attract back talent. For instance, today, Indian IT companies such as Infosys, TCS and Wipro are big brand names globally. They have grown significantly and have established a global presence by setting up offices across the world, by listing themselves on Nasdaq and the New York Stock Exchange, and through overseas acquisitions. These companies are seen as comparable and sometimes better employment options than multinationals overseas. Many Indian professionals are choosing to give up multinational jobs to take up employment in Indian companies as they perceive they can do more meaningful work and move up to management positions more rapidly. [23] And finally, rising standards of living and improved facilities for families of returning migrants are making it easier for overseas Indians to return.

In other important source sectors such as healthcare, the incidence of return migration is more limited. However, some surveys conducted among overseas Indian doctors suggest that there is high interest in

---

[21] See, http://www.indiadaily.com/editorial/07-21c-04.asp , "The new trend of 2004 – Indian Americans returning back to India to lead US and Indian Corporations in the outsourcing market", Peter Oberoi (July 21, 2004)

[22] See, http://www.sharedxpertise.org/modules.php?file=article&name=News&op=modload&sid= 1327, "Outsourcing sparks reverse migration" for a discussion on the impact of recent economic conditions and offshoring by American companies on reverse migration.

[23] See, http://www.business-standard.com/general/storypage_test.php?&autono=174013 for a discussion of the growing brand equity of Indian IT companies and Indians quitting multinationals to join domestic IT companies.

Table 13 **Estimates of Indian doctors who have returned from overseas, 1998**

Country of destination	Total trained %	% Returned	Major specialties
United Kingdom	3,708	48.03	General medicine, surgery, veterinary science and pediatrics
USA	1,080	49.7	-Do-
Germany	82	41.46	-Do-
Other European countries	284	52.46	-Do-
Australia & New Zealand	60	23.33	-Do-
Canada	176	42.04	-Do-
Other	694	47.55	-Do-
Total	6,084		

Source: Ganguly (2003) (obtained from the Health Information of India).

return, especially among medical graduates from some of India's best institutions. A survey of All India Institute of Medical Sciences graduates settled abroad found that about 40 percent of the respondents were ready to return, mainly for personal reasons followed by their desire to give back to the country. Table 13 provides the findings of a survey on returnee doctors. The results indicate that on average about 43 percent of those trained and practicing abroad in selected developed countries, actually returned to India. For example, within the sample, of the 3,708 doctors trained in the UK, 48 percent returned. Of the 1,080 trained in the US, close to 50 percent returned. The absolute numbers were smaller for the other developed countries and the corresponding shares were comparable to those for the UK and the US. These doctors were trained in general medicine, surgery, veterinary sciences, and pediatrics. [24]

While it is difficult to provide overall estimates of the number of returning doctors to India, there are numerous examples of reputed health care establishments, such as the Apollo Group of Hospitals or Escorts, which have been set up by physicians formerly practicing in developed countries. Such establishments have in turn helped induce further return by Indian healthcare professionals based in other countries and have created opportunities for overseas doctors of Indian origin to contribute to India through visiting, research, and collaborative arrangements.

---

[24] Ganguly (2003).

Inflows of skilled foreigners

An interesting phenomenon that is emerging is the migration by skilled foreigners into India. Recruiting firms in India note that overseas professionals from sectors such as Information Technology, biotechnology, research and development, garments, hospitality, and BPO are increasingly seeking options in India. According to recruitment sources, most inquiries are for middle and senior level management positions, but people are interested in lower rank jobs too.[25] The BPO industry is one of the main driving forces behind this emerging phenomenon. A growing number of professionals from the US, the UK, and African countries are seeking jobs in India mainly on account of outsourcing and job cuts in their home countries. As noted by the CEO of Head Hunters (India), a top recruiting firm, the setting up of offshore offices and subsidiaries by foreign firms in India is helping to attract experienced professionals from other countries to India, although at present the numbers are not very large. The target destinations for the foreign professionals are BPO hubs such as Bangalore, Mumbai, and New Delhi, which are also the main destinations for returning expatriates. Recruiting firms indicate that there is growing interest by foreign workers from European countries like Germany and Italy and a call centre in New Delhi has employed people from Finland to answer queries for a leading travel portal in Europe.[26] Other factors that are seen to have contributed to such inflows include the changing perception among foreigners about India and the available opportunities in India, the growing possibilities for doing high value offshored work in India, the desire on the part of some foreigners to work and travel in an emerging economy, and India's overall economic and political stability.

Some BPO firms in India are also recruiting foreign professionals on temporary work visas in order to secure certain advantages in the BPO business. One such reason is to diversify their language-based operations and to cater to non-English speaking regions and markets. For example, Tecnovate, a BPO firm in India, which is a subsidiary of the London based online travel agency, ebookers Plc, has recently hired 30 foreigners (French, German, Finnish, Norwegian, Swedish, Dutch, Swiss and Irish nationals) in order to cater to their non-English business. Tecnovate, with its European and Indian team now can offer work in Finnish, French, German, Norwegian, and Swedish besides English. Company sources

---

[25] See, http://news.indiainfo.com/2004/02/11/1102jobs.html , "Foreign pros increasingly seeking jobs in India", (Wednesday, February 11, 2004) for further details.

[26] See, http://www.bpoindia.org/news/2003.shtml, "India Beckons".

note that there were 100 applications from foreigners for the five positions they advertised in Scandinavian papers for jobs in India, indicating that there is interest in taking up employment in India among foreigners. Tecnovate has plans to increase its European strength further. Similarly, when online bookstore Amazon asked Daksh eServices to offer German language work for its European customers, Daksh hired its first German-speaking professional. By end-2003, Daksh had over 100 non-English speaking foreign professionals to cater to their business in non-English speaking countries. Some Indian BPO providers are also hiring foreign professionals as the latter have destination specific knowledge, which can give them an edge with customers in certain countries and regions, knowledge that is difficult to replicate in Indian BPO workers even with substantial training. While such hiring of foreign professionals is still a very small part of total employment in India's BPO industry, this trend of employing foreigners is likely to increase as the industry diversifies its business to other languages and to parts of the world other than the US and the UK. [27]

Contribution of skilled migration to source sectors and the Indian economy

Skilled migration has contributed positively to the Indian economy in several ways. [28] The most important contribution has been through remittances and transfers and financial savings. Remittances have constituted between 1 to 2 percent of GDP in India. Throughout the 1980s, remittances accounted for about US$ 3 billion and rose to nearly US$ 12 billion in cash and kind in 1997-98. [29] Although the bulk of remittances to India have been from low skilled migrants in the Gulf and Middle East, skilled migrants in developed countries have also been an important source. For example, professional non-resident Indians (NRIs) have played an important role in channeling their savings to India. They helped support the country's foreign exchange position in the most recent economic crisis of 1991, by depositing their savings in special instruments such as Indian Development Bonds and specially targeted

---

[27] At present, many Indian BPO firms are outsourcing to third countries to cater to non-English speaking customers. See, http://in.jobstreet.com/aboutus/mreports43.htm, R. Leishemba, S. Neogi, S. Nair, "India shines for job seeking foreigners too", Financial Express (Sunday, February 1, 2004).

[28] Note that there have also been negative effects such as brain drain. There has been much discussion about the negative impact of migration by the best and brightest from India's premier educational institutions and the associated loss of public investments in higher education, fiscal revenues, and economic value.

[29] India Today (January 2003).

repatriable foreign accounts. The contribution made to foreign exchange earnings by service suppliers in sectors such as software, is well recognized. In fact, export earnings on the service account, mostly in the form of manpower-based exports, have helped the country to keep a comfortable current account position in recent years. But there have been many other channels of impact, including those of network externalities, investment, skill and knowledge transfer, influencing of education choices, and the growth of certain industries, which warrant discussion.

Investments and network externalities

Skilled Indian migrants have contributed to the Indian economy through *investments and through overseas networks* (though not yet as significant as in the case of China). For instance, returnee Indian doctor entrepreneurs from the UK, the US, and the Middle East as well as Indian Diaspora associations in the medical profession have helped set up world class corporate hospitals and superspeciality health care establishments in India. They have also helped procure the latest equipment and technology.[30] The reputed Apollo group of hospitals, India's first corporate hospital chain, was set up by Dr. Pratap Reddy, a returning Indian doctor from the US. Today, Apollo is one of Asia's largest health care establishments, the first to attract foreign investment in India and the first to set up hospitals outside the country. Evidence from regional studies in health care indicates that the growth of private hospitals in Hyderabad was in large part due to the return of doctors who had practiced in the Middle East, with one-third of the owners of general nursing homes having worked in that region. The emergence of such doctor entrepreneur hospitals has also helped raise the standard of health care within the private sector in India, including the introduction of processes such as counseling for patients, computerized medical records, seminars, education and training mechanisms, collaboration with overseas doctors and institutions, availability of the latest technology and infrastructural facilities, apart from cleanliness, hygiene, and better staffing and management practices.

Professionals in other areas such as in software and engineering services have helped in providing venture capital for startup companies in India. They have helped the development of their sectors by selling India as a safe destination for investments to foreign investors, by bringing in projects, facilitating the outsourcing of services to Indian companies,

---

[30] See Gupta (2002) and Baru (1998).

providing contacts to overseas clients, and facilitating further both inward and outward movement of service providers. For example, returning Indian IT professionals who have worked abroad for long periods and in senior and managerial capacities, help establish and manage subsidiaries of MNCs in the country. Often, they are instrumental in influencing foreign multinationals to set up operations in India and do offshore development work in India. Many returning IT professionals have also helped develop the IT industry by establishing their own operations in India, often out of their personal savings. They have made use of their overseas contacts, expertise, and networks to generate funds, get venture capital, and expand into new lines of business. In either instance, whether they set up their own operations or manage MNC operations in India, these professionals play a very important role by facilitating access to foreign capital, technology, personnel, and overseas clients, and by inducing return by other Indian IT professionals, given their prior work experience and networks.

Skill and technology transfer

Skilled migration and return has also contributed to skill and technology transfer. Surveys reveal that overseas experience in on-site projects in the IT industry helps employees to develop domain expertise in fields such as insurance, telecom, or energy, and domain knowledge in technology and applications. Such returnees are able to bring in specialization and depth, and are also better placed to lead and educate teams working on projects in specific areas. The exposure of returning professionals to overseas clients and to new technologies and applications helps Indian IT companies to undertake more diverse and up to date projects which require such expertise. Given their knowledge of overseas market conditions and expectations of clients, such professionals also play an important role by liaising with foreign clients. A recent survey of 225 IT firms in India confirms that on the whole, migration of Indian IT professionals has created possibilities for "brain gain", through Diaspora investment, networking for contacts and projects, technology transfer, information dissemination and exchange, and various forms of collaboration.[31]

In the health sector, returning doctors bring back specialized skills and expertise in rare and niche areas for which training opportunities and expertise are not available in India. Also, since the majority has received

---

[31] See, Commander et. al (2004).

further training abroad, there is upgrading of skills and knowledge by the returnees. There are other intangible benefits, including knowledge of quality processes, better ethics and attitudes towards work, greater professionalism and transparency, better management practices, and familiarity with the latest technology. Other intangibles include reputation and brand equity benefits as returning doctors also help in building the reputation of the institutions in which they work. The presence of returning superspecialists and overseas trained doctors helps these establishments convey an image of quality care and treatment of international standards to patients. Surveys also indicate that returning Indian doctors help improve the state of medical research and information in the health sector.

Education and training incentives

The prospect of migration, particularly in sectors such as IT, has led to increased demand for and supply of related education and training within India. The recent increase in demand for IT professionals in major developed countries and the resulting opportunities for overseas employment for Indian software professionals, has increased the demand for IT education and the corresponding supply of such education. The number of IT professionals in the country has risen from a mere 6,800 knowledge workers in 1985-86 to over 500,000 in 2002 due to rising enrolment for IT education. The number of students admitted for an IT degree in engineering programmes increased from 50,832 in 1992 to 89,957 in 1997 and further to 133,053 in 2001. The number of admissions for IT diplomas in engineering programmes increased from 46,591 in 1992 to 64,263 in 1997, and further to 73,465 in 2001.[32] In both cases, about half of those admitted into these IT degree or diploma programmes, graduated as IT professionals. This increase has in part been attributed to the increased scope for temporary and possibly permanent movement to overseas markets for providing on-site professional services in this sector, witnessed in recent years.

There has been a corresponding rise in the number of institutions for graduate and postgraduate training in the IT area and in related disciplines. Apart from the prestigious IITs which were earlier the main source of newly qualified graduates or postgraduates in this field, today, there are more than 250 universities and engineering colleges providing computer education at the degree/diploma level. There are also thousands

---

[32] Based on Nasscom (2002).

of private training institutions and polytechnics that provide computer education all over the country. Some of these private institutions, such as NIIT and Aptech, have acquired brand value. They have become an attractive choice for students seeking higher education after leaving school, for mid career professionals interested in changing or diversifying their career path, and for those seeking professional development and upgrading in the IT area. Degree and diploma colleges accounted for 90,867 new IT professionals who entered the labour market in 2001-02, of which 57,000 were IT degree professionals and about 34,000 were IT diploma professionals, across the computer science, electronics, and telecommunications streams. These degree and diploma colleges also produced 35, 612 new non-IT professionals who entered the labour market in 2001-02. In terms of the total stock of professionals, these colleges accounted for 71,066 IT professionals and 118,707 non-IT professionals in 2001-02 (not all of whom entered the IT labour market). In addition, the number of IT professionals produced by engineering schools stood at 71,000 in 2001, up from about 43,000 in 1997. [33] Thus, it is evident from the large annual output of graduates in IT and non-IT fields and the variety of training institutions available, that that there has been a significant increase in training and education opportunities in this area.

Growth of the BPO industry

While the BPO industry in India is still nascent, there is evidence to indicate that one of the positive fallouts of skilled migration, both earlier from the 1960s and 1970s as well as more recently (following the growth of the internet and the Y2K problem), has been the growth of India's BPO industry. According to a study conducted by the research firm, Evalueserve for the World Bank Institute, the growing influence and expertise of India's Diaspora in the US, UK, and Canada will help India to retain its edge and move up the value chain in outsourcing. As stated in this study, "Riding the wave of growing reputation and visibility of Indians in the IT sector, many well-placed senior executives (of Indian origin) in big corporations who had moved to these countries in 1960s influenced outsourcing-related decisions in India's favour. As the networking and mentoring role of Diaspora increases, India will continue to retain the edge in outsourcing." [34] According to this study, by the

---

[33] See, Nasscom (2002).

[34] See, "NRI's from UK, Canada to help India retain BPO edge" (Thursday, September 30 2004) and http://www.infoworld.com/article/04/10/04/HNindiandiaspora_1.html, John Ribeiro, "Indian diaspora helped outsourcing movement", IDG News Service (October 04, 2004) for further details on this study.

1990s, many Indian engineers, who had started moving to the US in the 1960s, have since become entrepreneurs, venture capitalists, or senior executives in large and medium-size companies. These expatriates have played an important role in setting up BPO companies in India or in convincing their companies to hire Indian IT professionals and offshore work to India, and have performed mentoring and troubleshooting functions for their companies.

The Indian Diaspora has also provided capital through investments in India's BPO industry and is facilitating the emergence of the high-end knowledge services sector within the Indian BPO industry. Some venture capitalists in the US, of Indian origin, are actively funding Indian companies that have back-end operations in India, so that they can save on research and development costs for their companies. Networking organizations like the IndUS Entrepreneurs have helped mobilize capital for investment in India's BPO sector and are helping increase the brand equity of this sector in India.

Government policy towards skilled migration

The Indian government has not had any coherent policy to regulate skilled migration or to benefit in any directed manner from such labour flows. Unlike countries such as South Korea, Taiwan, and South Africa, which have provided special incentives to attract back talent to the home country, there has not been any concerted effort to induce return migration in India, except in some indirect and limited ways. This is possibly due to the large domestic supply of skilled and unskilled labour (employed and unemployed) despite migration, which reduces the need to attract back migrants to the country and which also makes it difficult to significantly raise wages to levels that would make return attractive. There has also not been any major effort to retain skilled workers in the country, except for some policies to delay emigration or to recover government resources spent on training and education, although proposals have on occasion been mooted for retaining professionals in the health and engineering fields.

Remittances by overseas Indian service providers have also not been regulated by the government and channeled towards specific developmental purposes such as the building of local infrastructure or for investments in health and education. These remittances and their positive contributions to the home economy have mostly been driven by individual decision making and not government policies, barring some state level initiatives.

There have been a few initiatives to benefit from the overseas Indian Diaspora and to develop this network in the past. For instance, since 1980, there has been a nationally executed, UNDP sponsored TOKTEN (Transfer of Knowledge Through Expatriate Nationals) programme which encourages distinguished expatriate nationals of Indian origin who have expert knowledge in frontier areas of science, technology, industrial applications, and management to undertake short-term assignments in India on a voluntary basis. This programme, which is implemented by the Council for Scientific and Industrial Research (CSIR), aims to obtain technical inputs from expatriates for R&D, industrial enterprises, and academic institutions. Another programme, INRIST (Interface for NRI Scientists and Technologists), has been in operation since 1990, again implemented by CSIR. This programme aims to serve as a focal point of contact in India to establish linkages between expatriates and Indian organisations, and to connect various institutional and voluntary organisations abroad with all the scientific, technical, and economic departments of the Central and State Governments and with industries in the public and private sectors. The INRIST Centre has a database of expatriate scientists and technologists and promotes joint ventures and investments in industrial projects with expatriates. These programmes have, however, not been very successful due to bureaucratic, administrative, and budgetary problems.[35] These schemes have lacked an overall institutional framework and holistic approach to knowledge and skill transfer.

In the past, there have also been a few initiatives to develop collaborative ventures between expatriates and local investors to stimulate investment. But again, these have mostly been of an ad hoc nature. Some state governments in India have initiated measures to facilitate contributions by expatriates to the state and local economy. The states of Kerala, Punjab, and Gujarat have, for example, created special institutional structures to liaise with their overseas population and to deal with problems faced by temporary or permanent migrants from their states. But such state government initiatives are not common. Periodically, NRIs have been encouraged to invest in India though special incentives and attractive savings schemes. Following the economic crisis of 1991, the Indian government targeted NRIs through a variety of deposit schemes to build up its foreign exchange reserves and restore financial stability. For example, the Resurgent India Bond scheme helped the government to tap

---

[35] See, http://sunsite.tus.ac.jp/asia/india/jitnet/csir/tokten.html for more details on these programmes and their implementation.

US$ 4.2 billion in 1998. The government has also made some efforts to secure the involvement of affluent NRIs in setting up industries in the post-1991 period. However, most of these efforts have lacked an underlying framework and philosophy in dealing with skilled migration. The general consensus is that India has not effectively exploited its Diaspora for investment, as is evident from the fact that to date FDI by overseas Indians accounts for less than US$ 0.5 billion a year, or less than 10 percent of total FDI in the country.

On balance, the Indian government has not really been very effective in reaping the gains from skilled migration, whether temporary or permanent, whether involving overseas expatriates or returnees, to get technology, bring in foreign capital and expertise, facilitate business contacts, and stimulate research and development. It has also not been that effective in implementing the special incentives and schemes offered to this target group, due to problems with institutional mechanisms, follow up, and governance. Corruption, bureaucracy, and lack of administrative follow up or tracking mechanisms are among the most common complaints of overseas Indians who are interested in contributing to the Indian economy.

Sector-specific approaches to skilled migration

The Indian government's approach towards skilled migration has varied across sectors and also over time, reflecting both brain gain and brain drain considerations. This sector-specific approach is evident from the cases of the IT and health sectors.

IT sector

In recognition of the important role played by the IT sector in terms of employment and export earnings, and the significance of cross border movement of professionals for India's IT sector, the Indian government has on the whole tried to facilitate the temporary migration of Indian IT workers to other markets. Its liberal position towards migration of knowledge workers is also evident from the various incentives it has given the software export segment through tax breaks, setting up of export processing zones and software technology parks with single window clearance for investment approvals. The setting up of the National IT Task Force and the recent establishment of a separate Ministry of Information Technology to promote the growth of the IT sector and of software exports, including on-site services, also reflect the government's general support of manpower based exports in this sector.

The government has also been proactive in supporting the industry lobby for greater market access for Indian software professionals in bilateral negotiations with important destination countries like the US and in multilateral negotiations such as the mode 4 discussions under the General Agreement on Trade in Services. For instance, the government has endorsed the industry position on quicker and simpler procedures for issuance of work permits and visas, on removal of wage parity requirements, on greater transparency in labour certification requirements, greater inter-firm and inter-project mobility for on-site professionals, and on exemption from social security taxes. India's mode 4 and Service Provider Visa proposal under the GATS is largely driven by the interests of its IT industry. One of the most important features of the recently signed Indo-Singapore Comprehensive Economic Cooperation Agreement is the facilitation of temporary movement of Indian professionals to Singapore, through modification of requirements concerning equivalent wages, a change which will benefit Indian IT professionals in particular.

The government has also made limited attempts in recent years to retain IT talent in the country, mainly through the educational system, in collaboration with industry associations. For instance, there is an Indian expatriate investment outreach plan that is being executed by the National Association of Software Services Companies (NASSCOM) in association with Indian Universities. Under this plan, graduates (especially in the IT and technical sectors) are appealed to stay back and develop their skills in India and to not leave for foreign destinations. This plan is targeted at IT graduates with entrepreneurial proclivity who are urged to commence their ventures in India. Thus the education sector is being used to retain talent, with NASSCOM helping to set up IT focused courses and universities to enable skill development in India and meet the growing demand for IT workers in India. Indian Institutes of Information Technology (IIITs) have been set up in several cities in India, either as joint initiatives between the government and the IT industry or solely as government initiatives. The IIITs give computer software engineering degrees and also conduct short term courses, thus producing degree holders and also training professionals and industry sponsored candidates in short duration courses.[36] In many parts of the country, particularly in the South, state governments have supported the establishment of private training institutions through provision of physical infrastructure. Such government support to promote training and education in the IT sector is in large part a response to the industry's need for a

---

[36] See, http://www.eninteractive.com/tiki-print.php?page=Why+Choose+India for details.

continued stream of low cost and high quality IT workers if it is to remain cost competitive in providing on-site and offshore professional services.[37] Thus, it is a step to enable continued provision of manpower-based exports in this sector, while also ensuring that such outflows do not hurt the industry in the long run.

Talent in the IT and engineering sectors is also being retained and attracted by the growth in offshore development centers and the shift away from on-site to offshore provision of services. Although this trend is mainly driven by market forces, the government is indirectly supporting this shift in mode of service delivery by facilitating the establishment of offshore development centers in India, and by encouraging more higher value outsourcing, such as research, development, and analytical services to India. Some initiatives have been launched in this context to encourage FDI by overseas Indian IT professionals under the guidance of a High Level Committee on the Indian Diaspora.[38] Efforts are under way to tap overseas Diaspora networks such as The Indus Entrepreneur (TiE) and the International Association of Scientists and Engineers and Technologists of Bharatiya Origin in IT, for financial, technical, and organizational support to develop the IT and BPO sectors. However, such efforts are still at a preliminary stage and are few in number. Moreover, overseas as well as returning Indian entrepreneurs in the IT sector have cited difficulties in investing in India, due to bureaucratic hurdles in receiving investment clearances and approvals, inadequacies in supporting infrastructure, lack of institutional capacity at the government level, disconnect in policy intentions and their implementation between the central and state governments, and corruption and governance problems. But all these initiatives are essentially indirect ways of attracting and retaining talent, by developing the domestic industry and creating conducive working conditions at home. However, there is no explicit policy per se to attract knowledge workers back to India or to facilitate their integration into the domestic sector, unlike the case of countries like Taiwan and Korea which have actively wooed their IT workers through special incentives and privileges.

---

[37] However, questions can be raised about the quality and standards of many of these training institutions. The government has not made any concerted efforts to regulate training standards or to ensure that basic educational infrastructure requirements are met in these private institutes.

[38] See, Gupta (2002). More discussion on the recommendations of the High Level Committee on the Indian Diaspora is provided in the last section of this paper.

Health sector

The government's approach towards skilled migration in India's health sector has been largely guided by the concern over brain drain. In the past, the Indian government has taken some steps to discourage overseas movement of Indian health care personnel, chiefly for doctors. These steps date back to the 1960s. In 1969, the government banned the ECFMG examination in the country. Those interested in taking the exam would have to take it in other countries. The government also stipulated that doctors going to the UK and the US for further training would have to obtain a no-objection certificate declaring that the training was essential for developing the country's health care system. In addition, the government has not taken any steps to sign mutual recognition agreements with key markets like the US and the UK. Existing mutual recognition agreements are with countries in Africa, the Middle East, Central Asia, and in the region, where migration occurs mostly on a contractual, short-term basis. Thus, the overall approach has been to discourage the permanent outflow of service providers. However, steps such as the ECFMG ban in the country have not been successful in stemming outflows as Indian medical students have circumvented this ban by taking the exam in neighbouring countries like Thailand.[39] There have also been proposals to require a period of service or payback by those who have received medical education at government expense, before they can emigrate from the country. But such proposals have not been implemented.

There has also not been any concerted effort to attract health care providers back to the country or to help reintegrate returning health care providers into the sector. Such steps have, however, been taken by individual hospitals and institutions, which are the main employers for returning health care providers. These include schemes such as the "fee for service" programme instituted specially by the Apollo group of hospitals for returnees. Under this programme, returning doctors receive an equity stake in the hospital and receive not only their own consultation fees but also a part of the billing operations, thus enabling them to build a sense of ownership with the hospital while also helping to raise funds. Apollo also offers returnees a "guarantee money" program, which is valid for a one-year period, during which time the doctors do not have to worry about getting enough patients and so can use the time to integrate themselves into the system and build their own practice and network.[40]

---

[39] Ganguly (2003).

[40] Ibid 37.

There has, however, been some effort since the opening up of the economy in the 1990s, to attract investment by the Indian Diaspora in the health sector. Since 1996, hospitals and diagnostic centres have been accorded automatic approval for foreign equity participation of up to 51 percent. Investments by non resident Indian or migrant Indian investors have been given further special concessions, including automatic approval for investments of up to 100 percent foreign equity participation and exemption from import duties if at least 25 percent of the patients are offered free treatment. The recent report of the High Level Committee on Indian Diaspora, 2000 notes that NRIs and persons of Indian origin have to be targeted for developing tertiary health care services in the country, as neither the public nor the domestic private sector has the necessary resources to undertake such investment. However, surveys of NRI investors and returning professionals in India's healthcare sector indicate that the government has not done enough to create a supportive environment. Returning doctors cite problems in implementing investment projects in the health sector due to bureaucracy and corruption at the state government level, even after receiving clearance and approval from the investment authorities. There is also no specific development board or council which can facilitate the process of investment in this sector, such as by supplying information and helping with clearances and approvals. The government has also not given any special incentives in the form of subsidized land and infrastructure facilities to encourage investment directed at underserved areas. Entrepreneurs (and returning doctors) also cite problems with existing labour laws and poor quality and availability of trained support staff, which make it difficult for such establishments to function efficiently.[41]

Overall, the government has not had a holistic approach to addressing migration and its associated benefits or costs. While it has taken some steps to impede labour outflows in the health sector, these have had little effect. There have been some steps to encourage movements on a short-term basis under contracts with developing country hospitals and governments. There has been an attempt to attract investments by the Diaspora, but without the necessary administrative and institutional support to facilitate this process. Incentives for return and reintegration into the labour market have been decentralized in nature and in the private sector, with no efforts in this regard by the government. The government has also failed to address the public-private balance in the health care system.

---

[41] Based on survey results in Ganguly (2003).

Greater market segmentation has resulted from return migration as well as the emergence of corporate hospitals established by former migrants. Nor has the government really tried to use the private sector to meet larger public health needs. Any efforts in the latter regard have been mainly voluntary on the part of private sector entities.

Recent government initiatives concerning skilled migration [42]

There has been a gradual shift in the Indian government's approach to skilled migration and the potential of its non-resident population, since the opening up of the Indian economy. The underlying perception of skilled migration as constituting "brain drain" is changing to one of "brain circulation". This shift in perception is largely due to the various positive contributions made by non-resident Indians and returning Indians to sectors like IT, BPO, and healthcare, some of which were discussed earlier. Recently, the Indian government has made explicit efforts to encourage Diaspora participation in the country, by streamlining investment procedures for them, consulting with them on technology and education policies, and by creating networks and institutional mechanisms to tap their human and financial capital more effectively.

Status of skilled migrants

The first of these initiatives was in March 1999, with the launching of the People of Indian Origin (PIO) Card by the Ministry of Home Affairs. The aim was to reinforce the emotional bonds of Indians who have made other countries their homes, but who now wish to renew their ties with their land of origin. [43] Persons of Indian origin up to the fourth generation settled anywhere in the world, except for a few specified countries, are eligible to avail themselves this facility. The foreign spouse of a citizen of India or PIO is also covered under the scheme. This scheme entails a host of facilities to PIOs, which were generally open to Non-Resident Indians (NRIs). For instance, PIO Card holders would get facilities for acquisition, holding, transfer and disposal of immovable properties in India, except agricultural/plantation properties, admission of children in educational institutions in India under the general category

---

[42] Discussion of government policy is based on an unpublished note by the Protectors of Emigrants, Ministry of Labour, Government of India and various articles on the recently set up High Level Committee on the Indian Diaspora and various online articles.

[43] According to estimates, the NRI population is about 6.7 millions and that of PIOs is around 15 millon. Around 2.35 lakh applications are expected for the PIO Card. See, C. Bhat, "India and the Indian Diaspora", and C. Bhat, K. Laxmi Narayan, S. Sahoo, "Indian Diaspora: A Brief Overview", Centre for Study of Indian Diaspora, University of Hyderabad.

quota for NRIs, various housing schemes of Life Insurance Corporation of India, state governments and other government agencies. PIO Card holders would not need to get visas to visit India or to register with the Foreigner's Registration Officer if their period of stay does not exceed 180 days (on a continuous basis). Also, by investing US$ 310, PIOs can secure a multiple entry visa permit for 10 years.

In September 2000, the Ministry of External Affairs constituted a High Level Committee on the Indian Diaspora. The role of this committee was to examine the role of PIOs and NRIs in India, the rights and facilities to be extended to them in India, and to recommend a broad and flexible policy framework to encourage their participation in the Indian economy. Specifically, the terms of reference of the committee were:

(1) To review the status of PIOs and NRIs in the context of the Constitutional Provisions;

(2) Examine laws and rules applicable to them, both in India and the countries of their residence;

(3) Study the characteristics, aspirations, attitudes, requirements, strengths and weaknesses of the Indian Diaspora and its expectations from India;

(4) Study the role PIOs and NRIs could play in the economic, social and technological development of India; and

(5) Examine the current regime governing the travel and stay of PIOs and investments by PIOs in India.

The aim was to benefit from the network of migrants abroad and to given them a greater say in the country's economic and political decision making process.

The High Level Committee examined major issues pertaining to the Indian Diaspora, such as culture, education, media, economic development, health, science and technology, philanthropy, and dual citizenship. Based on this study, it brought out a report in January 2002 in which it recommended measures to forge a mutually beneficial relationship with NRIs and PIOs and to facilitate their interaction and participation in India's economic development, in an institutionalized manner. Some of the recommendations included: (1) charging a lower fee for the PIO Card but for a shorter validity of 10 years (rather than 20 years of validity for a fee of US$ 1000); (2) observation of *Pravasi Bharatiya Divas (Overseas Indians Day)* on January 9th of every year (the day Mahatma Gandhi returned to India from South Africa) in India and abroad, to recognize and appreciate the role of the Indian Diaspora in the promotion of India's interest; and (3) the institution of Pravasi Bharatiya Samman Awards for eminent PIOs and NRIs. The report also suggested that the Central and state governments remove all obstacles for promoting philanthropic and voluntary or welfare activities of NGOs that the members of Indian Diaspora wish to pursue in India.[44]

On the controversial issue of dual citizenship, the Committee made significant recommendations. Demand for dual citizenship had been made by the Indian community in North America and a few other advanced countries for many years, in order to facilitate investments, trade, tourism, and philanthropic contributions by NRIs in India. The High Level Committee recommended issuing of 'dual citizenship' after taking appropriate safeguards pertaining to India's security concerns, besides carrying out necessary amendments in the Citizenship Act of 1955. (According to the Citizenship Act of 1955, an Indian forfeits the Indian citizenship when he/she acquires the citizenship of a foreign country.) Based on these recommendations, the Citizenship (Amendment) Bill was passed by the Indian Parliament in December 2003 and the Citizenship Amendment Act was passed into law by the Indian government in January 2004. The Act grants Overseas Citizenship of India to PIOs from 16 countries and for those Indian citizens who choose to acquire citizenship of any of these 16 countries at a later date.[45] However, it denies holders of such dual citizenship any participation in electoral process or civil services in India. The philosophy guiding the granting of dual citizenship is that this would help India maintain its connection with emigrants, free up movement between the 16 countries and India, enabling more spontaneous feedback/transfers that promote economic development and in the long term possibly inhibiting migration and helping attract back skilled Indian migrants.[46] There have, however, been some criticisms of the dual citizenship act, mainly on the grounds that it is available to PIOs from only selected countries and that it does not extend voting, civil participation, and public employment rights.[47] Whether or not this policy encourages emigrants to make more trips to India and to start business ventures in India, remains to be seen.

---

[44] See, Employment News, Vol.XXVII No.38. New Delhi (21-27 December 2002).

[45] http://www.murthy.com/news/n_duacit.html , "India Passes Bill on Dual Citizenship for Certain PIOs", (Dec 6, 2003).

[46] http://www.globalpolicy.org/nations/citizen/2003/0118india.htm, Prashanth Lakhilal, "Dual Citizenship Greeted With Mixed Feelings" *India Tribune*, (January, 18, 2003).

[47] http://www.murthy.com/news/n_duacit.html , "India Passes Bill on Dual Citizenship for Certain PIOs", (Dec 6, 2003).

Networking

In line with one of the recommendations of the High Level Diaspora Committee, in January 2003, the government celebrated the Overseas Indian's Day (Pravasi Bharatiya Divas-PBD day) for the first time, to express its gratitude to Indian migrants based abroad for their contributions to the economy and to motivate them to participate more actively in India's future development. The PBD day was also held in January 2004. Over 2,500 delegates including 1,500 overseas Indians from 61 countries participated in each year.[48] Eminent Indians from all over the world, including Nobel Laureates, business leaders, scientists and innovators, academicians, and political leaders attended the conference. Representatives at the highest level from the government of India, including the President, Vice President, Prime Minister, Deputy Prime Minister, Cabinet Ministers, and Chief Ministers from different states interacted with the delegates. The third PBD day was held in Mumbai from January 7-9, 2005, in collaboration with the Federation of Indian Chambers of Commerce and Industry (FICCI). There were discussions on Education, Knowledge-Based Industry, Science and Technology, Healthcare, Rural Development, Ethnic Media and Entertainment, NRIs in the Gulf, Finance, and Tourism, as well as interactive parallel sessions with state governments. The Indian Prime Minister and President conferred special awards to expatriate Indians to recognize their contributions.[49]

Some institutional initiatives have also been taken to oversee work relating to the Indian Diaspora. In line with the High Level Committee's recommendations, an autonomous and empowered body, similar to India's Planning Commission and a Standing Committee of Parliament have been instituted. The latter would introduce interested Diaspora members to the country's Parliamentary procedures and practices and would serve as a means to reach out to influential persons in the Diaspora and convene biennial conventions of PIO Parliamentarians. Apart from these institutional initiatives, the government through the University Grants Commission (one of the chief regulatory agencies in India's education system) has set up a Centre at the University of Hyderabad to carry out research on the Indian Diaspora.[50]

---

[48] See, http://www.cgidubai.com/press57.htm, "The Third Pravasi Bharatiya Divas", Mumbai, January 7-9, 2005.

[49] See, http://indiandiaspora.nic.in/The%20Pravasi%20Bharatiya%20Divas.doc, for details on this event.

[50] See, C. Bhat, "India and the Indian Diaspora", and C. Bhat, K. Laxmi Narayan, S. Sahoo, "Indian Diaspora: A Brief Overview", Centre for Study of Indian Diaspora, University of Hyderabad.

Special initiatives are being taken in the area of science and technology in view of the large pool of Indian science and technology professionals overseas. The objective is to strengthen networking with Scientists and Technologists of Indian Origin (STIOs) based abroad, including persons in industries, research laboratories, universities and scientific departments located in various countries as well as those successfully working as entrepreneurs in technology intensive business and as venture capitalists.[51] As part of this effort, the Ministry of Science and Technology has set up a special website for "S&T" professionals of the Indian Diaspora as part of the overall Diaspora initiatives of the Ministry of External Affairs. This website aims at tapping the contributions of STIOs abroad for:

(1) Human resources and research capacity development to augment collaboration for strengthening Indian education, research, and human resource capabilities in frontier areas of basic sciences and cutting edge technologies;

(2) Technology entrepreneurship to enhance India's competence in this area, utilize venture financing and mentoring the younger generation for creating wealth from knowledge;

(3) Establishing India as an international science center by catalyzing the participation of Indian scientists and institutions in major international science projects and in programs of major advanced research facilities abroad;

(4) Establishing India as a global research and development platform as a preferred R&D outsourcing destination; and

(5) Alma mater relationship to connect alumni abroad with their alma mater for purposeful and sustainable relationships.

The Department of Science and Technology is taking steps to interact with Indian academia, research institutes, laboratories, industry, and enterprises, to facilitate collaboration, disseminate information on specific science and technology institutions and programs, and opportunities that may be of interest to STIOs based abroad.

---

51 For further details on the initiatives regarding scientists and technology professionals, see http://stio.nic.in, Government of India, "S&T Professionals of Indian Diaspora".

Conclusion

It is apparent that the Indian government is increasingly trying to realize the benefits of its huge overseas Diaspora population through investments, technology and skill transfer, networking and collaboration. It is still too early to assess the impact of such initiatives. There is, however, no concerted and direct effort to attract back talent. All attempts in that direction have been indirect and long-term in nature. The main focus is on attracting Diaspora investment rather than on return and retention.

Overall, the Indian government's policy on skilled migration is undergoing an important change. But it is at an incipient stage, perhaps more at the conceptual and public relations level rather than at the practical implementation level. Surveys of return migrants and Diaspora members suggest that much more needs to be done to address many of the institutional and governance related problems faced by returning Indians and Diaspora investors. Economic liberalization and growing employment and business opportunities are still the main forces driving return migration to India. Only time will tell to what extent these forces can be aided by the recent government initiatives.

References

Baru, Rama V., *Private Healthcare in India: Social Characteristics and Trends*, Sage Publications, New Delhi, 1998.

Bhat, C. "India and the Indian Diaspora", Centre for Study of Indian Diaspora, University of Hyderabad.

—, K. Laxmi Narayan, S. Sahoo, "Indian Diaspora: A Brief Overview", Centre for Study of Indian Diaspora, University of Hyderabad.

Chanda, R., "Movement of Services Suppliers and India: A Case Study of the IT and Health Sectors", Working Paper No. 206, Indian Institute of Management, Bangalore, April 2003. Based on paper written for the UNDP's Asia Pacific Trade and Human Development Report.

—, "Movement of Natural Persons from South Asian Countries", written for the Consumer Unity Trust Society, Jaipur, September 2004.

Commander, S., M. Kangasniemi, and A. Winters, "The Brain Drain: Curse or Boon? A Survey of the Literature", Report prepared for the CEPR/NBER/SNS, International Seminar on International Trade, Stockholm, May 24-25, 2002.

Commander, S., R. Chanda, M. Kangasniemi, and A. Winters, "Must Skilled Migration be a Brain Drain?: Evidence from the Indian Software Industry", London Business School, November 2004.

Commonwealth Secretariat, "Human Resource Development for Health", unpublished draft report, 1997.

D'Sami, B., Migration in India, unpublished note, Chennai, 2001.

Economic Survey (2000-01), Ministry of Finance, Government of India, New Delhi, 2001.

Economic Times, "Lure of the Home Turf Brings back NRI Doctors", Bangalore edition, April 6, 2001.

——, "Boom Time for Indian Nurses as US Open up", Bangalore, May 4, 2004.

Employment News, Vol.XXVII No.38. New Delhi, 21-27 December 2002.

Findlay, A., "From Brain Exchange to Brain Gain: Policy Implications for the UK and Recent Trends in Skilled Migration from Developing Countries", International Migration Papers No. 43, International Migration Programme, ILO, Geneva, December 2001.

Ganguly, D., draft note on "Barriers to Movement of Natural Persons from India in the US", prepared for the Indian Council for Research on International Economic Relations under the Ratan Tata Trust funded project on Movement of Natural Persons, July 2004.

——, *Return Migration and Diaspora Investment: Case Study of the Indian IT and Health Sectors*, doctoral dissertation, Indian Institute of Management, Bangalore, July 2003.

Gish, O., *Doctor Migration and World Health: The Impact of the International Demand for Doctors on Health Services in Developing Countries*, G. Bell & Sons, London, 1971.

Government of India, Report of the High Level Committee on the Indian Diaspora, Non Resident Indians and Persons of Indian Origin Division, Ministry of External Affairs, New Delhi, 2002.

——, unpublished note on emigration policy, Protectors of Emigrants, Ministry of Labour, New Delhi.

Gupta, D.B., "The Role of NRIs and PIOs in Health Sector Development", mimeo, Paper prepared for the Ministry of External Affairs and the Department of Health, Government of India, New Delhi, 2002.

Gupta, I. and B. Goldar (2001), "Commercial Presence in the Hospital Sector under GATS: A Case Study of India", mimeo paper for WHO/SEARO, New Delhi.

Hindu, "Malaysia expresses regret over ill treatment of Indians", Bangalore, March 15, 2003.

Hindu Business Line, "Indian IT pros heading back on home attraction", December 17, 2004.

http://www.scalabrini.asn.au/atlas/india99.htm

http://www.scalabrini.asn.au/atlas/india00.htm

http://www.cic.gc.ca/english/pub/facts2002/immigration/immigration_5.html

http://www.cic.gc.ca/english/pub/facts2002/workers/workers_6.html

http://www.gic.ca/english/monitor/issue05/02-immigrants.html#table2

http://www.gic.ca/english/monitor/issue05/03-workers.html

http://www.canadaimmigrants.com/statistics.asp

http://indiandiaspora.nic.in/The%20Pravasi%20Bharatiya%20Divas.doc

http://stio.nic.in, Government of India, "S&T Professionals of Indian Diaspora".

http://www.cgidubai.com/press57.htm, "The Third Pravasi Bharatiya Divas", Mumbai, January 7-9, 2005.

http://www.bpoindia.org/news/2003.shtml, "India Beckons".

http://www.sharedxpertise.org/modules.php?file=article&name=News&op=mod-load&sid=1327 , "Outsourcing sparks reverse migration".

http://www.business-standard.com/general/storypage_test.php?&autono=174013

http://news.indiainfo.com/2004/02/11/1102jobs.html, "Foreign pros increasingly seeking jobs in India", Wednesday, February 11, 2004.

http://www.murthy.com/news/n_duacit.html, "India Passes Bill on Dual Citizenship for Certain PIOs", December 6, 2003.

http://www.globalpolicy.org/nations/citizen/2003/0118india.htm, Prashanth Lakhilal, "Dual Citizenship Greeted With Mixed Feelings" India Tribune, January, 18, 2003.

http://sunsite.tus.ac.jp/asia/india/jitnet/csir/tokten.html

http://www.eninteractive.com/tiki-print.php?page=Why+Choose+India

http://www.sipa.org/about/about.cfm

Hunger, U., "The "Brain Gain" Hypothesis: Third World Elites in Industrialized Countries and Socioeconomic Development in their Home Country", Working Paper No. 47, Center for Comparative Immigration Studies, University of Muenster, Germany, January, 2002.

ILO, International Labour Migration Data Base (ILM), Emigration Country-Stocks and Ouflows of Employed Nationals, Pakistan Tables 11 and 13, 1986-2001, Geneva.

ILO, "The Indian Software Industry" in *Labour in the New Economy: Case of the Indian Software Labour Market*, Geneva, 2002, pp. 22-62.

India Today, "The Diaspora: How do we get them to Help", New Delhi, October 14, 2002.

—, "Special Report on the Diaspora", New Delhi, January 13, 2003.

International Organization for Migration, World Migration 2003: Managing Migration Challenges and Responses for People on the Move, Volume 2, World Migration Report Series, IOM, Geneva, 2003.

Kapur, D., "Diasporas and Technology Transfer", *Journal of Human Development*, 2 (2), 2001, pp. 265-84.

—, "Indian Diaspora as a Strategic Asset", Economic and Political Weekly, Mumbai, February 1, 2003, pp. 445-51.

Khadria, B., "Skilled Labour Migration from Developing Countries: Study on India", International Migration Papers No. 49, International Migration Programme, ILO, Geneva, June 2002.

—, *The Migration of Knowledge Workers: Second Generation Effect of India's Brain Drain*, Sage Publications, New Delhi, 1999.

Leishemba, R., S. Neogi, S. Nair, "India shines for job seeking foreigners too", Financial Express, Sunday, February 1, 2004. http://in.jobstreet.com/aboutus/mreports43.htm.

Lowell, B. Lindsay and A. Findlay, "Migration of Highly Skilled Persons from Developing Countries: Impact and Policy Responses", Synthesis Report, International

Migration Papers No. 44, International Migration Programme, ILO, Geneva, December 2001.

Martin, P., "Highly Skilled Labour Migration: Sharing the Benefits", International Institute for Labour Studies, Geneva, May 2003.

Mejia, A., H. Pizurki, and E. Royston, *Physician and Nurse Migration: Analysis and Policy Implications*, WHO, Geneva, 1979.

Meyer, Jean-Baptiste and M. Brown, "Scientific Diasporas: A New Approach to the Brain Drain, prepared for the *World Conference on Science*, UNESCO - ICSU Budapest, Hungary, June 26-July 1, 1999.

Migration Research Unit, "International Migration and the UK", Draft Final Report to the UK Home Office, London, 2001.

Nair, "Indian IT Pros are Homeward Bound", December 1, 2004.

NASSCOM, *The IT Industry in India: Strategic Review 2002*, New Delhi, 2002.

Nielson, J. And O. Cattaneo, "Current Regimes for the Temporary Movement of Service Providers: Case Studies of Australia and the United States" in Mattoo and Carzaniga (eds.), *Moving People to Deliver Services*, World Bank and Oxford University Press, Washington DC, 2003.

"NRI's from UK, Canada to help India retain BPO edge", Thursday, September 30 2004.

Oberoi, P., "The new trend of 2004 – Indian Americans returning back to India to lead US and Indian Corporations in the outsourcing market", July 21, 2004. http://www.indiadaily.com/editorial/07-21c-04.asp

OECD, "Service Providers on the Move: Labour Mobility and the WTO General Agreement on Trade in Services", Policy Brief, OECD Observer, Paris, August 2003.

—, "International Mobility of the Highly Skilled", Paris, 2002.

Ribeiro, J, "Indian diaspora helped outsourcing movement", IDG News Service, October 04, 2004. http://www.infoworld.com/article/04/10/04/HNindiandiaspora_1.html

Saxenian, A. *Local and Global Networks of Immigrant Professionals in Silicon Valley*, Public Policy Institute of California, Berkeley, 2002.

SOPEMI-OECD, *Trends in International Migration*, Paris, 2001.

Sukhatme, *The Real Brain Drain*, Orient Longman, Mumbai, 1994.

UNCTAD/WHO, *International Trade in Health Services: A Development Perspective*, (ed.) Zarilli S. and C. Kinnon, Geneva, 1998.

USINS, Statistical Yearbook of the Immigration and Naturalization Service, various years.

Vertovec, S., "Transnational Networks and Skilled Labour Migration", Working Paper, WPTC, February 2002. http://www.transcomm.ox.ac.uk/working%20papers/WPTC-02-02%20Vertovec.pdf

Wickramasekara, P., "Asian Labour Migration: Issues and Challenges in an Era of Globalization", International Migration Papers No. 57, International Migration Programme, ILO, Geneva, August 2002.

List of acronyms

IT	Information Technology
BPO	Business Process Outsourcing
Nasscom	National Association of Software Services Companies
UK	United Kingdom
US	United States
AIIMS	All India Institute of Medical Sciences
IIT	Indian Institute of Technology
IIIT	Indian Institute of Information Technology
NRI	Non Resident Indian
INRIST	Interface for NRI Scientists and Technologists
CSIR	Council for Scientific and Industrial Research
PIO	Persons of Indian Origin
TOKTEN	Transfer of Knowledge through Expatriates Network
UNDP	United Nations Development Programme
R&D	Research and Development
H1-B	specialty occupation visas (in the United States)

Part III: International Relations and global talent

Competing for global talent in an Age of Turbulence

Christopher R. Counihan
and Mark J. Miller

A new theory is beginning to emerge in the study of world politics that is gaining momentum in academic circles but whose influence has not yet been felt in the examination of some of the most serious issues facing the globe today. In this increasingly influential view, called Global Governance or "GG", experts often point to the processes of international migration as one of the clearest manifestations of globalization – the rapid increase in movements of people, goods and ideas between and across sovereign states. While GG does not deny that states are at the center of the current structure of the global system and are the primary actors on the world stage, it holds that this state-centric structure exists along side a developing multi-centric global structure. By emphasizing this split, this bifurcation, of the global political system, GG gives equal priority to the non-state actors that appear to be increasingly influential and powerful – actors ranging from global social movements to multinational corporations, from non-governmental organizations to terrorist groups. The tensions that emerge from this uneasy coexistence gives rise to the turbulence that defines the current age of world politics. In the worldview of GG, both state and non-state actors participate equally in the mutual construction of the political, economic, cultural landscapes within which they operate. States are just one of several types of actors which help to create the structures which influence the actions of the actors in the system and that are in turn formed by the actions of those actors in a continual and interactive process of creation and re-creation. While many GG scholars have used examples drawn from migration studies, there have not been many migration studies that have been built upon the framework provided by this new paradigm of world politics.

We believe using a Global Governance framework to study highly skilled migration will allow us to more accurately describe the phenomenon revealed in the data collected from recent studies in this area and will give us a deeper understanding of the impact that this phenomenon has on the workings of the global system. In recent years, scholars investigating highly skilled migration have made great strides in increasing our knowledge about the scale and scope of these vitally important, yet difficult to perceive, patterns of movement. Beginning primarily from an intuition that skilled international migration was an important process creating and created by the global system, scholars in this field have gone on to build an impressive storehouse of information. The quantity and quality of this data is especially remarkable in light of the difficulties often cited in accumulating these figures. These are real difficulties arising as much from the measures that states use to define both who qualifies as a "highly skilled migrant" and what qualifies as "migration" as they are derived from the design of institutions and statistical systems intended to capture the large scale movements of relatively low-skilled people rather than the smaller flows of the highly skilled. Despite these difficulties and limitations, those studying highly skilled migration have been able to develop a solid empirical base from which to build a more complete understanding of the movement of the highly talented across the globe. This empirical tradition is seen a source of strengths for all fields of migration studies, "while no 'grand theory' of international migration has emerged, nor is it likely to, the empirical tradition, still strong, has a better base on which to build" (Gould 1988, p. 382). Yet while we appreciate the value of this empirical tradition, we believe that there is much to be gained by placing this empirical data within the emerging framework of Global Governance theory.

Emerging conceptions of Global Governance

For the majority of the writings in the area of highly skilled migration, the phenomenon has been cast largely within a broadly Liberal conception of a global political and economic system, particularly within a framework of neoliberal institutionalism. In this state-centric conception of the global system, nation-states are presented as the central actors shaping the global system, with individuals and groups acting strategically to maximize their self-interests by rationally weighing the costs and benefits of alternative routes of action in anticipation of the possible responses by other actors in the system. While this worldview exists in the deep background of most studies in skilled international migration, it is often unarticulated, existing mainly in the form of assumptions referred to, but left largely unexplored. When engaging directly in the articulation of theory, the majority of highly skilled migration scholars tend to confine themselves to the realm of mid- and low-range theories. Organizational decision-making, individual career paths, internal labor markets of MNCs, personal and employment networks, channels of migration, and other mid- to low-level processes have become the focus of most of the writings in highly skilled migration. While this focus on the "nuts and bolts" of highly skilled migration has allowed writers to develop a clearer understanding of the details of the movement of talent around the globe, it has done so at the detriment of the development of a larger understanding of the relevance of the migration of talent to the global political, economic and social system.

The exception to this tendency of the majority towards low- to mid-range theory has been found in the writings of a small but prolific group of skilled international migration scholars focusing on the role played by highly skilled migrants in the creation and maintenance of a worldwide network of "global cities" that are believed to be the command and control centers at the heart of a new international division of labor. While investigating this network of global cities, these scholars have mined vast fields of statistics to compile some of the strongest empirical data on the phenomenon of highly skilled migration. Partially due to the inability of state-centric perspectives to fully capture the complexities and wide ranges of actors involved in the movement of talent around the globe, these scholars have made a conscious break with the unspoken assumptions upon which most scholars in this field have based their studies. Instead of interpreting the movement of the highly skilled within the structures of a neoliberal global system, these scholars have explored highly skilled migration as a means to investigate the larger structures that they see operating in the global system. However, this overarching vision of a network of global cities and the new international division of labor does not come without its own, also often unspoken and unexplored, assumptions. This global cities thesis entails the tacit acceptance of a series of normative assumptions that, among other things, purports to know which of the actors in the system stands on the "right" and which stands on the "wrong" side of History. These normative assumptions have cast these highly skilled migrants as the new bourgeoisie, the latest incarnation of a globally cosmopolitan Capitalist class. While this assumption may or may not be accurate, it is problematic in that it gives readers of these studies the impression of an inherent bias against highly skilled migrants, thereby casting doubts upon the objectivity of these scholarly studies.

Despite their shortcomings, both groups of scholars, the neoliberal majority and this small but prolific left-leaning group, have succeeded in creating a wealth of empirical data from which we can build a deeper understanding of highly skilled migration. Despite these achievements, however, we believe that both of these groups have been stymied in their quest for understanding by the theoretical frameworks that they employ. The neoliberal framework is held back by its overemphasis on the actions of states while it is simultaneously undermined by its overly rationalist conceptions of decision-making processes. While the global cities framework is heavily burdened with overarching normative and teleological assumptions that threaten to obscure rather than illuminate the subject of our study. We advocate replacing these theoretical requirements that see states as the primary actors in the global system and wherein economic models are seen as accurate vision of the procedures that individuals and groups use to make decisions. Instead, we advocate embracing a broader range of purposeful, independent actors on the world stage engaging in the mutual construction of social reality, as we believe that such a GG perspective will allow us to gain a deeper understanding of this vitally important facet of the current global system.

We agree with Findlay and Gould when they declared that "a new framework is required for the analysis of contemporary skilled international migration" (Findlay & Gould 1989, p. 5). However, while some scholars have sought to utilize a new theoretical framework drawn from the Marxian structures of global cities and a new international division of labor, we seek to take the study of highly skilled migration in a different direction. We seek to offer a new framework drawn from the emerging theories of Global Governance, based on a new understanding of the structure of the global political system – Rosenau's spheres of authority operating in an Age of Turbulence – and a view of intersubjective reality (a "reality" that exists somewhere between the subjective realm of ideas and the objective realm of material things) based on the social theories of Constructivism. A turn towards the rapidly emerging theories of Global Governance is especially warranted in this field as these new theories embrace the cultural, social, political, and economic complexities that surround the investigation of highly skilled migration while avoiding both the state-centric views favored by traditional theories of International Relations as well as the normative and teleological biases of Marxist analysis.

One of the creators and greatest thinkers of GG, James Rosenau, structures this new framework for understanding Global Governance around a force that he terms "fragmegration", the organizing principle of the Age of Turbulence in which we live. The turbulence of our day arises out of the dual existence of a relatively weakening state-centric understanding of global politics as it overlaps with an emerging multi-centric structure wherein non-state actors are beginning to take a more prominent role in our understanding of world politics. Rosenau's organizing principle of fragmegration – an admittedly ungraceful term to denote the even more inelegant process it describes – is the combination of the simultaneous centripetal forces of globalizing integration operating along side centrifugal forces of an ever more localizing fragmentation. The very awkwardness of this term emphasizes the inherent "messiness" of these two concurrent and opposing processes that are actively shaping today's global system. Through the dynamics of fragmegration, the global system is moving in two directions at once – towards an ever more tightly integrated and interdependent global structure on one hand, while it is simultaneously fragmenting apart into a myriad of fiercely independent units – a process that is creating a new landscape of authority (Rosenau 1983). Rosenau uses the example of highly skilled migration as an illustration of the ways in which there has been a revolution in the skill levels of individuals in the face of the challenges wrought by this Age of Turbulence:

> "Another insightful illustration of the extent to which fragmegration has occurred in the social realm is provided by the changing practices through which families adjust to overseas assignments. Rather than children being left 'home' to go to school, today the family joins the breadwinner on his or her foreign assignment. In effect, for such people the meaning of 'home' has changed. It is anywhere the occupation of parents take them, while the meaningful, long-term 'home' to which deep emotional ties are attached remains only 'a second away in communications and a day away in reality'." (Rosenau 1997, p.110)

In line with the emphasis on the process of the mutual construction of social ("intersubjective") reality, highly skilled migration is both a carrier and a creation of fragmegration, both shaping and being shaped by the simultaneous globalizing and localizing forces at work in our turbulent global system.

The traditional "sovereignty-bound" actors found in the mental and political maps of traditional theories of International Relations are not used to organize the new landscapes of authority found in Global Governance theories. Instead, the landscape of GG is organized around spheres of authority ("SOAs"), Rosenau's conception of the place (defined in terms of geography or in terms of functional issues) where politics happens. While the landscape of the state-centric world of traditional theories of International Relations are based on the separation of territory into sovereign states through the lines drawn on our political maps, Rosenau's spheres of authority are based on the mental maps of power and compliance that individuals carry around in their heads.

> "Stated differently, instead of initially positing a world dominated by state and national governments, the new ontology [theoretical landscape] builds on the premise that the world is comprised of spheres of authority (SOAs) that are not necessarily consistent with the division of territorial space and are subject to considerable flux. They are distinguished by the presence of actors who can evoke compliance when exercising authority as they engage in the activities that delineate the sphere. Authority, in other words, is conceived not as a possession of actors, nor as embedded in roles. Authority is relational; its existence can only be observed when it is both exercised and complied with." (Rosenau 1999, p. 295)

In these spheres of authority, states can be (and often are) the dominant actors shaping and controlling the processes that take place within them. However, the "actors who can evoke compliance" are not necessarily limited to nation-states. Spheres of authority can also be created by the interaction of actors outside of, above, or below the sovereign state. The phenomenon of highly skilled migration is an ideal example of such a sphere. Skilled international migration can be thought of as a realm of action where states and their interests are one of the agents influencing the movements of highly skilled people, yet it is also a sphere wherein other authority figures play an influential, if not dominant, role in that process.

One of the results (and causes) of the fragmegration of authority that has shaped this Age of Turbulence has been the skills revolution that has occurred at the personal level in persons around the globe:

> "People have become increasingly more competent in assessing where they fit in international affairs and how their behavior can be aggregated into significant collective outcomes. Included among these newly refined skills, moreover, is an expanded capacity to focus emotionally as well as to analyze the causal sequences that sustain the course of events." (Rosenau 1999, p. 59)

This skills revolution is not just limited to the upper echelons of the social hierarchy, the key decision-makers and opinion-leaders of the global system. Instead, it extends downward to all levels of national development and through all the rungs of the labor force. The increasing complexity of the global system is not merely confined to the lives of those at the top income brackets, but extends down to the every individual on earth, as these fragmegrative dynamics touch the lives of every person. While some individuals may become "unmoored" and lose their bearings in this increasingly complex world, most individuals have been able to alter their worldviews to match the growing density and fluidity of relationships that surround and bind them to the world beyond their everyday lives. While this is an admittedly optimistic appraisal of the ability of humans to cope with the complexities of the global system, and while numerous counter-examples abound of people retreating into comforting and simplistic understandings of the world, the notion of a skills revolution remains a valuable contribution to our understanding of world politics. Highly skilled migration is an obvious illustration of the relevance of this skills revolution not just in the lives of those sent on expatriate assignments, but also in the skills transferred between expatriates and the locals with whom they interact on a daily basis.

The skills revolution is as much a cultural revolution as it is a political transformation. The social revolutions that form the backdrop for GG's conception of world politics cannot be adequately interpreted through traditional theories of International Relations. These traditional theories often do not dare to cross into the realm of social relationships unmediated by political institutions. More often than not, these relationships are said to be outside of the "proper scope of inquiry" for International Relations scholarship, residing instead within the realms of sociology and psychology. Most IR scholars prefer to limit their investigations to the level of the political and the economic, fearing to tread beyond the range of their rationalist models of human decision-making derived from economic theory. In order to move into the worldview of Global Governance, one must move into new understanding of the creation and maintenance of social realities. The social theories of Constructivism occupy the middle ground between the rationalist models of decision-making found in most theories of International Relations (including most variants of Liberalism, Realism, and Marxism) and the interpretivist viewpoints of postmodernist, poststructuralist, critical, and feminist theorists that doubt the potential for rational human behavior.

Constructivism attempts to bridge the divide between the view that it is possible to achieve an objective understanding of reality and the conviction that the differences between our subjective understandings are too wide to be overcome in such a way as to create a single, shared vision of reality. More generally, "Constructivism is the view that the manner in which the material world shapes and is shaped by human action and interaction depends on dynamic normative and epistemic interpretations of the material world" (Adler 1997, p. 322). The concept that Constructivists use to bridge the difference between objective and subjective realities is the realm of intersubjective reality; the shared understandings

265

of social realities that we loosely hold in common with those that share our social and cultural spaces. It is through this interactive process of mutually constructing intersubjective realities that common ground can be forged between the rationalist and interpretivist understandings of human behavior and meanings (Adler 1997).

Constructivist social theory is built around social "norms" as the primary organizing principle and as key to deciphering the ways in which particular groups have mutually constructed their intersubjective realities. However, these norms are not seen as a set of unchanging "givens", but rather as a set of continually evolving shared beliefs that change according to their location in time and space. Constructivists share the interpretivist's belief that people within the social groups defined by shared norms have come to see these norms as "natural" facts, as real as rocks or flesh and blood, instead of being merely "social facts, which are facts only by human agreement" (Adler 1997, p. 323). Norms become the causal variables to explain the behaviors of people, the stories that we tell ourselves to justify our actions, stories so automatic that the very process of telling them to ourselves is no longer necessary. The dynamic aspect of intersubjective reality arises out of the ongoing construction of social reality created by the interaction of agents with each other and with the structures within which they are embedded. Norms are the "rules" by which these interactions take place, but norms are not given any content by the social theories of Constructivism. Traditional theories of International Relations often define the interactions of actors in a system by the rules that the system is believed to impose on them. While Liberalism or Marxism are both deliberately normative in outlook, and while Realism tends to downplay the importance of normative considerations (thereby assuming the preferability of the status quo); Constructivism does not presuppose any set of normative assumptions. Instead, Constructivism allows the interactions of the agents at certain times and places in history to reveal the unspoken normative biases that motivate and give meaning to their actions.

Highly skilled migration, we believe, is a phenomenon that can be best understood thorough the analytic lens of Constructivist social theory. The presumption that intersubjective realities are under constant and mutual reconstruction through the actions of the agents that participate in their creation is an apt vehicle for investigating the cultural and social effects of highly skilled migration. Highly skilled migration involves the influential decision-makers and opinion-leaders of global society; it brings together individuals from a vast array of cultures and forces them to directly interact. This social interaction creates new intersubjective meanings and realities, meanings that in turn have to be continually re-negotiated and re-created by those who have participated in their creation. While many studies of highly skilled migration bring with them a particular normative perspective on the relative value of the cultures and societies that are brought together in the process of highly skilled migration, investigations based upon a Constructivist vision of social theory should not. A Constructivist vision should not present societies as static "objects", but rather expects that all social realities will be subject to constant reappraisal and reinvention. An investigation of highly skilled migration informed by Constructivism, should not see the cultural and social interaction that accompanies the migration of expertise as either a zero-sum game which contrasts the gains of one culture by the losses of the other or as a clash between cultures whose result is predetermined by the relative power positions of the two. In a Constructivist view of the cultural interaction that accompanies the process of highly skilled migration, there are no "sides" but only a constantly shifting interpretation shared by all those interacting in one particular point in history and at one location in space.

Re-imagining highly skilled migration through Global Governance

While the data that has been collected utilizing today's dominant theoretical frameworks are vital and important, we believe that they can be made more useful by reinterpreting them using the tools provided by Constructivism and Global Governance. While this may merely seem to be a case of "pouring old wine into new bottles", it is our contention that such a shift of theoretical perspective will help develop a richer understanding of the processes which drive highly skilled migration and the impacts that this phenomenon has on the current and future structure of the world political system. Old data can yield new information when placed within the context of new theoretical approaches. Scholars working from both the neoliberal and Marxian perspectives have built a strong empirical body of evidence, but we feel that these perspectives have limited our investigations of highly skilled migration due to the assumptions that are inherent in their worldviews. Forging a new framework for investigating this phenomenon will hopefully carry our knowledge of this area further towards understanding its place in the anatomy of the global system.

As an example of the value of such a new theoretical framework, consider the most commonly told "story" of the approaches that multinational corporations ("MNCs") have taken towards managing their foreign subsidiaries and their interactions with local cultures, a story told by many skilled international migration and International Business scholars. This standard narrative speaks of the evolution from a period in which multinational enterprises duplicated the then predominant imperial/colonial model to the current fashion of envisioning global corporations as utilizing a set of inter-cultural management skills. This story of the evolution of MNCs' approach to their overseas affiliates, suppliers, and customers is the story of the ways in which we have described the interaction between local cultures and the multinational corporations that have entered into these new marketplaces bringing with them foreign institutions, products and (of course) highly skilled migrants. This standard story follows a trajectory that roughly mirrors the story told by traditional IR scholars when discussing the evolution of the diplomatic histories of the Great Powers and the developing world. The traditional theories of International Relations assume a level of rationality derived from economic models of decision-making. They assume that the vast majority of behavior in world politics is strategic, goal-oriented action in which the interests of the actors are taken as givens, as a set of beliefs that are both pre-existing and well understood by those working in the name of their institution. Susan Sell describes the "mainstream analyses of international politics, neorealism and neoliberal institutionalism" as treating "interests as exogenous ... either [assuming] that ideas are a product of the structure of the system, or that ideas must be viewed in opposition to interests" (Sell 1998, p. 11), while the main leftist alternatives, "world systems theory and structural Marxism ... [both] emphasize structure over agency, neglect the role of ideas, and are indeterminate" (*ibid*, p. 12). As Constructivist social theorists have argued, however, the interests that traditional IR theorists take for granted are neither stable nor self-evident.

> "By contrast, interpretivist neoliberal theories[1] focus on the role of ideas and learning. I call it 'interpretive' because it addresses the intersubjective dimension of international politics and treats interests as endogenous. In other words, these theories pay attention to how the actors themselves interpret their circumstances. Power and interests are not 'given' but rather must be interpreted and are periodically redefined." (Sell 1998, p. 13)

As such, investigations of the impact of highly skilled migrants on local cultures informed by Constructivist social theory needs to focus on the dynamics of interaction and social learning that take place beneath the surface of the story of differentiated phases told by traditional theorists.

---

[1] Sell's term for her conception of Constructivist theory.

The prevailing story of the evolution of MNCs' approach towards their overseas affiliates, suppliers and customers is a story told in several phases that describe the changing patterns of interaction between rational actors using strategic, goal-oriented behavior to achieve their pre-existing and well understood interests. According to this standard story (as outlined in Moore & Lewis 2000), the evolution of global corporations is told in several historical periods that reflect the broader geopolitical landscape of Great Power politics and technological capabilities. Prior to the development of chartered trading companies, the multinational interests of businesses were handled primarily through trusted family members who ran satellite offices in foreign lands. The first true wave of global business began in the early 1500s with the rise of the great European chartered trading companies, such as the Dutch and English East Indies Companies, the Hudson Bay Company, and others. These charted trading companies traveled in tandem with their royal patrons supplying the mercantilist economic sinews that fleshed out the military might of the Imperial body politic. During this period, the relationship between the home office and foreign subsidiaries was a mirror of the imperial connection between metropol and colony, a decidedly master-servant relationship wherein managers of foreign subsidiaries oriented their activities exclusively towards the needs and interests of the home office.

The second wave began after the end of the Napoleonic Wars with the rise of free trade ideology, with private corporations serving as the "national champions" of their homelands. These national champions were privately established (but publicly lauded, promoted, and protected) corporations that replaced chartered trading companies at the vanguard of the global economic system. While these national champions enjoyed a special relationship with their home state, they were not state-controlled entities. As such they were left to their own devices to create a diplomatic corps of employees on nearly permanent assignment abroad in order to represent the company's interests overseas. This "foreign service" model (Gonzalez & Negandhi, 1967) of foreign subsidiary management depended upon the creation of a small, dedicated cadre of expatriate managers serving as "our man" abroad. Interactions between the home office and the overseas markets were kept to a minimum and knowledge of local conditions was contained within this narrow cadre of expatriate managers.

The third phases in the evolution of global business (Jones 1996) began as World War II ended, as the United States and U.S. companies came to dominate the economies of the "free world". This phase continued into and beyond the Sixties as Europe and Japan rebuilt and began to reassert their economic power in the global marketplace. During this phase, the story of global business portrays the interactions between local cultures and the foreign corporations who penetrated their marketplaces as attempts to "convert" local employees and populations to modern ways, towards increasing "Americanization" or towards a more broad form of "Westernization". This culturally paternalistic phase of the evolution of global business is said to have ended in the face of growing resentment that produced economic and political backlashes launched by locals against the corporations who sought to replace indigenous cultures with "foreign" ways.

In the fourth phase of the evolution of global business, beginning in the mid-Seventies, efforts were made to "cherry pick" the best social traits from the home and host cultures to create a hybrid yet distinctly new organizational culture. The goal of this attempt to create a "neutral" and hybrid institutional culture was an attempt to move away from the imperial past that seemed to follow the movement of MNCs around the globe. It was to eliminate (at least on the rhetorical level) the power relations implied by the efforts to "impose" an alien culture on emerging markets, to create at least the appearance of an equal relationship. As a part of this change in the managerial style of MNCs, corporations sought to move the global business experience and expatriate management skills that had been isolated within a narrow core group into the corporate organization as a whole (Weeks 1992).

The final (or at least the latest) phase in the standard story of the evolution of global business is presented as a change in strategy in response to the expansion of the global economic marketplace that coincided with the fall of the Soviet Union's sphere of influence, as well as to the limited and declining success of the prior management models. In this most recent phase of global business evolution, scholars and practitioners often present cultural diversity as a positive source of comparative economic advantage, to the extent that it is often cited as the motivation behind the initial decisions of MNCs to move beyond their domestic marketplaces. Inter-cultural skills are honed not just within the internationally mobile core of the global management group, but across the entire global business organization and throughout at all levels of authority and functional areas. These inter-cultural skills are presented as being essential to survive the challenges of global competition as they reorient their vast organizations towards the demands and opportunities of the global marketplace (Marquardt 1999 & Ali 2000). This standard narrative tells the story of corporate leaders purposefully altering the behaviors of their employees in response to the resistance (in the form of poor economic performance and public image) that they encountered from the local marketplaces where they operated. Efforts in support of the earlier cultural transformation strategies continued up until the point where it became obvious that the attempted alterations were no longer meeting the goals that had been established. Once the difficulty was noted, a new model and strategy was devised to put into its place, with the end of one phase and the beginning of a new phase marked by clear delineations of business strategy and organizational culture.

The story of the anti-globalization movement tells the tale of the reaction of local inhabitants towards the international activities of multi-national corporations is also a story of a group pursuing a cogent strategy to achieve their own goals – goals derived from interests that are as equally pre-existing and well-understood as the shared interests of their MNC antagonists. In the stories of resistance told by world system, dependency and anti-globalization theorists, global social movements and local non-governmental organizations who stand against the encroaching tide of corporate invasion are acting in purposeful ways to further their interest in protecting their indigenous cultures. In most studies by both sides of this debate, the alterations in local resistance and MNC behaviors are presented as a set of rational counter-strategies designed to achieve what is presented to be each group's permanent interests and goals. Furthermore, the range of possible behaviors of both sides is presented as being constrained by the political structures within which the theoretical frameworks place the antagonists. The political structure within which this interplay between these opposing groups is presented as taking place is a state-centric model that channels the activities of the lesser actors (in this case, the MNCs and the local resistance) through the legal and economic structures erected by sovereign states.

> "… Although the economic and technical substructure partially determines and interacts with the political superstructure, political values and security interests are crucial determinants of international economic relations. Politics determines the framework of economic activities and channels it in directions that tend to serve the political objectives of dominant political groups and organizations. Throughout history each successive hegemonic power has organized economic space in terms of its own interests and purposes." (Gilpin 1971, p. 403)

While Gilpin was speaking from a Realist point of view, this statement could also be applied to a Liberal or even a Marxist view. For although these worldviews might give sub-state actors roles to play in world politics, they reserve the primary causal roles to states as they are

271

presented the actors doing the majority of the action that shapes the global political system.

However, as the empirical data carefully gathered by scholars investigating skilled international migration has shown, states do not always appear as the dominant actors that determine the movements of the highly skilled. Instead, it appears from the data that states are often either unable or unwilling to control the movement of the highly skilled across their borders. When states are concerned with highly skilled migrants, it appears that they are mainly concerned with attracting and retaining as many of these migrants as possible. Where they have become the focus of migration policy, states seem mainly to be interested in competing with other states in an attempt to retain their own skilled citizens while seeking to attract those from overseas. Yet, since the majority of the movements of highly skilled workers takes place within the internal labor markets of multinational corporations, the attempts by states to attract and retain skilled personnel often seems to be of secondary importance in relation to the interests of multinational corporations in determining the size, direction and duration of skilled international migration.

While the data on highly skilled migration does not appear to easily conform to a state-centric worldview, Rosenau's conception of spheres of authority allows MNCs and other non-state entities (such as global social movements and local NGOs) to rise up the causal chain as independent and purposeful actors on par with sovereign states. Within a GG framework the concept of SOAs empowers non-state actors and enables scholars to present them as worthy of examination in their own right. In the traditional state-centric stories of skilled international migration, states control the tone and tempo of migratory flows; however, these stories bear little resemblance to the empirical data collected by researchers in this area. A theoretical landscape comprised of spheres of authority allows us to follow the relationships that create the context of skilled international migration. In following these relationships, investigators may be able to discover the identities and interests of the actors involved in this phenomenon as they develop and define themselves in relation to the other actors with whom they interact. If we can trace the relationship which create and define the areas of activity that constitute the sphere of authority, we may be able to discover both the full range of the actors that inhabit these spheres and the rules, the norms, by which they interact.

A Constructivist understanding of identity- and interest-creation allows researchers to investigate the interplay between the changing behaviors all the actors involved in highly skilled migration. In GG approach to highly skilled migration, the historical processes of skilled international migration and the parallel evolution of global business should not be presented as a jagged progression of separate and distinct "phases" of development. Instead, they should be thought of as a smooth progression that builds upon the social learning and the mutual construction of social reality created by the interplay of all actors. If a Constructivist narrative speaks in terms of "phases" at all, these phases are presented as intellectual constructs that participants used to describe what they believed they were doing. The "foreign service" model, the attempts towards "Americanization" and/or "Westernization", and the current attempt to foster inter-cultural skills are all stories that employees of MNCs tell themselves in order to make their surroundings more sensible and to guide their actions in foreign environs. Equally, the stories that local societies tell themselves, the narratives of anti-colonialism, neo-colonialism, and anti-globalization, are also constructs that attempt to give structure and meaning to their actions in the face of what they believe is an overwhelmingly unequal power relationship. Yet underneath these conflicting alternate self-narratives of human behavior is a far more dynamic and complex relationship between "local" and "foreign" cultures and norms as they interact and blend together in an on-going process that results in the mutual construction of social reality.

In our traditional conceptions of the impact of highly skilled migrants on local national cultures, the two "sides" are seen as separate and distinct objects that exist in a stable and internally consistent manner. When these two "separate" groups meet, it is often presented as a clash in which one must be subsumed or surpassed by the other. In a Constructivist conception of this "culture clash", our very notion of culture becomes less concrete and stable. Cultures become defined by the actions of their members while also helping to give meaning to those actions. Norms are causal in that they guide behaviors, but they are also dynamic in nature, being altered in subtle but vital ways as they move across specific times and places. Norms are constructed out of the prior experiences and lessons of the actors who inhabit a particular social space thereby becoming substantially altered by the migration of agents across cultural boundaries. Local national cultures are indeed changed by the inclusion of highly skilled migrants into their midst. However, they have always been and will likely always be subject to such changes caused by contacts between cultures. Skilled international migration merely becomes a new instance in a long-existing pattern of mutual construction in the meetings between supposedly "local" and "distinct" cultures. While the stories that we tell ourselves to describe these instances and to guide our behaviors within them may change over time, the mutual construc-

273

tion of interests and identity continues unabated among groups and individuals.

Research into the phenomenon of skilled international migration has undergone an immense period of development in recent years. It has moved from relative obscurity to become a vital component in the broader field of migration studies. While the empirical data that has been gathered by scholars in this area is a vast improvement over what had previously existed and while we now know far more about the movement and impact of skilled transients; we believe that the theoretical frameworks that scholars have used to interpret to data have limited our ability to answer vital questions. The state-centric landscapes of traditional IR theories have limited our ability to study the role of non-state actors in shaping flows of skilled workers within and across the internal labor markets of multinational enterprises. Constructivist social theory and a view of a global system comprised of spheres of authority, free scholars from such seemingly predetermined normative outlooks. By employing a framework drawn from GG and Constructivism, we may be able to follow the linkages created by the relationships between actors as they create their own realms of activity and meaning while participating in the mutual construction of their shared social realities. While there is not enough space here to provide a full example of the ways in which such a new theoretical viewpoint would reinvigorate the study of skilled international migration, we hope that we have provided a tantalizing glimpse at the ways in which we might be able to reach a new understanding of the competition for global talent in an Age of Turbulence.

References

Adler, Emanuel. 1997. "Seizing the Middle Ground: Constructivism in World Politics." *European Journal of International Relations* 3(3): pp. 319 – 363.

Ali, Abbas J. 2000. *Globalization of Business: Practice and Theory.* International Business Press; New York, NY.

Findlay, Allan M. and W T. S. Gould. 1989. "Skilled International Migration: A Research Agenda." Area 21(1): pp. 3 – 11.

Gilpin, Robert. 1971. "The politics of transnational economic relations." *International Organizations,* Special Issue 25 (3): pp. 398 – 419.

Gonzalez, Richard and Adant Negandhi. 1967. *The United States Overseas Executive: His Orientation and Career Pattern.* Michigan State University Press; East Lansing, MI.

Gould, William T.S. 1988. "Skilled International Labour Migration: An Introduction." *Geoforum* 19(4): pp. 381 – 385.

Jones, Geoffrey. 1996. *The Evolution of International Business: An Introduction.* Routledge; New York, NY.

Marquardt, Michael J. 1999. *The Global Advantage: How World-Class Organizations Improve Performance Through Globalization.* Gulf Publishing Company; Houston, TX.

Moore, Karl and David Lewis. 2000. *Foundations of Corporate Empire: Is History Repeating Itself?* Prentice Hall; New York, NY.

Rosenau, James N. 1983. "'Fragmegrative' Challenges to National Security" in *Understanding U.S. Strategy: A Reader* edited by Terry Heyns. National Defense University; Washington, D.C.

Rosenau, James N. 1997. *Along the Domestic-Foreign Frontier: Exploring Governance in a Turbulent World.* Cambridge University Press; New York, NY.

Rosenau, James N. 1999. "Towards an Ontology for Global Governance" in *Approaches to Global Governance Theory* edited by Martin Hewson and Timothy J. Sinclair. State University of New York Press; Albany, NY.

Sell, Susan K. 1998. *Power and Ideas: North-South Politics of Intellectual Property and Anti-Trust.* State University of New York Press; Albany, NY.

Weeks, David A. 1992. *Recruiting and Selecting International Managers.* The Conference Board; New York, NY.